The Rich Get Richer and the Poor Get Prison

The Rich Get Richer and the Poor Get Prison

Ideology, Class, and Criminal Justice
Third Edition

Jeffrey Reiman

The American University
Washington, D.C.

Macmillan Publishing Company
New York

Editor: Christine Cardone
Production Supervisor: George Carr
Production Manager: Nick Sklitsis
Text and Cover Designer: Blake Logan
Cover illustration: Kenny Beck

This book was set in Aster by Huron Valley Graphics, and printed and bound by Fairfield Graphics. The cover was printed by Phoenix Color Corp.

Macmillan Publishing Company
866 Third Avenue, New York, New York 10022

Collier Macmillan Canada, Inc.

Library of Congress Cataloging-in-Publication Data

Reiman, Jeffrey H.
   The rich get richer and the poor get prison: ideology, class, and criminal justice / Jeffrey Reiman.—3rd ed.
      p.   cm.
   Includes index.
   ISBN 0-02-399241-7
   1. Criminal justice, Administration of—United States.   2. Social classes—United States.   3. United States—Social policy.
I. Title.
HV9950.R46   1990
364.973—dc20   89-32307
                                                          CIP

Printing: 1 2 3 4 5 6 7   Year: 0 1 2 3 4 5 6

For Sue

Preface to the Third Edition

In revising *The Rich Get Richer and the Poor Get Prison*, my overriding aim has been to show that recent developments still support the main arguments made in the original edition of the book. I have resisted the temptation to make the book into the one I might write now were I starting from scratch. Nonetheless, bringing the research findings and statistics up to date and sharpening points here and there have required many changes. I have tried to introduce these changes with as little violation of the original edition's style and argument as possible.

This new edition reports findings of studies published as recently as 1988. However, where I compare the relative danger to the public of criminal versus noncriminal harms (such as occupational and environmental hazards), I have generally used figures for 1986 because this was the latest year for which I could find adequate statistics on both types of harm. When new statistics were not available, I have, where it seemed plausible, assumed that earlier statistics reflect continuing trends and enable projections from the past into the present. In all cases, I have tried to keep my assumptions as conservative as possible in order to keep the argument on the firmest ground.

Although things have changed (some even for the better) since the last edition of the book, the main thesis of the original edition is still supported by the facts. It is still true that acts that are not treated as crimes (or if treated as crimes, not treated as serious crimes) pose at least as great a danger to the public as the acts that are treated as (serious) crimes—and often a significantly greater danger. In spite of the comparability of the dangers, it remains true that those responsible for noncriminal dangers are treated far more gently than those responsible for criminal dangers. It is still true that those well-off folks who are guilty of white-collar crimes are treated more gently than those poor ones who are guilty of nonviolent property crimes. It also is still true that better-off offenders are less likely to end up behind bars than poor offenders, even when they have committed the same offense. In short, it is still true that *the rich get richer and the poor get prison.*

There are two substantial changes I have made in the book in the hope of making it more useful for classroom teachers. First, I have added summaries and study questions to the chapters after the Introduction. The study questions require the student both to recall what he or she has read and to think critically about it. Accordingly, the questions can be used by instructors for the purpose of testing and review and by students as a way of making sure they have covered and thought about the most important issues in each chapter. Second, I have added as an appendix a short essay on Marxian theory and criminal justice. The essay attempts to cover the ground from a general statement of Marxian theories of capitalism, ideology, and law to a Marxian theory of criminal justice. I hope that some instructors may find this a handy and compendious way of introducing their students to Marxian theory and its relation to criminal law and criminology. The essay addresses some of the same issues discussed in the main text of *The Rich Get Richer* and thus offers an alternative theoretical framework for understanding those issues. Nevertheless, although this framework is compatible with that developed in the main text, the argument of *The Rich Get Richer* stands alone without it.

Because I have revised rather than rewritten *The Rich Get Richer*, I am still indebted to those who helped me with the original edition (see acknowledgments). For this third edition, however, I have incurred some new debts. My thanks go to Professors Jim Fyfe, Jim Lynch, and Pat Gunning of The American University Department of Justice, Law, and Society, each of whom generously gave me extensive criticisms and recommendations based on the previous edition. Although doing full justice to their comments would have required a new and longer book, I have tried where possible to cast my revisions in ways that took their thoughts into consideration. Needless to say, they are not to blame for my mistakes. I am also grateful to Marcia Trick, who served as my research assistant during the summer and fall of 1988 (as she did in 1982 when I was preparing the second edition), and to Jean Landis, who helped me when Ms. Trick's tenure was over. They gathered most of the data I used in updating the book. Much in the new edition reflects their hard work and good judgment.

As before, I am grateful to The American University for providing me with a supportive and lively intellectual environment in which to pursue my work. I thank also Chris Cardone, my editor at Macmillan, for her encouragement and good advice. I am grateful for the comments of Peter J. Benekos (Mercyhurst College) and Duane A. Matcha (Findlay College). I incorporate many of their recommendations in the final version.

Finally, because of her unflagging passion for justice, and for all the earlier reasons as well, this edition, like the first and the second, is dedicated to my wife, Sue Headlee.

Jeffrey Reiman

Acknowledgments for the First Edition

This book is the product of seven years of teaching in the School of Justice (formerly, the Center for the Administration of Justice), a multidisciplinary criminal justice education program at The American University in Washington, D.C. I have had the benefit of the school's lively and diverse faculty and student body. And, although they will surely not agree with all that I have to say, I have drawn heavily on what I have learned from my colleagues over the years and stand in their debt. In addition, more than is ordinarily recognized, a teacher receives guidance from students as they test, confirm, reject, and expand what they learn in class in the light of their own experience. Here, too, I am deeply in debt. My thanks go to the hundreds of students who have shared some part of their world with me as they passed through The American University, and in particular to three students whose encouragement, loyalty, and wisdom are very much a part of the development of the ideas in this book: Elizabeth Crimi, Bernard Demczuk, and Lloyd Raines.

I express my gratitude to The American University for providing me with a summer research grant that enabled me to devote full time to the book in the summer of 1976 when most of the actual writing was done. I am also grateful to Bernard Demczuk who was my research assistant during the academic year 1975 to 1976 and who gathered much of the research data. I owe thanks as well to Cathy Sacks for ably and carefully typing the final manuscript.

Drafts of the manuscript for this book were read in whole or in part by (or at) Bernard Demczuk, Sue Hollis, Richard Myren, Lloyd Raines, Phillip Scribner, I. F. Stone, and John Wildeman. I am grateful for their many comments and I incorporate many of their recommendations in the final version. I have made my mistakes in spite of them.

Finally, for teaching me about artichokes, the meaning of history, and countless other mysteries, this book is dedicated to Sue Headlee Hollis.

J. R.

Contents

Introduction: Criminal Justice Through the Looking Glass, or Winning by Losing

The inescapable conclusion is that society secretly wants *crime, needs crime, and gains definite satisfactions from the present mishandling of it.*

Karl Menninger, *The Crime of Punishment*

A criminal justice system is a mirror in which a whole society can see the darker outlines of its face. Our ideas of justice and evil take on visible form in it, and thus we see ourselves in deep relief. Step through this looking glass to view the American criminal justice system—and ultimately the whole society it reflects—from a radically different angle of vision.

In particular, entertain the idea that the goal of our criminal justice system is not to reduce crime or to achieve justice but to project to the American public a visible image of the threat of crime. To do this, it must maintain the existence of a sizable or growing population of criminals. To do this, it must fail in the struggle to reduce crime. Crime may, of course, occasionally decline, as it has in recent years—but not because of criminal justice policies.

You will rightly demand to know how and why a society such as ours would tolerate a criminal justice system designed to fail in the fight against crime. Indeed, a considerable portion of this book is devoted to answering this question. Right now, however, a short explanation of how this upside-down idea of criminal justice was born will best introduce it and myself.

Some years ago, I taught a seminar for graduate students, titled "The Philosophy of Punishment and Rehabilitation." Many of the students were already working in the field of corrections as probation officers or prison guards or halfway-house counselors. First we examined the various philosophical justifications for legal punishment, and then we directed our attention to the functioning of the actual correctional system. For much of the semester we talked about the myriad inconsistencies and cruelties and overall irrationality of the system. We discussed the arbitrariness with which offenders are sentenced to prison and the arbitrariness with which they are treated in prison. We discussed the lack of privacy and the deprivation of sources of personal identity and dignity, the ever-present physical violence, as well as the lack of meaningful counseling or job training within prison walls. We discussed the harassment of parolees, the inescapability of the "ex-con" stigma, the refusal of society to let a person finish paying his or her "debt to society," and the near-total absence of meaningful noncriminal opportunities for the ex-prisoner. We confronted time and again the bald irrationality of a society that builds prisons to prevent crime knowing full well that they do not and that does not even seriously try to rid its prisons and post-release practices of those features that guarantee a high rate of *recidivism:* the return to crime by prison alumni. How could we fail so miserably? We are neither an evil nor a stupid nor an impoverished people. How could we continue to bend our energies and spend our hard-earned tax dollars on cures we know are not working?

Toward the end of the semester I put before the students an idea that appears from time to time in the literature of sociology: Imagine that instead of designing a correctional system to reduce and prevent crime, we had to design one that would maintain and encourage the existence of a stable and visible "class" of criminals. What would it look like? The response was electrifying. In briefer and somewhat more orderly form, here is a sample of the proposals that emerged in our discussion:

First. It would be helpful to have a number of irrational laws on the books, such as laws against heroin or prostitution or gambling—

laws that prohibit acts that have no clear victim and that really do not prevent the acts they make illegal. This would make many people "criminals" for what they regard as normal behavior and would increase their need to engage in *secondary* crime (the drug addict's need to steal to pay for drugs, the prostitute's need for a pimp, because police protection is unavailable, and so on).

Second. It would be good to give police, prosecutors, and judges broad discretion to decide who got arrested, who got charged, and who got sentenced to prison. This would mean that almost anyone who got as far as prison would know of others who committed the same crime but who either were not arrested or were not charged or were not sentenced to prison. This would assure us that a good portion of the prison population would experience their confinement as arbitrary and unjust and thus respond with rage, which would make them more "antisocial," rather than respond with remorse, which would make them feel more bound by social norms.

Third. The prison experience should be not only painful but also demeaning. The pain of loss of liberty might deter future crime. But demeaning and emasculating prisoners by placing them in an enforced childhood characterized by no privacy and no control over their time and actions, as well as by the constant threat of rape or assault, is sure to overcome any deterrent effect by weakening whatever capacities a prisoner had for self-control.

Fourth. It goes almost without saying that prisoners should neither be trained in a marketable skill nor provided with a job after release. Of course, their prison records should stand as a perpetual stigma to discourage employers from hiring them. Otherwise, they might be tempted *not* to return to crime after release.

Fifth. The ex-offenders' sense that they can never pay their debt to society, that they will always be different from "decent citizens," should be reinforced by the following means. They should be deprived for the rest of their lives of rights, such as the right to vote. They should be harassed by police as "likely suspects" and be subject to the whims of parole officers who can at any time threaten to send them back to prison for things no ordinary citizens could be arrested for, such as going out of town or drinking or fraternizing with the "wrong people."

And so on.

In short, *asked to design a system that would maintain and encourage the existence of a stable and visible "class of criminals," we "constructed" the American criminal justice system!*

What is to be made of this? First, it is, of course, only part of the truth. Some prison officials do try to treat their inmates with dignity and to respect their privacy and self-determination to the greatest extent possible within an institution dedicated to involuntary confinement. Minimum security prisons and halfway houses are certainly moves in this direction. Some prisons do provide meaningful job training, and some parole officers are not only fair but go out of their way to help their "clients" find jobs and make it "legally." Of course, plenty of people are arrested for doing things that no society ought to tolerate, such as rape, murder, assault, or armed robbery, and many are in prison who might be preying on their fellow citizens if they were not. *All of this is true.* Complex social practices are just that: *complex.* They are neither all good nor all bad. For all that, though, the "successes" of the system, the "good" prisons, the halfway houses that really help offenders make it, are still the exceptions. They are not even prevalent enough to be called the beginning of the trend of the future. *On the whole, most of the system's practices make more sense if we look at them as ingredients in an attempt to maintain rather than to reduce crime!*

This statement calls for an explanation. The one I will offer is that the practices of the criminal justice system keep before the public the *real* threat of crime and the *distorted* image that crime is primarily the work of the poor. The value of this *to those in positions of power* is that it deflects the discontent and potential hostility of middle America away from the classes above them and toward the classes below them. If this explanation is hard to swallow, it should be noted in its favor that it not only explains our dismal failure to reduce crime, but it also explains why the criminal justice system functions in a way that is biased against the poor at every stage from arrest to conviction. Indeed, even at the earlier stage, when crimes are defined in law, the system primarily concentrates on the predatory acts of the poor and tends to exclude or deemphasize the equally or more dangerous predatory acts of those who are well off. In sum, I will argue that *the criminal justice system fails to reduce crime while making it look like crime is the work of the poor.* It does this in a way that conveys the image that the real danger to decent, law-abiding Americans comes from below them, rather than from above them, on the economic ladder. This image sanctifies the status quo with its disparities of wealth, privilege, and opportunity and thus serves the interests of the rich and powerful in America—the very ones who could change criminal justice policy if they were really unhappy with it.

Therefore, it seems appropriate to ask you to look at criminal justice "through the poking glass." On one hand, this suggests a reversal of common expectations. Reverse your expectations about criminal justice and entertain the notion that the system's real goal is the very reverse of its announced goal. On the other hand, the figure of the looking glass suggests the prevalence of image over reality. Indeed, my argument is that the system functions the way it does *because it creates a particular image of crime: the image that it is a threat from the poor.* Of course, for this image to be believable there must be a reality to back it up. The system must actually fight crime—or at least some crime—but only enough to keep it from getting out of hand and to keep the struggle against crime vividly and dramatically in the public's view—never enough to reduce or eliminate crime.

I call this outrageous way of looking at criminal justice policy the *Pyrrhic defeat* theory. A "Pyrrhic victory" is one in which a military victory is purchased at such a cost in troops and treasure that it amounts to a defeat. The Pyrrhic defeat theory argues that the failure of the criminal justice system yields such benefits to those in positions of power that it amounts to success. In what follows, I will try to explain the failure of the criminal justice system to reduce crime by showing the benefits that accrue to the powerful in America from this failure. I will argue that from the standpoint of those with the power to make criminal justice policy in America: *Nothing succeeds like failure.* I challenge you to keep an open mind and determine for yourself whether the Pyrrhic defeat thesis does not make more sense out of criminal justice policy and practice than the old-fashioned idea that the goal of the system is to reduce crime.

The Pyrrhic defeat thesis has several components. Above all, it must provide an explanation of *how* the failure to reduce crime could benefit anyone—anyone other than criminals, that is. This is the task of Chapter 4, which is titled "To the Vanquished Belong the Spoils: Who Is Winning the Losing War Against Crime?" I argue there that the failure to reduce crime broadcasts a powerful *ideological* message to the American people, a message that benefits and protects the powerful and privileged in our society by legitimating the present social order with its disparities of wealth and privilege and by diverting public discontent and opposition away from the rich and powerful and onto the poor and powerless.

To provide this benefit, however, not just any failure will do. It is necessary that the failure of the criminal justice system take a particular shape. *It must take a dive in the fight against crime while*

*making it look like serious crime and thus the real danger to society is
the work of the poor.* Indeed, the system accomplishes this both by
what it does and by what it refuses to do. In Chapter 2, "A Crime by
Any Other Name . . . ," I argue that the criminal justice system
refuses to label and treat as crime a large number of acts that
produce as much or more damage to life and limb as the so-called
crimes of the poor. In Chapter 3, ". . . And the Poor Get Prison," I
show how, even among the acts that are treated as crimes, the
criminal justice system is biased from start to finish in a way that
guarantees that *for the same crimes* members of the lower classes
are much more likely than members of the middle and upper
classes to be arrested, convicted, and imprisoned—thus providing
living "proof" that crime is a threat from the poor. (A statement of
the main propositions that form the core of the Pyrrhic defeat
theory is found in Chapter 2 in the section titled "Criminal Justice
as Creative Art.")

One caution is in order: The argument in Chapters 1 through 4 is
not a "conspiracy theory." It is the task of social analysis to find
patterns in social behavior and then explain them. Naturally, when
we find patterns, particularly patterns that serve someone's interests, we are inclined to think of these patterns as *intended* by those
whose interests are served, as somehow brought into being *because*
they serve these interests. This way of thinking is generally called a
"conspiracy theory." Later I will have more to say about the shortcomings of this way of thinking and will explain in detail how the
Pyrrhic defeat theory differs from it. For the present, however, note
that although I have (and will) speak of the criminal justice system
as "not wanting" to reduce crime and of the failure to reduce crime
as resulting in benefits to the rich and powerful in our society, *I am
not maintaining that the rich and powerful intentionally make the
system fail in order to gather up the resulting benefits.* A closer approximation is this: The criminal justice system we have is characterized by beliefs about what is criminal and about what to do
about crime that predate industrial society. Rather than being anyone's conscious plan, the system reflects attitudes so deeply embedded in tradition as to appear natural. To understand why it persists
even though it fails to protect us, all that is necessary is to recognize that, on one hand, those who are most victimized by crime are
not those in positions to make and implement policy. Crime falls
more frequently and more harshly on the poor than on those who
are better off (see Chapter 4). On the other hand, there are enough
benefits to the wealthy from the identification of crime with the

poor and the system's failure to reduce crime (see Chapter 4, the section called "The Poverty of Criminals and the Crime of Poverty") that those with the power to make profound changes in the system feel no compulsion nor see any incentive in making them. In short, the criminal justice system came into existence in an earlier epoch and persists in the present because, even though it is failing, indeed because of the way it fails, it generates no effective demand for change. When I speak of the criminal justice system as "designed to fail," I mean no more than this. I call this explanation of the existence and persistence of our failing criminal justice system the *historical inertia* explanation. In Chapter 4, I shall spell this explanation out in greater detail.

In the concluding chapter, I present an argument that the conditions described in Chapters 1, 2, and 3 (whether or not one accepts my explanation for them in Chapter 4) have the effect of undermining the essential moral difference between criminal justice and crime itself. In this chapter, called *"Criminal* Justice or Criminal *Justice,"* I make some recommendations for reform of the system. However, these are not offered as ways to "improve" the system but as the minimal conditions necessary to establish the moral superiority of that system to crime itself.

It will prevent confusion later if the reader remembers that when I speak of the criminal justice system I mean more than the familiar institutions of police, courts, and prisons. I mean the entire system that runs from the decisions of lawmakers about what acts are criminal all the way to the decisions of judges and parole boards about who will be in prison to pay for these acts.

I claim no particular originality for the Pyrrhic defeat theory. It is a child of the marriage of several streams of western social theory. Although this will be discussed at greater length in what follows, it will serve clarity to indicate from the start the parents and the grandparents of this child. The idea that crime serves important functions for a society comes from Emile Durkheim. The notion that public policy can be best understood as serving the interests of the rich and powerful in a society stems from Karl Marx. From Kai Erikson is derived the notion that the institutions that are designed to fight crime serve instead to contribute to its existence. From Richard Quinney comes the concept of the "reality" of crime as *created* in the process that runs from the definition of some acts as "criminal" in the law to the treatment of some persons as "criminals" by the agents of the law. The Pyrrhic defeat theory combines these ideas into the view that the failure of criminal justice policy becomes intelligible when we see that it creates the "reality" of crime as the work of the poor and thus projects an image that serves the interests of the rich and powerful in American society.

The Pyrrhic defeat theory veers away from traditional Marxist accounts of legal institutions insofar as such accounts generally emphasize the *repressive* function of the criminal justice system, whereas my view emphasizes its *ideological* function. On the whole, Marxists see the criminal justice system as serving the powerful by *successfully* repressing the poor. My view is that the system serves the powerful by its *failure* to reduce crime, not by its success. Needless to add, insofar as the system fails in some respects and succeeds in others, these approaches are not necessarily incompatible. Nevertheless, in looking at the ideological rather than the repressive function of criminal justice, I will focus primarily on the image its *failure* conveys rather than on what it actually *succeeds* in repressing. To these remarks should be added the recognition that since the 1960s, a new generation of Marxist theorists, primarily French, has begun to look specifically at the ideological functions performed by the institutions of the state. Most noteworthy in this respect is the work of Louis Althusser and Nicos Poulantzas.[1] (The Appendix contains a general statement of the relationship between Marxian theory and criminal justice.)

Having located the Pyrrhic defeat theory in its family tree, a word about the relationship between crime and economics is in order. It is my view that the social order (shaped decisively by the economic system) causes or promotes most of the crime that troubles us. This is true of all classes in the society, because a competitive economy that refuses to guarantee its members a decent living places pressures on all members to enhance their economic position by whatever means available. Nevertheless, these economic pressures work with particular harshness on the poor because their condition of extreme need and their relative lack of access to opportunities for lawful economic advancement vastly intensify for them the pressures toward crime that exist at all levels of our society.

These views lead to others that, if not taken in their proper context, may strike you as paradoxical. Evidence will be presented showing that there is a considerable amount of crime in our society at all socioeconomic levels. At the same time, it will be argued that poverty is a *source* of crime—I say "source" rather than "cause" because the link between poverty and crime is not like a physical relationship between cause and effect. Many, perhaps most, poor people do not commit serious crimes. Nevertheless, there is evidence suggesting that the particular pressures of poverty lead poor people to commit a higher proportion of the crimes that people fear (such as homicide, burglary, and assault) than their number in the population. There is no contradiction between this and the recognition that those who are well off commit many more crimes than is generally acknowledged, both the crimes widely feared and those not widely feared (such as "white-collar" crimes). There is no contradiction here, because, as will be shown, the poor are arrested far more frequently than those who are well off when they have committed the same crimes; and the well-to-do are almost never arrested for white-collar crimes. Thus, if arrest records were brought in line with the real incidence of crime, it is likely that those who are well off would appear in the records far more than they do at present, even though the poor would still probably appear in numbers greater than their proportion of the population in arrests for the crimes people fear. In addition to this, it will be argued that those who are well off commit acts that are not defined as crimes and yet that are as or more harmful than the crimes people fear. Thus, if we had an accurate picture of who is really dangerous to society, there is reason to believe that those who are well off would receive still greater representation. On this basis, the following propositions will be put forth, which may appear paradoxical if these various levels of analysis are not kept distinct.

1. Society fails to protect people from the crimes they fear by (among other things, documented in Chapter 1) refusing to alleviate the poverty that breeds them.
2. The criminal justice system fails to protect people from the most serious dangers by failing to define the dangerous acts of those who are well off as crimes (documented in Chapter 2) and by failing to enforce the law vigorously against the well-to-do when they commit crimes (documented in Chapter 3).
3. By virtue of these and other failures, the criminal justice system succeeds in creating the image that crime is almost exclusively the work of the poor, an image that serves the interests of the powerful (argued in Chapter 4).

The view that the social order is responsible for crime does not mean that individuals are wholly blameless for their criminal acts or that we ought not have a criminal justice system able to protect us against them. To borrow an analogy from Ernest van den Haag, it would be foolhardy to refuse to fight a fire because its causes were suspect. The fact that society produces criminals is no reason to avoid facing the realization that these criminals are dangerous and must be dealt with. Also, although blaming society for crime may require that we tone down our blame of individual criminals, it does not require that we deny entirely that they are responsible for their crimes. This is particularly important to remember in view of the fact that so many of the victims of the crimes of the poor are poor themselves. To point to the unique social pressures that cause the poor to prey on one another is to point to a mitigating, not an excusing, factor. Even the victims of exploitation and oppression have moral obligations not to harm those who do not exploit them or who share their oppression.

1

Crime Control in America: Nothing Succeeds Like Failure

My love she speaks softly
She knows there's no success like failure
And that failure's no success at all.

Bob Dylan, *Love Minus Zero/No Limit*

DESIGNED TO FAIL

Something in the American grain keeps us from admitting defeat both to ourselves and to others. Perhaps it is the heady air of the long-closed frontier trapped in our lungs; whatever it is, it keeps us from confessing to anything more serious than the temporary elusiveness of victory. Americans never confess to having lost a war, although we do admit there are a few we did not win. Domestically, no public policy ever fails, although some do not succeed. Hence President Ronald Reagan's remarks about crime control in America can only be read as a confession of failure, *American style:*

> *The frightening reality—for all of the speeches of those of us in government, for all of the surveys, studies, and blue ribbon panels, for all of the 14-point programs and the declarations of war on crime, crime has advanced and advanced steadily in its upward climb, and our citizens have grown more and more frustrated, frightened, and angry.*[1]

11

Of course, we do not need a presidential announcement to know that our assaults on the crime problem are a failure anymore than we need a presidential announcement to know that Monday follows Sunday. Everyone knows that for all our efforts, intelligence, and money, serious crime remains an enormous social problem. Although rates for some crimes do occasionally decrease from one year to the next, the overall trend in recent decades has been *up*. In that same speech, Mr. Reagan said:

> *In the past decade, violent crime reported to the police has increased by 59 percent. Fifty-three percent of our citizens say they're afraid to walk the streets alone at night. Eighty-five percent say they're more concerned today than they were five years ago about crime.*
>
> *Crime is an American epidemic. It takes the lives of nearly 25,000 Americans, it touches nearly one-third of American households, and it results in at least . . . $8.8 billion per year in financial losses.*
>
> *Just during the time that you and I are together today, at least 1 person will be murdered, 9 women will be raped, 67 other Americans will be robbed, 97 will be seriously assaulted, and 389 homes will be burglarized.*

Indeed, President Reagan's remarks themselves no more than hint at the enduring and abysmal nature of our failure. In 1960, the average citizen had less than a one-in-fifty chance of being a victim of one of the crimes on the FBI Index (murder, forcible rape, robbery, aggravated assault, burglary, larceny, or auto theft). In 1970, that chance grew to one-in-twenty-five. In 1986, the FBI reported nearly 5,500 Index crimes per 100,000 citizens, a further increase in the likelihood of victimization to a one-in-eighteen chance. This only counts the crimes that are *reported*. Based on "victimization studies" (asking randomly selected citizens if they or anyone in their household had been a victim of a crime reported to the police or not), experts estimate that *unreported* crime is at least double the number of reported crimes, and in some cases as much as six times as great. For example, the FBI reported 1,029,580 crimes of violence in 1977 and 1,488,140 in 1986. Victimization surveys, however, reported 5,902,000 crimes of violence in 1977 and 5,515,000 in 1986.[2] Although FBI reports show a rapidly increasing amount of crime, victimization reports show a stable, even slightly declining, but much larger amount of crime persisting through the period of intense criminal justice activity and expenditure. Whichever way you take it—a smaller amount of crime rapidly increasing or a larger amount remaining stable or even slightly declining—criminal justice policy is failing to make our lives substantially safer.

How are we to comprehend this failure? It appears that our government is failing to fulfill the most fundamental task of governance: keeping our streets and homes safe, assuring us of what the Founding Fathers called "domestic tranquility," providing us with the minimal requirement of civilized society. It appears that our new centurions with all their modern equipment and know-how are no more able than the old Roman centurions to hold the line against the forces of barbarism and chaos.

One way to understand this failure is to look at the *excuses* that are offered for it. This we will do—but mainly to show that they do not hold up! In general, these excuses fall into two categories. Some apologists point to some feature of modern life, such as urbanization or population growth (particularly the rapid increase in the number of individuals in the crime-prone ages of fifteen to twenty-four), and they say that this feature is responsible for the growth in crime. This means that crime cannot be reduced unless we are prepared to return to horse-and-buggy days or to abolish adolescence. *Translation:* We are failing to reduce crime because it is impossible to reduce crime.

The second batch of excuses tries to argue that we simply do not know how to reduce crime. *Translation:* Even though we are doing our best, we are failing to reduce crime because our knowledge of the causes of crime is still too primitive to make our best good enough.

These excuses simply do not pass muster. Although increasing urbanization and a growing youth population account for some of the increase in crime, they by no means account for all the increase, and certainly not for the impossibility of reducing crime. Crime rates vary widely (and wildly) when we compare cities of similar population size and density. Some very large and densely populated cities have lower crime rates than small and sparse ones. Some cities are high in one type of crime and low in another, and so on. What this means is that growing crime is not a simple, unavoidable consequence of increasing urbanization. If crime rates vary between large cities, urbanization cannot explain away our inability to reduce crime *at least* to *the lowest* rates prevalent in large cities. Similarly, the crime rate has increased far more rapidly than the youth population has both in absolute numbers and as a fraction of the total population. This means that growing crime is not a simple, unavoidable consequence of a growing youth population. If crime rates are increasing faster than the young themselves are, then increasing youth itself is not the cause of increasing crime. We have to know why fifteen- to twenty-four-year-old young people are committing more crimes now than they did in the past, and it is no answer to point to their youth. A growing youth population cannot explain away our inability to reduce crime *at least* down to the rate at which the young are increasing (or, more recently, decreasing) in our population.

On the other hand, the excuse that we do not know how to reduce crime also does not hold up. The bald truth is that we *do* know some of the sources of crime and *we obstinately refuse to remedy them!* We know that poverty increases the pressures to commit crimes in pursuit of property and that crimes to obtain property account for about 90 percent of the crime rate—and yet we do little to improve the conditions of our impoverished inner-city neighborhoods beyond clicking our tongues over the strange coincidence that these are also the neighborhoods with the highest crime rates. We know that our prisons undermine human dignity and the the "ex-con" stigma closes the door to many lawful occupations—and yet we do little to improve these conditions beyond shaking our heads over the fact that so much crime is committed by *recidivists:* people who have already enjoyed the hospitality of our jails and penitentiaries. We know that heroin addiction "forces" people into crime *because* of the high prices of illegal heroin—and yet we refuse to make cheap heroin legally available. We know that guns figure in most murders and make possible many thefts—and yet we refuse to adopt effective gun control. In other words, we may not know how to eliminate crime, but we certainly know how to reduce crime and the suffering it produces. The simple truth is that, as with crime, so with crime reduction, *ignorance is no excuse.*

Since the excuses do not explain our failure to reduce crime, we are back at square one. The question "How will we comprehend this monstrous failure?" still stares us in the face. Examining the excuses has been of little avail. Indeed, it has produced a result opposite from the one hoped for. It has suggested that our failure is an avoidable one. What has to be explained is not why *we cannot* reduce crime *but why we will not!* Oddly enough, this parodoxical result points us in the direction of an answer to our question.

Failure is, after all, in the eye of the beholder. The last runner across the finish line has failed in the race only if he or she wanted to win. If the runner wanted to lose, the "failure" is, in fact, a success. Here, I think lies the key to understanding our criminal justice system.

If we look at the system as "wanting" to reduce crime, it is an abysmal failure—and we cannot understand it. If we look at it as *not* wanting to reduce crime, it's a howling success—and all we need to understand is why the goal of the criminal justice system is to fail to reduce crime. If we can understand this, then the system's "failure," as well as its obstinate refusal to implement the policies that could remedy that "failure," becomes perfectly understandable.

In other words, I propose that we can make more sense out of criminal justice policy by assuming that its goal is to maintain crime than by assuming that its goal is to reduce crime!

In the remainder of the present chapter, I explore in some detail the excuses for the failure to reduce crime and show that they will not suffice. In addition, I offer evidence to back up my assertion that there are policies that could reduce crime that we refuse to implement. I then briefly outline the relationship between the Pyrrhic defeat theory and the criminological theory of Kai Erikson and Emile Durkheim, to which it is akin.

THREE EXCUSES THAT WILL NOT WASH, OR HOW WE COULD REDUCE CRIME IF WE WANTED TO

On July 23, 1965, President Lyndon Johnson signed an Executive Order establishing the President's Commission on Law Enforcement and Administration of Justice to investigate the causes and nature of crime, to collect existing knowledge about our criminal justice system, and to make recommendations about how that system might better meet "the challenge of crime in a free society." The commission presented its report to the president early in 1967, thick with data and recommendations. Because we are a nation higher on commissions than on commitments, it should come as no surprise that for all the light cast on the crime problem by the President's Commission, little heat has been generated and virtually no profound changes in criminal justice policy have taken place in the nearly twenty years since the report was issued.

During this period, however, more and more money has been poured into crime control with the bleak results I have already outlined. When the commission wrote, it estimated that more than $4 billion was being spent annually at the national, state, and local levels to pay for police, courts, and correction facilities in the fight against crime.[3] Since that time the total number of reported Index crimes grew from 4,710,000 in 1965 to a staggering 13,210,800 in

1986.[4] The annual cost to the public of this brand of domestic tranquility reached $45,607,142,000 for fiscal year 1985, with over a million and quarter persons employed by the criminal justice system.[5] Needless to say, dollar-for-dollar crime control is hardly an impressive investment.

Nevertheless, multiplying almost as fast as crime and anticrime dollars are excuses for our failure to stem the rapid growth of crime (not to say the failure to actually reduce it) in the face of increased expenditure, personnel, research, and data. Three excuses (or, more charitably, "explanations") have sufficient currency to make them worthy of consideration as well as to set in relief the Pyrrhic defeat thesis, which I propose in their place.

First Excuse

One excuse is that crime is an inescapable companion of any complex, populous, industrialized society. As we become more complex, more populous, more industrialized, and particularly more *urbanized*, we will have more crime as inevitably as we will have more ulcers and more traffic. These are the costs of modern life, the benefits of which abound and clearly outweigh the costs. Growing crime, then, takes its place alongside death and taxes. We can fight it, but we cannot win, and we should not tear our hair out about it.

It takes little reflection to see that this is less an explanation than a recipe for resignation. Furthermore, it does not account for the fact that other complex, populous, and highly industrialized nations such as Japan have crime rates that are not only lower than ours but that do not accelerate as quickly as ours. In 1971, the total number of criminal offenses known to the police in Japan was 1,244,168, a little more than 1,000 offenses for every 100,000 inhabitants. In other words, about *one-fifth* the number of serious offenses known to the police in America that year occurred in a country with *half* the population of the United States crowded onto a land less than *one-twentieth* the size of the United States. More striking, however, is that while American crime was soaring in the 1970s, Japan reports that offenses known to the police decreased to 1,191,549 in 1973.

Reporting the results of her study of the relationship between crime and modernization around the world, Louise Shelley writes,

Although both societies have undergone urbanization and industrialization, Japan and Switzerland have been exempt from many of the crime problems that currently plague the other developed countries. . . . Most

*other developed countries have considerably higher rates of crime com-
mission than these two societies, but few developed countries have as
high rates of crime commission as the United States.*[6]

This generalization is borne out strikingly by comparing homicide
rates in the United States with those in other modern nations. In
1981–1982, Japan had a homicide rate of 1 (per 100,000 inhabitants), England and Wales had a rate of 2, Belgium and Australia
each had a rate of 3, and West Germany 5. For 1982, the homicide
rate in the United States was 9.1.[8]

Moreover, the "costs of modern life" or urbanization excuse does
not account for the striking differences in the crime rates *within*
our own modern complex, populous, and urbanized nation. Within
the United States in 1986, the homicide rate ranged from 1 per
100,000 inhabitants in North Dakota to 13.5 in Texas and 17.9 in
Puerto Rico.[9] Discussing the homicide rate in a 1968 issue, *Time*
magazine reported that

*in some Northern ghettos it hits 90, just as it did some years ago in the
[Martin Luther] King murder city of Memphis. Texas, home of the shoot-
out and divorce-by-pistol, leads the U.S. with about 1000 homicides a year,
more than 14 other states combined. Houston is the U.S. murder capital:
244 last year, more than in England, which has 45 million more people.*[10]

By 1986, however, Texas (with 2,258 homicides) was in second
place behind California (with 3,038). New York (with 1,907) was
close behind Texas—and Houston's glory as the murder capital had
clearly faded. Houston reported 408 homicides in 1986, roundly
outdone by Los Angeles with 834 and Chicago with 744 and left far
behind by New York City, which captured the 1986 murder title
with an astounding 1,582 (30 killings a week!).[11]

Such variations are not limited to murder. A comparison of
crime rates (incidence of FBI Index crimes per 100,000 inhabitants)
for standard metropolitan statistical areas (areas "made up of a
core city with a population of 50,000 or more inhabitants and the
surrounding county or counties which share certain metropolitan
characteristics") reveals a striking *lack* of correlation between
crime rate and population size (which we can take as a reasonable,
though rough, index of urbanization and the other marks of modernity, such as complexity and industrialization, that are offered as
explanations for the intractability of crime). Citizens of the New
York City metropolitan area (population 8,394,246) have only a
slightly greater chance of being victimized by an Index crime
(8,121 per 100,000 population) than citizens living in and around

New Orleans, where the population is 1,330,143 and the crime rate is 8,049.4 per 100,000, and a slightly smaller chance than citizens in the area of Des Moines, Iowa, where the population is 369,470 and the crime rate is 8,238.3 per 100,000.[12]

Some people prefer the figures reported in the Justice Department's National Crime Survey (NCS) to those in the FBI's *Uniform Crime Reports* (UCR), because the UCR's figures reflect crimes reported to the police and are thus subject to the vagaries of people's reporting practices. The NCS is thought to get a fuller picture of crime incidence because it is mainly a telephone survey asking recipients about victimization experiences whether reported or not. The NCS figures are even less supportive of the notion that crime increases with urbanization because it reports a 19 percent decline in the number of households touched by rape, robbery, or assault from 1975 to 1986, a period during which the nation's overall population as well as the number of cities with populations more than a quarter million increased.[13] Incidentally, I have generally used the UCR figures rather than the NCS figures because there is some reason to believe that the UCR figures are more accurate for assessing trends in violent crimes. Violent crimes have a high and generally stable rate of being reported to the police, thus making the UCR figures a reasonably accurate indicator of the trends in their occurrence. Moreover, because victims of violent crimes may be in the hospital, such crimes may be underreported in a telephone survey.

It might reasonably be thought that population density (number of persons per square mile) is a better indicator of urbanization. Thus, if crime is an ineluctable product of urbanization, we should see a clear correlation between population density and crime rates. The facts, however, do not bear this out. Instead, they indicate a striking lack of correlation between cities' population densities and their crime rates. (See Table 1, in which ten large cities are ranked by population density and then by their crime rates.)[14]

In other words, classifying crime with death and taxes and saying that it is an inevitable companion of modernity or urbanization just will not explain our failure to reduce it. Even if death and taxes are inevitable (although unfortunately not in that order), some die prematurely and some die suspiciously and some pay too much in taxes and some pay none at all. None of these variations is inevitable or unimportant. So too with crime. Even if crime is inevitable in modern societies, its rates and types vary extensively—and this is

TABLE 1

Large Cities by Population Density and Crime Rates (per 100,000 population)

Cities and Population per Square Mile	Overall Crime Rank and Rate	Violent Crime Rank and Rate	Property Crime Rank and Rate
New York City (24,089)	6th 8,847	5th 1,995	7th 6,852
Philadelphia (12,080)	10th 5,234	8th 1,046	10th 4,188
Miami (10,902)	1st 14,830	1st 2,948	1st 11,882
Washington, D.C. (9,984)	7th 8,332	6th 1,505	8th 6,827
Detroit (8,010)	2nd 12,800	2nd 2,487	2nd 10,313
Los Angeles (6,996)	5th 9,550	4th 2,036	5th 7,514
Cleveland (6,783)	8th 8,087	7th 1,301	9th 6,786
Milwaukee (6,316)	9th 7,851	10th 985	6th 6,866
Phoenix (2,314)	4th 9,641	9th 997	4th 8,645
Kansas City (Mo.) (1,395)	3rd 12,138	3rd 2,159	3rd 9,979

Source: UCR-1987 and StatAbst-1988.

neither inevitable nor unimportant. Indeed, the variations in crime rates between modern cities and nations is proof that the *extent* of crime is not a simple consequence of urbanization. Other factors must explain the differences. It is these differences that suggest that although some crime may be an ineradicable consequence of urbanization, this in no way excuses our failure to reduce crime at least to the lowest rates reported in modern cities and nations.

Second Excuse

A second excuse takes the form of attributing the growth in crime to young people—particularly young men between the ages of fifteen and twenty-four. This explanation goes as follows: Young people in our society, especially males, find themselves emerging from the security of childhood into the frightening chaos of adult responsibility. Little is or can be done by the adult society to ease the transition by providing meaningful outlets for the newly bursting youthful energy aroused in still immature and irresponsible youngsters. Hence, these youngsters both mimic the power of manhood and attack the society that frightens and ignores them by resorting to violent crime. Add to this the rapid increase of people in this age group since the baby boom of the 1940s, and we have another explanation that amounts to a recipe for resignation: We can no more expect to reduce crime than we can hope to eradicate adolescence. We can fight crime, but it will be with us until we figure out a way for people to get from childhood to adulthood without passing through their teens.

There can be no doubt that youngsters show up disproportionately in arrest figures. In 1965, persons between the ages of eleven and twenty-four constituted 23.4 percent of the nation's population. They represented, however, 50 percent of those arrested for willful homicide, rape, robbery, and aggravated assault and a staggering 75.2 percent of those arrested for larceny, burglary, and motor vehicle thefts.[15] Using more recent statistics, *Time* reports that "forty-four percent of the nation's murderers are 25 or younger, and 10 percent are under 18. Of those arrested for street crimes, excluding murder, fully 75 percent are under 25 and 45 percent are under 18."[16]

However, there are problems with this explanation. The most important is that crime rates have grown faster than either the absolute number of young people or their percentage of the population. Compare, for example, 1981, the post-war year with both the highest UCR crime totals and the highest NCS survey reports of violent victimizations, with 1973, the first year for which we have NCS survey results. In 1973, the number of people aged sixteen to twenty-four was 34,967,000, and in 1981, their number had increased 10 percent to 38,591,000. As a percentage of the national population they went from 16.5 to 16.8 (that is, their percentage of the population increased by slightly under 2 percent). During that same period, the UCR's crime total increased *54 percent,* from 8,718,100 to 13,423,800. The supposedly more accurate NCS shows an increase in reported violent victimizations of *23 percent,* from 5,351,000 to 6,582,000—more than twice the increase in the absolute number of sixteen- to twenty-four-year-olds, more than ten times the increase in their fraction of the population. Or, compare

1975 and 1984, years in which the number of sixteen- to twenty-four-year-olds are nearly the same (36,544,000 and 36,677,000, respectively). NCS reports an increase in violent victimizations of *8 percent* from 1975 (5,573,000 victimizations) to 1984 (6,582,000). Nineteen eighty-four had 133,000 more sixteen- to twenty-four-year-olds than 1975 had, but it had 448,000 more violent victimizations.[17]

Note that I am not denying that a large number of crimes are committed by young people. Thus, there is undoubtedly truth in the claim that some of the decreases in crime rates that have recently been noted can be attributed to the end of the "baby boom" and the resultant decrease in the number of persons in the fifteen- to twenty-four-year-old group.[18] This truth is easily overstated. The period of decline in the youth population has coincided with an increase in serious crime in New York City, and although crime rates have recently gone down, they have still not returned to the levels they were at in the 1940s when the percentage of young people sixteen to twenty-four years old was about 14, roughly comparable to what it is now.[19] Says Charles Murray, senior research fellow at the Manhattan Institute for Policy Research,

> *However one reads the data, the* level *of crime today remains at least at the plateau reached in the 1960s—which means that despite the recent decline, crime is still drastically greater today than it was in the 1950s.*[20]

All of this suggests that although the number of youngsters in the populace has an important effect on the crime rates, it cannot fully explain them or explain them away. When this group was growing, the crime rates were growing faster than it was. If crime has increased faster than the youth population, then that increase cannot be explained by the increase in youths. If crime *among* these youngsters has increased, then this certainly is not explained by their youth. Something other than their youth or their numbers must explain why they are committing more crimes than people their age did in other periods. For example, some observers have suggested that increased youth population increases crime exponentially by, among other things, increasing the competition for jobs. This in turn increases unemployment, which predictably leads to crime.[21] But from this it doesn't follow that the increased crime results from the increased youth population, because at least part of the responsibility must be ascribed to the failure of the economy to provide jobs for the new youthful candidates. In any case, the increase in young people provides no excuse for failing to reduce the growth of crime at least to the rate at which the number of young people is (or was) growing. Moreover, this remains a failure even when a declining youth population leads to declining crime rates because neither decline can be credited to criminal justice polices. So another excuse for our failure fails to excuse.

Third Excuse

The third excuse is the hardest to swallow. This excuse, in its crudest form, is that we simply are not yet smart enough to solve the problem. We have tried and continue to try in good faith, but we can only go as far as our own lights, and they have not yet lit the path to the solution of the crime problem. In differing forms and in differing degrees of despair, this excuse is proffered by experts—both academic and professional—in the various divisions of the criminal justice system. An article by Joel D. Weisman, titled "Chicago Reflects Police Frustration in Fight Against Crime," in the *Washington Post* gives a good sampling of this view among experts on the police:

> There is controversy over whether police departments can significantly affect crime. Boston Police Commissioner Robert J. diGrazia claims police can only displace crime—not reduce or eliminate it. "It's like squeezing a balloon," said [David] Fogel [executive director of the Illinois Law Enforcement Commission]. "You push the air away from where you're squeezing but it expands the rest of the balloon."
> James Q. Wilson, a professor of political science at Harvard University and author of the book Thinking About Crime, said police can contribute to reducing crime but it is unclear by how much. The data are too unreliable, he contended.
> "All those answers the sociologists had for us in the 1960s aren't so definite now," said [Franklin] Zimring [head of the University of Chicago's Center for Studies in Criminal Justice]. "For that matter, all of the law enforcement answers weren't so right either."[22]

An article by Leroy Aarons, also in the *Washington Post*, titled, "U.S. Penal System 'Truths' Questioned," reflects similar bewilderment among correctional officials. Reporting the conclusions of a "recent issue of *Corrections* magazine," which "devoted 27 pages to an article on the current ferment in the field," Aarons writes:

> The article concluded, based on interviews with wardens, administrators and students of corrections around the country that:
>
> • There is little or no evidence that correctional "treatment" programs work.

• *The gradual restructuring of the correctional system over the last 50 years around the notion of individualized and enforced treatment for all offenders was a mistake.*

• *A radically new approach is needed that will provide both better protection for the public and a more realistic view of what can and cannot be done to cut recidivism, the return to criminal behavior.*

"*What the new approach should include is a matter of dispute,*" the article said.

Aarons concludes his own article with an observation drawn from current doubts among corrections experts but applicable to the whole criminal justice system:

It seems clear that, in the long run, solutions to the age-old problem of what to do with those individuals deemed law-breakers still elude society.[23]

This excuse says, in short, that growing crime is not inherently intractable, as is claimed by the partisans of excuses one and two— but it might as well be. It might as well be because we simply do not know what to do about it. So we fail, and we cannot be blamed for our failure.

To believe this excuse, you must believe the following: The United States, with virtually limitless resources, capable of spending hundreds of billions of dollars to fight a hardly believable "threat" in Vietnam, cannot summon the resources and will to do battle with a threat that haunts almost everyone in our society and makes them fearful to walk the streets and hardly more secure at home; that the United States, with technology and information beyond the dreams of any previous generation, indeed any previous civilization, capable of placing a human being on the moon and a heart in a human being, cannot figure out at least *some* of the causes of some crime and eliminate those causes; and that the United States, with more than a million law enforcement and criminal justice personnel with training and literally billions of work hours of experience in the "fight against crime," has not developed the expertise even to dent the rising crime rate, much less actually to reduce it. This is just too much to swallow.

But there is more. There are, in fact, things that we do know about the sources of crime. Note that I have said "sources" rather than "causes," because the kind of knowledge we have is far from the precise knowledge that a physicist has about how some event *causes* another. We know that poverty, slums, and unemployment are *sources* of street crime. We do not know if (or how) they *cause* crime, because we know as well that many, if not most, poor, unemployed slum-dwellers do not engage in street crime. Yet to say that this means we do not know that such conditions increase the likelihood of an individual resorting to violent crime is like saying that we do not know that a bullet in the head is deadly because some people survive or because we do not fully understand the physiological process that links the wound with the termination of life.

Those fifteen- to twenty-four-year-olds who figure so prominently in arrest statistics are not drawn equally from all economic strata. Although there is much reported and even more unreported crime among middle-class youngsters, the street crime that is attributed to this age group and that makes our city streets a perpetual war zone is largely the work of poor ghetto youth. This is the group at the lowest end of the economic spectrum. This is a group among whom unemployment approaches 50 percent with underemployment (the rate of persons either jobless or with part-time, low-wage jobs) still higher. This is a group with no realistic chance (for any but a rare individual) to enter college or amass sufficient capital (legally) to start a business or to get into the union-protected, high-wage, skilled job markets. This much we do know, just as we know that of the more than 1 million persons processed through the criminal justice system on any given day, fully 80 percent come from the lowest 15 percent of the economic spectrum.[24] We know that poverty is a *source* of crime, even if we do not know how it *causes* crime—and yet we do virtually nothing to improve the life chances of the vast majority of the inner-city poor. They are as poor as ever and are facing cuts in welfare and other services.

Indeed, the gap between rich and poor widened during the seventies and eighties. Lawrence Mishel and Jacqueline Simon write in *The State of Working America:*

> *The gap between rich and poor has grown. Those at the very top, the upper 20 percent but particularly the upper 5 percent, have enjoyed substantial income growth since 1979. The bottom 40 percent of families saw their incomes fall, with those at the very bottom suffering the most. . . . Overall, income inequality is now at its highest levels since 1947. Income inequality along racial lines has also increased.[25]*

Mishel and Simon indicate that real family income (measured in 1987 dollars) declined by 7.5 percent among the poorest fifth of the population, whereas it grew by 9.7 percent among the best-off fifth and by 11.9 percent among the richest 5 percent of Americans.[26] In

1986, the poorest fifth of the nation's families received 4.6 percent of the aggregate income, and the richest fifth received 43.7 percent.[27] Moreover, the Reagan administration's strategy of fighting inflation by cutting services to the poor while reducing the taxes of the wealthy only accelerated this process. In September 1982, a group of thirty-four prominent economists sharply criticized Reagan's economic policy as "extremely regressive in its impact on our society, redistributing wealth and power from the middle class and the poor to the rich, and shifting more of the tax burden away from business and onto low- and middle-income consumers."[28] In that same month, a study released by the Urban Institute concluded that "the Reagan administration's policies are not only aiding upper-income families at the expense of the working poor, but also are widening the gulf between affluent and poorer regions of the country."[29] The study maintained that Reagan's tax cuts required sacrifices of low-income families, while yielding small gains for middle-income families and large gains for the upper-income families; and that the combined effect of the administration's tax and social service spending cuts was "to penalize working families near the poverty line who receive some federal benefits . . . creating 'major work disincentives.' " Moreover, as unemployment has gone up and down over the past decades, unemployment at the bottom of society remains strikingly worse than the national average. For example, over the past twenty years black unemployment has remained slightly more than twice the rate of white unemployment. In 1967, when 3.4 percent of white workers were unemployed, 7.4 percent of black workers were jobless. By January 1988, 5.8 percent of white workers were unemployed and 12.2 percent of blacks were. (Bear in mind that these figures are for workers of all ages: As of 1986, *Time* magazine reported that unemployment for black teens was more than 40 percent!) Other indicators show a relative worsening of conditions. For example, in 1965, nonwhite infants (under one month old) died at a rate 58 percent higher than the rate for white infants, whereas in 1984 nonwhite infants died at a rate 65 percent higher than for whites.[30]

There are other things we know as well. We know that prison produces more criminals than it cures. We know that more than 70 percent of the inmates in the nation's prisons or jails are not there for the first time. We know that prison inmates are denied autonomy and privacy and subjected to indignities, mortifications, and acts of violence as regular features of their confinement. The result, as delineated by Robert Johnson and Hans Toch in *The Pains of*

Imprisonment, "is that the prison's survivors become tougher, more pugnacious, and less able to feel for themselves and others, while its nonsurvivors become weaker, more susceptible, and less able to control their lives."[31] Prisoners are thus bereft of both training and capacity to handle daily problems in competent and socially constructive ways, inside or outside of prison. Once on the outside, rarely trained in a marketable skill and burdened with the stigma of a prison record, they find few opportunities for noncriminal employment open to them. Should we then really pretend that we do not *know* why they turn to crime? Can we honestly act as if we do not know that our prison system (combined with our failure to ensure a meaningful post-release noncriminal alternative for the ex-con) is a *source* of crime? Recidivism does not happen because ex-cons miss their alma mater. In fact, if prisons are built to deter people from crime, one would expect that ex-prisoners would be most deterred because the deprivations of prison are more real to them than to the rest of us. Recidivism is thus a doubly poignant testimony to the job that prison does in preparing its graduates for crime—and yet we do little to change the nature of prisons or to provide real services to ex-convicts.

We know that it is about as difficult to obtain a handgun in the United States as a candy bar. We know that there are more than 100 million guns in private use in this country. In 1968 Franklin Zimring tried to estimate the numbers of guns in civilian hands by using both the results of public opinion polls and the available figures on domestic production, as well as foreign import of firearms for civilian use. He concluded that:

> *Survey results thus indicate ownership of approximately 80 million firearms, while production and import totals indicate approximately 100 million. We can do no better than average these two figures and conservatively estimate the number of firearms now in civilian hands in this country . . . 35 million rifles, 31 million shotguns, and 24 million handguns—in 60 million households.*[32]

Speaking before the Law Enforcement Executives Narcotics Conference, former Attorney General Edward Levi estimated that the number of handguns in the United States is more than 40 million "and that the number increases each year by 2.5 million."[33] The President's Crime Commission reported that in 1965, "5,600 murders, 34,700 aggravated assaults and the vast majority of the 68,400 armed robberies were committed by means of firearms. All but 10 of 278 law enforcement officers murdered during the period

1960–65 were killed with firearms." The commission concluded over a decade ago that

> *more than one-half of all willful homicides and armed robberies, and almost one-fifth of all aggravated assaults, involve use of firearms.* As long as there is no effective gun-control legislation, violent crimes and the injuries they inflict will be harder to reduce than they might otherwise be.[34]

The situation has worsened since the commission's warning. The FBI reported that 20,613 Americans were murdered in 1986, 59 percent of them by firearms and 44 percent by handguns.[35] In the face of these facts—indeed, in the face of his own nearly fatal shooting by a would-be assassin—President Reagan refused to support any legislative attempts to control the sale of handguns.[36]

Can we believe that a president sincerely wants to cut down on violent crime and the injuries it produces when he opposes even as much as *registering* guns or *licensing* gun owners, much less actually restricting the sale and movement of guns as a matter of national policy? Are we to believe that the availability of guns does not contribute to our soaring crime rate? Zimring's study indicates that areas with a high number of privately owned guns have more crimes involving guns than do areas with lower numbers of privately owned firearms. His data also indicate that cities that experience an increase in legal gun sales also experience an increase in gun-related suicides, accidents, and crimes.[37]

This is hardly more than what common sense would lead us to expect. Can we really believe that if guns were less readily available, violent criminals would simply switch to other weapons to commit the same amount of crimes and do the same amount of damage? Is there a weapon other than the handgun that works as quickly, that allows its user so safe a distance, or that makes the criminal's physical strength (or speed or courage for that matter) as irrelevant? Could a bank robber hold a row of tellers at bay with a switchblade? Would an escaping felon protect himself from a pursuing police officer with a hand grenade? In fact, Zimring's studies also indicate that if gun users switched to the next deadliest weapon—the knife—and attempted the same number of crimes, we could still expect *80 percent fewer fatalities* because the fatality rate of the knife is roughly one-fifth that of the gun. In other words, even if guns were eliminated and crimes not reduced, we could expect to save as many as four out of every five persons who are now the victims of firearm homicide!

Finally, the United States has an enormous drug abuse and addiction problem. There is considerable evidence, however, that our attempts to cure it are worse than the disease itself. Consider first heroin. The number of heroin users is hard to estimate because we only know of the ones who get caught and because there are a large but unknown number of individuals who (contrary to popular mythology) shoot up occasionally without becoming addicts—a practice known as "chipping." In his book *The Heroin Solution*, Arnold Trebach indicates that this number may be as high as 3.5 million.[38] Nevertheless, some reasonable methods of arriving at a ballpark estimate of the number of addicts—that is, regular users who have developed a physical need for heroin and who therefore experience painful withdrawal symptoms if they do not shoot up regularly— have been concocted, and the most conservative figure that emerges is 250,000, with estimates ranging as high as 600,000.[39]

As shocking as this statistic may be, it must be at least as shocking to discover that there is little evidence proving that heroin is a *dangerous* drug. There is no evidence conclusively establishing a link between heroin and disease or tissue degeneration such as that established for tobacco and alcohol. On the basis of the scientific evidence available, there is every reason to suspect that we do our bodies more damage, more *irreversible* damage, by smoking cigarettes and drinking liquor. Most of the physical damage that is associated with heroin use is probably attributable to the trauma of withdrawal—and this, of course, is a product not so much of heroin but of its unavailability.

It might be said that the evil of heroin is that it is *addicting*, because this is a bad thing even if the addicting substance is not itself harmful.[40] It is hard to deny that the image of a person enslaved to a chemical is rather ugly and is repugnant to our sense that the dignity of human beings lies in their capacity to control their destinies. More questionable, however, is whether this is, in the case of adults, anybody's business but their own. Even so, suppose we agree that addiction is an evil worthy of prevention. Doesn't that make us hypocrites? What about all our other addictions? What about nicotine addiction, which is, like heroin, a physical need the body develops for a chemical that, unlike heroin, we know contributes to cancer and heart disease? What about the 9 or 10 million alcoholics in the nation who are working their way through their livers and into their graves? What about the people who cannot get started without a caffeine fix in the morning and those who, once started, cannot slow down without their alcohol fix in the evening? Are they not addicts? Suffice it to say, then, at the very least, our attitudes about heroin are inconsistent and irrational, and there is reason to believe they are outrageous and hypocritical. Even if this were not so, even if we could be much more certain that heroin addiction was a disease worth preventing, the fact would remain that the "cure" we have chosen is worse than the disease. We *know* that treating the possession of heroin as a criminal offense produces more crime than it prevents.

In its report titled *Social Cost of Drug Abuse*, the Special Action Office for Drug Abuse Prevention uses figures on the average cost per day of a heroin habit to estimate the amount of theft that heroin addicts must engage in to support their habits. They compute a variety of totals using a combination of different assumptions and then average them to produce their final estimate. They assume that the average addict must supply his or her habit 255 days a year, allowing some time for being in jail or in the hospital; that they must resort to crime to obtain funds for between 33 and 60 percent of their drug needs; and that they must steal three times the dollar value they need, since they must convert their booty into cash through a fence. They assume, then, that there are between 250,000 and 600,000 addicts, who must steal to supply between 33 and 60 percent of habits costing between $43 and $51.50 per day. Using eight combinations of these assumptions, they calculate eight totals reflecting the combination of the lowest to the combination of the highest assumptions. Their totals range from a low of $2.7 billion to a high of $14.2 billion. They drop the lowest two and the highest two as unrealistic in both directions and then compute the average of the middle four:

The average cost of these alternatives is $6.3 billion, which we shall use as an approximation of cost due to theft related to heroin use.[41]

These figures should be seen in relation to the total dollar value of stolen property across the nation. In the *Uniform Crime Reports* for 1980, the FBI sets the value of stolen property at $8.6 billion. Moreover, the figure of $6.3 billion is a conservative one on many counts. First of all, it is an estimate of what it cost addicts to support their habits in 1974, without adjustment for the effects of inflation between 1974 and 1980, the year for which the FBI's figures on stolen property are given. Second, it does not take into account the expenses that addicts have other than their drugs. In 1977, Dr. Robert DuPont said,

> *Our latest data at NIDA [National Institute on Drug Abuse] suggest that, during the time the addict is involved in crime . . . [his] annual income exceeds $24,000—58 percent of which (or $14,000) is required to cover the cost of drugs. Of course, the actual value of goods stolen is generally estimated to be 3 to 4 times the amount obtained through fences. So we estimate that a single heroin addict may cost society up to $100,000 a year in property loss.*[42]

Trebach adds about these comments that if "DuPont's $100,000 loss figure were to be multiplied by 200,000, our minimum estimated number of addicts not in treatment, annual property loss would amount to $20 billion, an improbable figure."[43] Even if we accept that this is an improbable figure, and even if we also assume that the FBI's estimate of the value of stolen property would increase dramatically if we knew the value of unreported theft, we cannot escape the conclusion that theft by heroin addicts—who have no other means of supporting their habits—accounts for an astounding amount of property crime. Note that nearly 60,000 inmates of state corrections facilities in 1979 reported regular use of heroin prior to incarceration, and 23,000 inmates of local jails in 1978 reported daily use of heroin prior to incarceration.[44]

It is essential to recognize that it is not the "disease" of heroin addiction that leads to property crime. There is, writes Trebach, "nothing in the pharmacology, or physical and psychological impact, of the drug that would propel a user to crime."[45] Nor is there anything about heroin itself that makes it extremely costly. The heroin that an addict pays $50 or more a day for could be legally produced at a cost of a few cents for a day's supply. Thus, it is not the "disease" of heroin addiction but its "cure" that leads to property crime. *It is our steadfast refusal to provide heroin through legal sources that, for approximately a quarter of a million individuals on the streets, translates a physical need for a drug into a physical need to steal over $6 billion worth of property a year.*

Prior to 1914, when anyone could go into a drugstore and purchase heroin and other opiates the way we buy aspirin today, hundreds of thousands of upstanding law-abiding citizens were hooked.[46] Opiate addiction is not in itself a *cause* of crime—if anything, it is a pacifier.[47] However, once sale or possession of heroin is made a serious criminal offense, a number of consequences follow. First, because those who supply it face grave penalties, they charge wildly high prices to make the risk worthwhile. Because those who need it face grave pains of withdrawal and have no alternative source, they pay the wildly high prices. What an addict pays $50 a day for could be produced and sold legally for pennies (as is the case in Great Britain, where heroin is dispensed to addicts by government-controlled clinics). Second, because the supply (and the quality) of the drug fluctuates depending on how vigorously the agents of the law try to prevent it, the addict's life is continuously unstable. Addicts live in constant uncertainty about the next fix and must devote much of their wit and energy to getting it and to getting enough money to pay for it. They do not, then, fit easily into the routines of a 9-to-5 job even if they could get one that would pay enough to support their habits. Finally, all the difficulties of securing the drug add up to an incentive to be not merely a user of heroin but a dealer as well because this both earns money and makes one's own supply more certain. Addicts thus have an incentive to find and encourage new addicts, which they would not have if heroin were legally and cheaply available. If we add to this the fact that heroin addiction has increased in spite of all our law enforcement efforts, can we doubt that the cure is worse than the disease? Can we doubt that the cure is a *source* of crime?

Against this conclusion, it is sometimes countered that studies show that a large proportion of criminal heroin addicts were criminals before they were addicts. Such studies would only refute the claim that the illegality of heroin is a source of crime if the claim was that heroin addiction turns otherwise law-abiding citizens into thieves. Rather, the claim is that the illegality of heroin (and thus its limited availability and almost unlimited price) places addicts in situations in which they *must* engage in theft continually and at a high level in order to keep a step ahead of the pains of withdrawal. Thus, even for addicts who already were criminals, heroin addiction must increase the amount they need to steal and must work to make them virtually immune to any attempts to wean them from a life of crime. Consequently, even if all criminal heroin addicts were criminals before they were addicts, the illegality of heroin would still be a source of crime because of the increased pressure it places on the addict to steal much and often.

Recently, attention has shifted from heroin to "crack," a highly addictive derivative of cocaine. Having learned nothing from our experience with heroin, we have applied to cocaine and crack the same policy that failed with heroin—with predictable results: First of all, our large-scale attempts to reduce the flow of cocaine into the country have failed. Says Trebach,

After seven years of a multi-billion dollar drug war, our prisons are filled to record levels, violent drug traffickers pollute our cities, and drug abuse is rampant. Despite the most aggressive drug war campaign in history, so much cocaine has been imported since 1981 that the price has dropped to one-third its former level. While some of our children now find it more difficult to buy marijuana, many find it much easier to buy crack and cocaine.[48]

According to law enforcement officials, "the amount of cocaine coming into the country has soared from 1,872 kilograms in fiscal year 1981 to 35,970 in fiscal 1987."[49] The General Accounting Office reports that U.S. efforts to reduce cultivation of drug crops in Bolivia and Columbia "have been almost entirely ineffective and the cultivation of drug crops has increased dramatically in both countries."[50] The *Wall Street Journal* reports that a kilogram of cocaine that cost between $55,000 and $65,000 in 1981 cost between $20,000 and $40,000 in 1987. They even report a "rock-bottom" price in Miami of $14,000 for a kilo.[51]

In 1988, the *National Law Journal* surveyed 181 chief prosecutors or their top drug deputies throughout the United States and reported that "nearly two-thirds of the country's top state and local prosecutors say they are having little to no impact in the fight against illegal narcotics."[52] This failing drug war is now costing federal, state, and local governments approximately $8 billion a year for police, courts, and prisons.[53] To that must be added the *nonfinancial* costs, such as increased violence among competing drug traffickers and increased corruption among law enforcement officials on the front line in the drug war. Nineteen eighty-eight saw the nation's capital reach and overtake its annual homicide record, with all experts attributing the surge in murders to the struggle to capture the lucrative drug market.[54] The *New York Times* reports that "researchers say there are now more than 100 cases each year in state and Federal courts in which law enforcement officials are charged or implicated in drug corruption."[55] Says William Green, assistant commissioner for internal affairs at the U.S. Customs Service, "The money that's being offered by the drug dealers is so big it is just hard to visualize."[56]

Though many who would call for the legalization of heroin (and less dangerous drugs than it, such as marijuana) hesitate to call for legalization of crack, it seems clear that our efforts to fight crack are failing and costing us more than the drug itself. Moreover, as Trebach suggests, there is reason to believe that our policy is contributing to the popularity of crack. The crackdown on importation of marijuana has given drug traffickers an incentive to shift to cocaine because much smaller amounts of it are needed for intoxication and thus much smaller amounts are needed to make big money. It remains the case that most drug arrests are for marijuana use or possession and that marijuana is a relatively safe drug.[57] The 1988 surgeon general's report lists tobacco as a more dangerous drug than marijuana.[58] Experts maintain that there are no documented marijuana user fatalities, and that there is no amount of marijuana that a person could possibly eat or smoke that would constitute a lethal dose. By contrast, even aspirin causes hundreds of deaths a year from overdose.[59] With the drugs that can cause death from overdose, the dangers have been blown wildly out of proportion. Trebach points out that although federal authorities documented 2,177 deaths from the most popular illicit drugs in 1985, between 400,000 and 500,000 people died from alcohol and tobacco during that same year. He adds that fifty-nine children aged seventeen and under died from drug overdoses in 1987, while "408 American children (from infants through the age of 14) were murdered by their parents in 1983"![60]

In sum, we have an antidrug policy that is failing at its own goals and succeeding only in adding to crime. First, there are the heroin addicts, who must steal to support their habits. Then, there are the cocaine and crack merchants who are offered fabulous incentives to provide illicit substances to a willing body of consumers. Next, there are the law enforcement officials who, after risking their lives for low salaries, are corrupted by nearly irresistible amounts of money. Finally, there are the otherwise law-abiding citizens who are made criminals because they use cocaine, a drug less harmful than tobacco, and those who are made criminals because they use marijuana, a drug that is surely safer than alcohol and arguably less deadly than aspirin. (Evidence from the eleven states that decriminalized marijuana possession in the 1970s suggests that decriminalization does not lead to increased use.)[61] And all this is occurring at a time when there is increasing evidence that what does work to reduce substance abuse is public education. Because this has succeeded in reducing alcohol and tobacco consumption and, in some cases, marijuana and cocaine consumption as well, it's time that we took the money we are wasting in the "war on drugs" and spent it on public education instead. Because that would be far less costly than the "war," this would leave over money to fight a more effective war against muggers and rapists rather than recreational drug users. Some form of decriminalization of marijuana, heroin, and cocaine would reduce the criminalization of law-abiding users, would reduce the need for addicts to steal, would reduce incentives to drug traffickers and smugglers, and would free up personnel and resources for a more effective war against the crimes that people most fear.

In the face of all this, it is hard to believe that we do not know how to reduce crime at all. It is hard not to share the frustration expressed by Norval Morris, dean of the University of Chicago Law School: "It is trite but it remains true that the main causes of crime are social and economic. The question arises whether people really care. The solutions are so obvious. *It's almost as if America wished for a high crime rate.*"[62] If this is so, then the *system's failure is only in the eye of the victim: For those in control, it is a roaring success!*

HOW CRIME PAYS: ERIKSON AND DURKHEIM

Kai T. Erikson has suggested in his book *Wayward Puritans* that societies derive benefit from the existence of crime and thus there is reason to believe that social institutions work to maintain rather than to eliminate crime. Since the Pyrrhic defeat theory draws heavily upon this insight, it will serve to clarify my own view if we compare it with Erikson's.

Professor Erikson's theory is based on the view of crime that finds expression in one of the classic books on sociological theory, *The Division of Labor in Society*, by Emile Durkheim. Writing toward the end of the nineteenth century, Durkheim

> had suggested that crime (and by extension other forms of deviation) may actually perform a needed service to society by drawing people together in a common posture of anger and indignation. The deviant individual violates rules of conduct which the rest of the community holds in high respect; and when these people come together to express their outrage over the offense and to bear witness against the offender, they develop a tighter bond of solidarity than existed earlier.[63]

The solidarity that holds a community together, in this view, is a function of the intensity with which the members of the community share a living sense of the group's cultural identity, of the boundary between acceptable and unacceptable behavior that gives the group its distinctive nature. It is necessary, then, for the existence of a community *as a community* that its members learn and constantly relearn the location of its "boundaries." Erikson writes that these boundaries are learned in dramatic confrontations with

policing agents whose special business it is to guard the cultural integrity of the community. Whether these confrontations take the form of criminal trials, excommunication hearings, courts-martial, or even case conferences, they act as boundary-maintaining devices in the sense that they demonstrate to whatever audience is concerned where the line is drawn between behavior that belongs in the special universe of the group and behavior that does not.[64]

In brief, this means not only that a community makes good use of unacceptable behavior *but that it positively needs unacceptable behavior.* Not only does unacceptable behavior cast in relief the terrain of behavior acceptable to the community but also it reinforces the intensity with which the members of the community identify that terrain as their shared territory. On this view, *deviant behavior is an ingredient in the glue that holds a community together.* "This," Erikson continues,

raises a delicate theoretical issue. If we grant that human groups often derive benefit from deviant behavior, can we then assume that they are organized in such a way as to promote this resource? Can we assume, in other words, that forces operate in the social structure to recruit offenders and to commit them to long periods of service in the deviant ranks? . . .

Looking at the matter from a long-range historical perspective, it is fair to conclude that prisons have done a conspicuously poor job of reforming the convicts placed in their custody; but the very consistency of this failure may have a peculiar logic of its own. Perhaps we find it difficult to change the worst of our penal practices because we expect *the prison to harden the inmate's commitment to deviant forms of behavior and draw him more deeply into the deviant ranks.*[65]

In other words, based on Durkheim's recognition that societies benefit from the existence of deviants, Erikson entertains the view that societies have institutions whose unannounced function is to recruit and maintain a reliable supply of deviants. Modified for our purposes, Erikson's view would become the hypothesis that the American criminal justice system fails to reduce crime because a visible criminal population is essential to maintaining the "boundaries" that mark the cultural identity of American society and to maintaining the solidarity between those who share that identity. In other words, in its failure, the criminal justice system succeeds in providing some of the cement necessary to hold American society together as a society.

It is not my intention to do battle with the Durkheim-Erikson thesis. Rather, my aim is to acknowledge my debt to that thesis and state the difference between it and the view that I will defend. The debt is to the insight that societies may promote behavior that they seem to desire to stamp out, that failure to eliminate deviance may be a success of some sort.

The difference, on the other hand, is this: Both Durkheim and Erikson jump from the *general* proposition that the failure to eliminate deviance promotes social solidarity to the *specific* conclusion that the form in which this failure occurs in a particular society can be explained by the contribution the failure makes to promoting consensus on shared beliefs and thus feelings of social solidarity. This is a "jump" because it leaves out the important question of how it is that a social group forms its particular consensus around one set of shared beliefs rather than another. That is, Durkheim and Erikson implicitly assume that a consensus already exists (at least virtually) and that deviance is promoted in order to manifest and reinforce it. This leads to the view that social institutions reflect beliefs that are already in people's heads and already largely and spontaneously shared by all of them. In my view, even if it is granted that societies work to strengthen feelings of social solidarity, the set of beliefs about the world around which those feelings will crystallize are by no means already in people's heads and spontaneously shared. A consensus is made, not born, although, again, I do not mean that it is made intentionally. It is created by social institutions, not just reflected by social institutions. Thus, the failure to stamp out deviance does not simply reinforce a consensus that already exists; it is part of the process by which a very particular consensus is created. In developing the Pyrrhic defeat theory, I try to show how the failure of criminal justice works to create and reinforce a very particular set of beliefs about the world, about what is dangerous and what is not, who is a threat and who is not. This does not merely shore up general feelings of social solidarity; it allows those feelings to be attached to a social order characterized by striking disparities of wealth, power, and privilege; and considerable injustice.

SUMMARY

In this chapter, I have tried to establish the first part of the Pyrrhic defeat theory, namely, that the war on crime is a failure and an avoidable one: The American criminal justice system—by which I mean the entire process from lawmaking to law enforcing—has done little or nothing to reduce the enormous amount of crime that characterizes our society and threatens our citizens. Over the last several decades, crime has risen, although in recent years it has declined. No doubt demographic changes, most significantly the growth followed by the decrease in the number of youngsters in the crime-prone years, have played a role in this. This in itself suggests that criminal justice policy and practice cannot be credited with the recent decline. At the same time, however, neither can it be thought on this basis that criminal justice could not reduce (or reduce further) the crime we have. To support this, I have shown that crime is neither a simple and unavoidable consequence of the number of youngsters nor of the degree of urbanization. I have suggested that there are a number of things we have good reason to believe would succeed in reducing crime—effective gun control, decriminalization of illicit drugs, and, of course, amelioration of poverty—that we refuse to do. I conclude the chapter by showing that the Pyrrhic defeat theory shares, with the Durkheim-Erikson view of the functional nature of crime, the idea that societies may promote behavior that they seem to want to eliminate. My theory differs from their view in insisting that the failure to stamp out crime is functional for only a certain part of our society.

STUDY QUESTIONS

1. Why do crime rates rise and fall?

2. What causes crime?

3. What excuses have been given for our inability to reduce the amount of crime we have? How do you evaluate these excuses?

4. Do you think we could reduce the amount of crime? How?

5. What does it mean to say that "crime is functional for a society"? How does the Pyrrhic defeat theory differ on this from the Durkheim-Erikson theory?

6. Do you think that our current war on drugs is working? Do you think that legalizing all or some illicit drugs would reduce crime? If so, would you agree to legalization?

2

A Crime by Any Other Name . . .

*If one individual inflicts a bodily injury
upon another which leads to the death
of the person attacked we call it manslaughter; on the other hand, if the
attacker knows beforehand that the
blow will be fatal we call it murder.
Murder has also been committed if
society places hundreds of workers in
such a position that they inevitably
come to premature and unnatural ends.
Their death is as violent as if they had
been stabbed or shot. . . . Murder has been
committed if society knows perfectly
well that thousands of workers cannot
avoid being sacrificed so long as these
conditions are allowed to continue.
Murder of this sort is just as culpable
as the murder committed by an
individual.*

Frederick Engels, *The Condition of the Working Class in England*

WHAT'S IN A NAME?

If it takes you an hour to read this chapter, by the time you reach
the last page, two of your fellow citizens will have been murdered.

During that same time, at least four Americans will die as a result of unhealthy or unsafe conditions in the workplace! Although these work-related deaths could have been prevented, they are not called murders. Why not? Doesn't a crime by any other name still cause misery and suffering? What's in a name?

The fact is that the label "crime" is not used in America to name all or the worst of the actions that cause misery and suffering to Americans. It is primarily reserved for the dangerous actions of the poor.

In the March 14, 1976 edition of the *Washington Star*, a front-page article appeared with the headline: "Mine Is Closed 26 Deaths Late." The article read in part:

> *Why, the relatives [of the twenty-six dead miners] ask, did the mine ventilation fail and allow pockets of volatile methane gas to build up in a shaft 2,300 feet below the surface?*
>
> *Why wasn't the mine cleared as soon as supervisors spotted evidence of methane gas near where miners were driving huge machines into the 61-foot-high coal seam? . . .*
>
> *In Washington, Sen. Harrison Williams, D-N.J., said investigators of the Senate Labor and Welfare Committee which he chairs have found that there have been 1,250 safety violations at the 13-year-old mine since 1970. Fifty-seven of those violations were serious enough for federal inspectors to order the mine closed and 21 of those were in cases where federal inspectors felt there was imminent danger to the lives of the miners working there, he said. . . .*
>
> *Federal inspectors said the most recent violations found at the mine were three found in the ventilation system on Monday—the day before 15 miners were killed.*[1]

Next to the continuation of this story was another, headlined: "Mass Murder Claims Six in Pennsylvania."[2] It described the shooting death of a husband and wife, their three children, and a friend in a Philadelphia suburb. This was murder, maybe even mass murder. My only question is, "Why wasn't the death of the miners also murder?"

Why do twenty-six dead miners amount to a "disaster" and six dead suburbanites a "mass murder"? "Murder" suggests a murderer, whereas "disaster" suggests the work of impersonal forces. If more than 1,000 safety violations had been found in the mine— three the day before the first explosion—was no one responsible for failing to eliminate the hazards? Was no one responsible for *preventing* the hazards? If someone could have prevented the hazards and did not, does that person not bear responsibility for the deaths of twenty-six men? Is he less evil because he did not want them to die although he chose to leave them in jeopardy? Is he not a murderer, perhaps even a *mass* murderer?

These questions are at this point rhetorical. My aim is not to discuss this case but rather to point to the blinders we wear when we look at such a "disaster." Perhaps there will be an investigation. Perhaps someone will be held responsible. Perhaps he will be fined. But will he be tried for *murder?* Will anyone think of him as a murderer? *And if not, why not?* Would the miners not be safer if such people were treated as murderers? Might they not still be alive? Will a president of the United States address the Yale Law School and recommend mandatory prison sentences for such people? Will he mean these people when he says,

> These relatively few, persistent criminals who cause so much misery and fear are really the core of the problem. The rest of the American people have a right to protection from their violence[?][3]

Didn't those miners have a right to protection from the violence that took their lives? *And if not, why not?*

Once we are ready to ask this question seriously, we are in a position to see that the reality of crime—that is, the acts we label crime, the acts we think of as crime, the actors and actions we treat as criminal—is *created:* It is an image shaped by decisions as to *what* will be called crime and *who* will be treated as a criminal.

THE CARNIVAL MIRROR

It is sometimes coyly observed that the quickest and cheapest way to eliminate crime would be to throw out all the criminal laws. There is a thin sliver of truth to this view. Without criminal laws, there would indeed by no "crimes." There would, however, still be dangerous acts. This is why we cannot really solve our crime problem quite so simply. The criminal law *labels* some acts "crimes." In doing this, it identifies those acts as so dangerous that we must use the extreme methods of criminal justice to protect ourselves against them. This does not mean that the criminal law *creates* crime—it simply "mirrors" real dangers that threaten us. What is true of the criminal law is true of the whole justice system. If police did not arrest or prosecutors charge or juries convict, there would be no "criminals." This does not mean that police or prosecutors or juries create criminals any more than legislators do. They *react* to real dangers in society. The criminal justice system—from lawmakers to law enforcers—is just a mirror of the real dangers that lurk in our midst. *Or so we are told.*

How accurate is this mirror? We need to answer this in order to know whether or how well the criminal justice system is protecting us against the real threats to our well-being. The more accurate a mirror, the more the image it shows is created by the reality it reflects. The more misshapen a mirror is, the more the distorted image it shows is created by the mirror, not by the reality reflected. It is in this sense that I will argue that the image of crime is created: The American criminal justice system is a mirror that shows a distorted image of the dangers that threaten us—an image created more by the shape of the mirror than by the reality reflected. What do we see when we look in the criminal justice mirror?

On the morning of September 16, 1975, the *Washington Post* carried an article in its local news section headlined "Arrest Data Reveal Profile of a Suspect." The article reported the results of a study of crime in Prince George's County, a suburb of Washington, D.C. It read in part that

> *The typical suspect in serious crime in Prince George's County is a black male, aged 14 to 19, who lives in the area inside the Capital Beltway where more than half of the county's 64,371 reported crimes were committed in 1974. . . .*
>
> *[The study] presents a picture of persons, basically youths, committing a crime once every eight minutes in Prince George's County.*[4]

This report is hardly a surprise. The portrait it paints of "the typical suspect in serious crime" is probably a pretty good rendering of the image lurking in the back of the minds of most people who fear crime. Furthermore, although the crime rate in Prince George's County is somewhat above the national average and its black population somewhat above that of the average suburban county, the portrait generally fits the national picture presented in the FBI's *Uniform Crime Reports* for the same year, 1974. In Prince George's County, "youths between the ages of 15 and 19 were accused of committing nearly half [45.5 percent] of all 1974 crimes."[5] For the nation in 1974, the FBI reported that persons in this age group accounted for 39.5 percent of arrests for the FBI Index crimes (criminal homicide, forcible rape, robbery, aggravated assault, burglary, larceny, and motor vehicle theft.)[6] In 1980, this age group made up 39 percent of Index crime arrests.[7] In Prince George's County, where blacks make up approximately 25 percent of the population, "blacks were accused of 58 percent of all serious crimes."[8] In the nation, where blacks made up 11.4 percent of the population in 1974, they accounted for 34.2 percent of arrests for Index crimes.[9] In 1986, blacks made up 12 percent of the nation's population and 27 percent of Index crime arrests.[10] This, then, is the Typical Criminal, the one whose portrait President Reagan described as "that of a stark, staring face, a face that belongs to a frightening reality of our time—the face of a human predator, the face of the habitual criminal. Nothing in nature is more cruel and more dangerous."[11] This is the face that we see in the criminal justice mirror. Whose face is it? Let us look more closely.

He is, first of all, a *he*.[12] Second, he is a *youth*—most likely under the age of twenty. Third, he is predominantly *urban*—although increasingly suburban.[13] Fourth, he is disproportionately *black*—blacks are arrested for Index crimes at a rate three times that of their percentage in the national population. Finally, he is *poor*:

> *Of the 1.3 million criminal offenders handled each day by some agency of the United States correctional system, the vast majority (80 percent on some estimates) are members of the lowest 15-percent income level—that percent which is below the "poverty level" as defined by the Social Security Administration.[14]*

The President's Commission reports that

> *from arrest records, probation reports, and prison statistics, a "portrait" of the offender emerges that progressively highlights the disadvantaged character of his life. The offender at the end of the road in prison is likely to be a member of the lowest social and economic groups in the country.[15]*

This is the Typical Criminal feared by most law-abiding Americans. His crime, according to former Attorney General John Mitchell (who was by no means a typical criminal), is forcing us "to change the fabric of our society, . . . forcing us, a free people, to alter our pattern of life, . . . to withdraw from our neighbors, to fear all strangers and to limit our activities to 'safe' areas."[16] These poor, young, urban (disproportionately) black males comprise the core of the enemy forces in the war against crime. They are the heart of a vicious, unorganized guerrilla army, threatening the lives, limbs, and possessions of the law-abiding members of society—necessitating recourse to the ultimate weapons of force and detention in our common defense. They are the "career criminals" President Reagan had in mind when he told the International Association of Chiefs of Police, assuring them of the tough stance that the federal government would take in the fight against crime, that "a small number of criminals are responsible for an enormous amount of the crime in American society."[17]

How do we know who the criminals are who so seriously endanger us that we must stop them with force and lock them in prisons? "From the arrest records, probation reports, and prison statistics," the authors of *The Challenge of Crime in a Free Society* tell us, the " 'portrait' of the offender emerges."[18] *These sources are not merely objective readings taken at different stages in the criminal justice process: Each of them represents human decisions.* "Prison statistics" and "probation reports" reflect *decisions* of juries on who gets convicted and decisions of judges on who gets probation or prison and for how long. "Arrest records" reflect decisions about which crimes to investigate and which suspects to take into custody. All of these decisions rest on the most fundamental of all *decisions:* the decisions of legislators as to which acts shall be labeled "crimes" in the first place.

The reality of crime as the target of our criminal justice system and as perceived by the general populace is not a simple objective threat to which the system reacts: *It is a reality that takes shape as it is filtered through a series of human decisions running the full gamut of the criminal justice system*—from the lawmakers who determine what behavior shall be in the province of criminal justice to the law enforcers who decide which individuals will be brought within that province.

Note that by emphasizing the role of "human decisions," I do not mean to suggest that the reality of crime is voluntarily and intentionally "created" by individual "decision makers." Their decisions are themselves shaped by the social system, much as a child's decision to become an engineer rather than a Samurai warrior is shaped by the social system. Thus, to have a full explanation of how the reality of crime is created, we have to understand how our society is structured in a way that leads people to make the decisions that they do. In other words, these decisions are part of the social phenomena to be explained—they are not the explanation.

For the present, however, I emphasize the role of the decisions themselves for the following reasons: First, they are conspicuous points in the social process, easy to spot and verify empirically. Second, because they are decisions aimed at protecting us from the dangers in our midst, we can compare the decisions to the real dangers and determine whether they are responding to the real dangers. Third, because the reality of crime—the real actions labeled crimes, the real individuals identified as criminals, the real faces

we watch in the news as they travel from arrest to court to prison—
results from these decisions, we can determine whether that reality
corresponds to the real dangers in our society. Where that reality does correspond to the real dangers, we can say that the reality
of crime simply reflects the real dangers in society. Where the
reality of crime does not correspond to the real dangers, we can
say that it is a reality *created* by those decisions—although, ultimately this is a shorthand way of saying that it is a reality created
by the social system that leads people to make the decisions that
they do.

It is to capture this way of looking at the relation between the
reality of crime and the real dangers "out there" in society that I
refer to the criminal justice system as a "mirror." Who and what we
see in this mirror is a function of the decisions about who and what
are criminal, and so on. Our poor, young, urban, black male, who is
so well represented in arrest records and prison populations, appears not simply because of the undeniable threat he poses to the
rest of society. As dangerous as he may be, he would not appear in
the criminal justice mirror *if* it had not been decided that the acts
he performs should be labeled "crimes," *if* it had not been decided
that he should be arrested for those crimes, *if* he had access to a
lawyer who could persuade a jury to acquit him and perhaps a
judge to expunge his arrest record, and *if* it had not been decided
that he is the type of individual and his the type of crime that
warrants imprisonment. *The shape of the reality we see in the criminal justice mirror is created by all these decisions.* What we want to
know is how accurately the reality we see in this mirror reflects the
real dangers that threaten us in society.

It is not my view that this reality is created out of nothing. The
mugger, the rapist, the murderer, the burglar, the robber all pose a
definite threat to our well-being, and they ought to be dealt with in
ways that effectively reduce that threat to the minimum level possible (without making the criminal justice system itself a threat to
our lives and liberties). Of central importance, however, is that the
threat posed by the Typical Criminal is not the greatest threat to
which we are exposed. The acts of the Typical Criminal are not the
only acts that endanger us, nor are they the acts that endanger us
the most. We have a greater chance (as I show below) of being
killed or disabled, for example, by an occupational injury or disease, by unnecessary surgery, or by shoddy emergency medical
services than by aggravated assault or even homicide! Yet even
though these threats to our well-being are graver than that posed

by our poor, young, urban, black males, they do not shc
FBI's Index of serious crimes. The individuals who are
for them do not turn up in arrest records or prison statistics. *I n...y
never become part of the reality reflected in the criminal justice mirror,
although the danger they pose is at least as great and often greater
than those who do!*

Similarly, the general public loses more money *by far* (as I show
below) from price-fixing and monopolistic practices and from consumer deception and embezzlement than from all the property
crimes in the FBI's Index combined. Yet these far more costly acts
are either not criminal, or if technically criminal, not prosecuted,
or if prosecuted, not punished, or if punished, only mildly. In any
event, although the individuals responsible for these acts take
more money out of the ordinary citizen's pocket than our Typical
Criminal, they rarely show up in arrest statistics and almost never
in prison populations. *Their faces rarely appear in the criminal justice mirror, although the danger they pose is at least as great and often
greater than those who do.*

The inescapable conclusion is that the criminal justice system
does not simply *reflect* the reality of crime; it has a hand in *creating*
the reality we see.

The criminal justice system is like a mirror in which society can
see the face of the evil in its midst. Because the system deals with
some evil and not with others, because it treats some evils as the
gravest and treats some of the gravest evils as minor, the image it
throws back is distorted like the image in a carnival mirror. Thus,
the image cast back is false, not because it is invented out of thin
air, but because the proportions of the real are distorted: Large
becomes small and small large; grave becomes minor and minor
grave. Like a carnival mirror, although nothing is reflected that
does not exist in the world, the image is more a creation of the
mirror than a picture of the world.

If criminal justice really gives us a carnival-mirror image of
"crime," we are doubly deceived. First, we are led to believe that
the criminal justice system is protecting us against the gravest
threats to our well-being when, in fact, the system is only protecting us against some threats and not necessarily the gravest ones.
We are deceived about how much protection we are receiving and
thus left vulnerable. We are deceived about what threatens us and
are, therefore, unable to take appropriate defensive action. The
second deception is just the other side of this one. If people believe
that the carnival mirror is a true mirror—that is, if they believe

that the criminal justice system simply *reacts* to the gravest threats to their well-being—they come to believe that whatever is the target of the criminal justice system must be the greatest threat to their well-being. In other words, if people believe that the most drastic of society's weapons are wielded by the criminal justice system *in reaction to* the gravest dangers to society, they will believe the reverse as well: that those actions that call forth the most drastic of society's weapons *must be* those that pose the gravest dangers to society.

There is a strange alchemy that takes place when people uncritically accept the legitimacy of their institutions: What *needs* justification becomes *proof* of justification. People come to believe that prisoners must be criminals *because* they are in prison and that the inmates of insane asylums must be crazy *because* they are in insane asylums.[19] The criminal justice system's use of extreme measures—such as force and imprisonment—is thought to be justified by the extreme gravity of the dangers it combats. By this alchemy, these extreme measures become *proof* of the extreme gravity of those dangers, and the first deception, which merely misleads the public about how much protection the criminal justice system is actually providing, is transformed into the second, which deceives the public into believing that the acts and actors that are the target of the criminal justice system pose the gravest threats to its well-being. Thus, the system may not only fail to protect us from dangers as great or greater than those listed in the FBI Crime Index, it may do still greater damage by creating the false security of the belief that only the acts on the FBI Index really threaten us and require control.

In the following discussion, I describe how and why the criminal justice carnival mirror distorts the image it creates.

CRIMINAL JUSTICE AS CREATIVE ART

In Chapter 1, I introduced the Pyrrhic defeat explanation for the "failure" of criminal justice in America: Criminal justice *fails* (or, what amounts to the same thing, crime is maintained) in order to project a particular *image* of crime.

It is the task of this chapter and the next to prove that the reality of crime is *created* and that it is created in a way that promotes a particular *image* of crime: *The image that serious crime—and therefore the greatest danger to society—is the work of the poor.* The notion that the reality of crime is created is derived from

Richard Quinney's theory of the *social reality of crime*.[20] Because the meaning I attribute to this notion is different from the meaning Quinney gives it, it will help in presenting my view to compare it to Quinney's.

Quinney maintains that crime has a "social reality" rather than an objective reality. What he means can be explained with an example: Wherein lies the reality of money? Certainly not in the "objective" characteristics of green printed paper. It exists rather in the "social" meaning attributed to that paper and the pattern of "social" behavior that is a consequence of that meaning. If people did not act as if that green printed paper had value, it would be just green paper, not real money. The reality of a crime *as a crime* does not lie simply in the objective characteristics of an action. It lies in the "social" meaning attached to that action and the pattern of "social" behavior—particularly the behavior of criminal justice officials—that is a product of that meaning. I think Quinney is right in this. When I speak of the reality of crime, I am referring to much more than physical actions like stabbing or shooting. I mean the reality that a society gives those physical actions by labeling them and treating them as criminal.

Quinney further maintains that this reality of crime is *created*. By this he means that crime is a definition of behavior applied by lawmakers and other criminal justice decision makers. "Crime," Quinney writes,

> is a definition *of behavior that is conferred on some persons by others. Agents of the law (legislators, police, prosecutors, and judges), representing segments of a politically organized society, are responsible for formulating and administering criminal laws. Persons and behaviors, therefore, become criminal because of the* formulation *and* application *of criminal definitions. Thus,* crime *is* created.[21]

Now this is *not* what I have in mind when I say that the reality of crime is created. Here is the difference. Quinney's position amounts to this: Crimes are established by the criminal law and the criminal law is a human creation; ergo, crime is created. This is true, but it does not take us very far. After all, who can deny that crime is created *in this sense?* Only someone who has been hypnotized into forgetting that law books are written by lawmakers could deny that "crime" is a label that human beings apply to certain actions. What *is* controversial, however, is whether the label is applied appropriately. "Crime," after all, is not merely a sound—it is a word with a generally accepted meaning. It means roughly "an intentional action that is harmful to society." (Now, of course, "crime" has a technical definition, namely, "an act prohibited by a criminal law." The point of prohibiting an act by the criminal law is to protect society from an injurious act. Thus, though any act prohibited by criminal law is rightly labeled a crime in the technical sense, not every act so prohibited is rightly prohibited, and thus not every act labeled "crime" is appropriately labeled. To determine whether the label crime is applied appropriately, we must use the more general definition.) The label is applied appropriately when it is used to identify all, or at least the worst of, the acts that are harmful to society. The label is applied inappropriately when it is attached to any harmless act *or* when it is not attached to seriously harmful acts. When I argue that the reality of crime is created, what I mean is that the label "crime" has not been applied appropriately.

One might ask why the inappropriate use of the label "crime" is a reason for saying that crime is created. My answer is this: By calling something *created*, we call attention to the fact that human actors are responsible for it. By calling crime created, I point to human actors rather than objective dangers as determining the shape that the reality of crime takes in our society. If the label "crime" is consistently applied to the most dangerous or harmful acts, then it is misleading to point to the fact that human decision makers are responsible for how the label is applied because their decisions are dictated by compelling objective reasons. Rather than creating a reality, their decisions simply ratify a reality that already exists. On the other hand, if the label is not applied appropriately, it is sensible to assume that it is applied for reasons that lie with the decision makers and not in the realm of objective dangers. This means that when the label "crime" is applied inappropriately, it is essential to call attention to the fact that human actors are responsible for it. In other words, it is precisely when the label "crime" is applied inappropriately that it is important to point out that the reality of crime is *created*.

By calling crime created, I want to emphasize the human responsibility for the shape of crime, not in the trivial sense that humans write the criminal law, *but rather to call attention to the fact that decisions as to what to label and treat as crime are not compelled by objective dangers, and thus that to understand the reality of crime, we must look to the social processes that shape those decisions.*

By calling crime created, I suggest that our picture of crime—the portrait that emerges from arrest statistics, prison populations, politicians' speeches, news media, and fictionalized presentations, the portrait that in turn influences lawmakers and criminal justice policymakers—is not a photograph of the real dangers that threaten us. Its features are not simply traced from the real dangers in the social world. Instead, it is a piece of creative art. It is a picture in which some dangers are portrayed and others omitted. Because it cannot be explained as a straight reflection of real dangers, we must look elsewhere to understand the shape it takes.

This argument, which will occupy us in this chapter and the next leads to *five hypotheses* about the way in which criminal justice policy is made. To demonstrate that the reality of crime is created, that the criminal justice system is a carnival mirror that gives us a distorted image of the dangers that threaten us, I will try to prove that at each of the crucial decision-making points in criminal justice, the decisions made do not reflect the real and most serious dangers we face.

1. **Of the Decisions of Legislators** That the definitions of crime in the criminal law do not reflect the only or the most dangerous of antisocial behaviors.
2. **Of the Decisions of Police and Prosecutors** That the decisions on whom to arrest or charge do not reflect the only or the most dangerous behaviors legally defined as "criminal."
3. **Of the Decisions of Juries and Judges** That criminal convictions do not reflect the only or the most dangerous individuals among those arrested and charged.
4. **Of the Decisions of Sentencing Judges** That sentencing decisions do not reflect the goal of protecting society from the only or the most dangerous of those convicted by meting out punishments proportionate to the harmfulness of the crime committed.
5. **Of All These Decisions Taken Together** That what criminal justice policy decisions (in hypotheses 1 to 4) *do* reflect is the implicit identification of crime with the dangerous acts of the poor.

The Pyrrhic defeat theory is composed of these five hypotheses, *plus* the proposition that the criminal justice system is failing in avoidable ways to reduce crime (argued in Chapter 1), *plus* the *historical inertia* explanation of how this failure is generated and left uncorrected because of the ideological benefits it produces (argued in Chapter 4). In presenting this explanation, I try to show how the decisions that create the reality of crime are caused by historical forces and left unchanged because the particular distribution of costs and benefits to which those decisions give rise serves to make the system self-reinforcing.

A CRIME BY ANY OTHER NAME . . .

Think of a crime, any crime. Picture the first "crime" that comes into your mind. What do you see? The odds are you are not imagining a mining company executive sitting at his desk, calculating the costs of proper safety precautions and deciding not to invest in them. Probably what you do see with your mind's eye is one person physically attacking another or robbing something from another on the threat of physical attack. Look more closely. What does the attacker look like? It's a safe bet he (and it is a *he*, of course) is not wearing a suit and tie. In fact, my hunch is that you—like me, like almost anyone in America—picture a young, tough, lower-class male when the thought of crime first pops into your head. You (we) picture someone like the Typical Criminal described above. The crime itself is one in which the Typical Criminal sets out to attack or rob some specific person.

This last point is important. What it indicates is that we have a mental image not only of the Typical Criminal, but also of the Typical Crime. If the Typical Criminal is a young lower-class male, the Typical Crime is *one-on-one harm*—where harm means either physical injury or loss of something valuable or both. If you have any doubts that this is the Typical Crime, look at any random sample of police or private eye shows on television. How often do you see Jim Rockford or "The Equalizer" investigate consumer fraud or failure to remove occupational hazards? A study of TV crime shows by The Media Institute in Washington, D.C., indicates that, while the fictional criminals portrayed on television are on the average both older and wealthier than the real criminals who figure in the FBI *Uniform Crime Reports*, "TV crimes are almost 12 times as likely to be violent as crimes committed in the real world."[22] In short, TV crime shows broadcast the double-edged message that the "one-on-one" crimes of the poor are the typical crimes of all and thus not uniquely caused by the pressures of poverty; *and* that the criminal justice system pursues rich and poor alike—thus, when the criminal justice system happens mainly to pounce on the poor in real life, it is not out of any class bias.

In addition to the steady diet of fictionalized TV violence and crime, there has been an increase in the graphic display of crime on many TV news programs. A new breed of nonfictional "tabloid" TV show has appeared in which viewers are shown films of actual violent crimes, blood and screams and all, or reenactments of actual violent crimes, sometimes using the actual victims playing themselves! An article in *The Washingtonian* says that the word around two prominent local TV news programs is, "If it bleeds, it leads."[23] The *Wall Street Journal*, reporting on the phenomenon of tabloid TV, informs us that "Television has gone tabloid. The seamy underside of life is being bared in a new rash of true-crime series and contrived-confrontation talk shows."[24] Is there any surprise that a survey by *McCall's* indicates that its readers have grown more afraid of crime in the past five years—even though this period has witnessed a decrease in crime rates?[25]

It is important to identify this model of the Typical Crime because it functions like a set of blinders. It keeps us from calling a mine disaster a mass murder even if twenty-six men are killed, even if someone is responsible for the unsafe conditions in which they worked and died. In fact, I argue that this particular piece of mental furniture so blocks our view that it keeps us from using the criminal justice system to protect ourselves from the greatest threats to our persons and possessions.

What keeps a mine disaster from being a mass murder in our eyes is the fact that it is not one-on-one harm. What is important here is not the numbers but the *intent to harm someone*. An attack by a gang on one or more persons or an attack by one individual on several fits the model of one-on-one harm. That is, for each person harmed there is at least one individual who wanted to harm that person. Once he selects his victim, the rapist, the mugger, the murderer, all want this person they have selected to suffer. A mine executive, on the other hand, does not want his employees to be harmed. He would truly prefer that there be no accident, no injured or dead miners. What he does want is something legitimate. It is what he has been hired to get: maximum profits at minimum costs. If he cuts corners to save a buck, he is just doing his job. If twenty-six men die because he cut corners on safety, we may think him crude or callous but not a killer. He is, at most, responsible for an *indirect harm*, not a one-on-one harm. For this, he may even be criminally indictable for violating safety regulations—but not for murder. The twenty-six men are dead as an unwanted consequence of his (perhaps overzealous or undercautious) pursuit of a legitimate goal. So, unlike the Typical Criminal, he has not committed the Typical Crime—or so we generally believe. As a result, twenty-six men are dead who might be alive now if cutting corners of the kind that leads to loss of life, whether suffering is specifically intended or not, were treated as murder.

This is my point. Because we accept the belief—encouraged by our politicians' statements about crime and by the media's portrayal of crime—that the model for crime is one person specifically intending to harm another, we accept a legal system that leaves us unprotected against much greater dangers to our lives and well-being than those threatened by the Typical Criminal. Before developing this point further, let us anticipate and deal with a likely objection. The defender of the present legal order is likely to respond to my argument at this point with irritation. Because this will surely turn to outrage in a few pages, let us talk to him now while the possibility of rational communication still exists.

The Defender of the Present Legal Order (I'll call him "the Defender" for short whenever it is necessary to deal with his objections in the future) is neither a foolish nor an evil person. He is not a racist, nor is he oblivious to the need for reform in the criminal justice system to make it more evenhanded and for reform in the larger society to make equal opportunity a reality for all Americans. In general, his view is that—given our limited resources, particularly the resource of human altruism—the political and legal institutions we have are the best that can be. What is necessary is to make them work better and to weed out those who are intent on making them work shoddily. His response to my argument at this point is that the criminal justice system *should* occupy itself primarily with one-on-one harm. Harms of the sort exemplified in the "mine disaster" are really *not* murders and are better dealt with through stricter government enforcement of safety regulations. He would admit that this enforcement has been rather lax and recommend that it be improved. Basically, though, he thinks this division of labor is right because it fits our ordinary moral sensibilities.

The Defender maintains that, according to our ordinary moral notions, someone who wants to do another harm and does is really more evil than someone who jeopardizes others while pursuing legitimate goals but wishes no one harm. Being directly harmed by another person, he believes, is terrifying in a way that being harmed impersonally, say, by a safety hazard, is not—even if the resultant injury is the same in both cases. What's more, we should be tolerant of the one responsible for lax safety measures because he is pursuing a legitimate goal, that is, his dangerous action occurs as part of a productive activity, something that ultimately adds to social wealth and thus benefits everyone—whereas the doer of direct harm benefits no one but himself. Thus, the latter is rightfully in the province of the criminal justice system with its drastic weapons, and the former is appropriately dealt with by the milder forms of regulation.

Moreover, the Defender insists, the crimes identified as such by the criminal justice system are imposed on their victims totally against their will, whereas the victims of occupational hazards chose to accept their risky jobs and thus have in some degree consented to subject themselves to the dangers. Where dangers are consented to, the appropriate response is not blame but correction, and this is most efficiently done by regulation rather than with the guilt-seeking methods of criminal justice.

I think that the Defender's argument rests on three errors. First, he overestimates the reality of the "free consent" with which workers enter their jobs. Although no one is forced at gunpoint to accept any particular job, virtually everyone is forced by the requirements of necessity to take some job. Thus, at best, workers can choose among the dangers present at various worksites and not choose to face no danger at all. Moreover, workers can only choose jobs where there are openings, which means they cannot simply pick their place of employment at will. Consequently, for all intents and purposes, most workers *must* face the dangers of the jobs that are available to them.

Second, the Defender's argument errs by treating our ordinary notions of morality as a single consistent fabric rather than the crazy quilt of conflicting values and ideals it is. In other words, even if it fits some of our ordinary moral notions to believe that one-on-one harm is more evil than indirect harm, other aspects of our ordinary moral sensibilities lead to the opposite conclusion. For instance, it is a feature of both our moral sensibilities and our legal system that we often hold people culpable for harms they have caused through negligence or recklessness, even though they wished to harm no one—thus the kid-glove treatment meted out to those responsible for occupational hazards and the like is no simple reflection of our ordinary moral sensibilities, as the Defender claims. Moreover, compare the mine executive who cuts corners to the typical murderer. Most murders, we know, are committed in the heat of some passion like rage or jealousy. Two lovers or neighbors or relatives find themselves in a heated argument. One (usually it is a matter of chance *which* one) picks up a weapon and strikes the other a fatal blow. Such a person is clearly a murderer and rightly subject to punishment by the criminal justice system. Is this person more evil than the executive who chooses not to pay for safety equipment? I think a perfectly good case can be made that starts with our ordinary moral notions and ends up with the opposite conclusion.

The one who kills in a heated argument kills from passion. What he does he probably would not do in a cooler moment. He is likely to feel "he was not himself." The one he killed was someone he knew, a specific person who at the time seemed to him to be the embodiment of all that frustrates him, someone whose very existence makes life unbearable. I do not mean to suggest that this is true of all killers, although there is reason to believe it is true of many. Nor do I mean to suggest that such a state of mind justifies murder. What it does do, however, is suggest that the killer's action, arising out of passion, does not show general disdain for the lives of his fellows. Here is where he is different from the doer of *indirect harm.* Our absentee killer intended harm to no one in particular, but he *knew his acts were likely to harm someone*—and once someone is harmed, *he* (the victim) is someone in particular. Nor can our absentee killer claim that "he was not himself." His act is done, not out of passion, but out of cool reckoning. Precisely here his evil shows. In his willingness to jeopardize the lives of unspecified others who pose him no real or imaginary threat in order to make a few dollars, he shows his general disdain for all his fellow human beings. In this light, it is surely absurd to hold that he is less evil than one who kills from passion. My point will be made if you merely agree that both are equally wicked.

I think the Defender is right in believing that direct personal assault is terrifying in a way that impersonal harm is not. This difference is no stranger to the criminal justice system. Prosecutors, judges, and juries constantly have to consider how terrifying an attack is in determining what to charge and what to convict offenders for. This is why we allow gradations in charges of homicide or assault and allow particularly grave sentences for particularly grave attacks. In short, the difference the Defender is pointing to here might justify treating a one-on-one murder as graver than murder by lax safety, but it doesn't justify treating one as a grave crime and the other as a mere regulatory (or very minor criminal) matter. After all, although it is true that for the same level of injury it is worse to be injured with terror than without, it is still the injury that constitutes the worst part of violent crime. Given the choice, seriously injured victims of crime would surely rather have been terrorized and not injured than injured and not terrorized. If that is so, then the worst part of violent crime is still shared by the indirect harms that the Defender would relegate to regulation.

There is also something to the Defender's claim that indirect harms, such as ones that result from lax safety measures, are part of productive and thus generally beneficial activities, whereas one-on-one crimes are not. Here, too, the difference can be overstated. What the Defender calls productive is any activity that produces something that other people are willing to buy. For him, the manufacture of cancer-causing cigarettes is as much a productive activity as the manufacture of cancer-curing medicines. If that is what is meant by productive activity, then it covers a great deal of the crimes that people fear. For example, many of these crimes are committed in the course of the commerce in illicit drugs or prostitution. Moreover, even if we must or should tolerate the risks that are necessary ingredients of productive activity, that doesn't imply that we shouldn't identify those risks, or levels of danger, that are not necessary and use the law to protect innocent people from them. Needless to say, this will require identifying such risks or levels clearly in advance so that the executives who will be held responsible for them can know in advance what they may and what they may not do.

The Defender's argument errs a third time by overlooking the role of legal institutions in shaping our ordinary moral notions. Many who defend the criminal justice system do so precisely because of its function in educating the public about the difference between right and wrong. The great historian of English law, Sir James Fitzjames Stephens, held that a

> great part of the general detestation of crime which happily prevails amongst the decent part of the community in all civilized countries arises from the fact that the commission of offences is associated in all such communities with the solemn and deliberate infliction of punishment wherever crime is proved.[26]

In other words, one cannot simply appeal to ordinary moral notions to defend the criminal law because the criminal law has already had a hand in shaping ordinary moral notions. At least one observer has argued that making narcotics use a crime in the beginning of this century *caused* a change in the public's ordinary moral notions about drug addiction, which prior to that time had been viewed as a medical problem.[27] It is probably safe to say that in our own time, civil rights legislation has sharpened the public's moral condemnation of racial discrimination. Hence, we might speculate that if the criminal justice system began to prosecute—and if the media began to portray—those who inflict *indirect harm* as serious criminals, our ordinary moral notions would change on this point as well.

I think this disposes of the Defender for the time being. We are left with the conclusion that there is no moral basis for treating *indirect harm* as less evil than *one-on-one harm*. What matters, then, is whether the purpose of the criminal justice system will be served by including, in the category of serious crime, actions that are predictably likely to produce serious harm, yet that are done in pursuit of otherwise legitimate goals and without the desire to harm someone.

What is the purpose of the criminal justice system? No esoteric answer is required. Norval Morris and Gordon Hawkins write that "the prime function of the criminal law is to protect our persons and our property."[28] *The Challenge of Crime in a Free Society*, the report of the President's Commission on Law Enforcement and Administration of Justice, tells us that "any criminal justice system is an apparatus society uses to enforce the standards of conduct necessary to protect individuals and the community."[29] Whatever else we think a criminal justice system should accomplish, I doubt if anyone would deny that its central purpose is to protect us against the most serious threats to our well-being. I argue that this purpose is seriously undermined by taking one-on-one harm as the model of crime. Excluding harm caused without the intention to harm prevents the criminal justice system from protecting our persons and our property from dangers at least as great as those posed by one-on-one harm. This is so because, as I will show, there are a large number of actions that are not labeled *criminal* but that lead to loss of life, limb, and possessions on a scale comparable to those actions that are represented in the FBI Crime Index—and a crime by any other name still causes misery and suffering.

*   *   *

In the remainder of this section I identify some acts that are *crimes by any other name*—that is, acts that cause harm and suffering comparable to that caused by acts called crimes. My purpose is to confirm the first hypothesis: that the definitions of crime in the criminal law do not reflect the only or the most dangerous behaviors in our society. To do this, we will need some measure of the harm and suffering caused by crimes with which we can compare the harm and suffering caused by noncrimes. Our measure need not be too refined because my point can be made if I can show that there are some acts that we do not treat as crime but that cause harm *roughly comparable* to that caused by acts that we do treat as crimes. Thus, it is not necessary to compare the harm caused by noncriminal acts to the harm caused by *all* crimes. I need only show that the harm produced by some noncriminal acts is comparable to the harm produced by *any* serious crime. Because the harms caused by noncriminal acts fall into the categories of death, bodily injury (including the disabling effects of disease), and property loss, I will compare these harms to the injuries caused by the crimes of murder, aggravated assault, and theft.

According to the FBI's *Uniform Crime Reports*, in 1986 there were 20,613 murders and nonnegligent manslaughters. During that year, there were 834,322 reported cases of aggravated assault. "Murder and nonnegligent manslaughter" includes all "willful (nonnegligent) killing of one human being by another." "Aggravated assault" is defined as an "attack by one person on another for the purpose of inflicting severe or aggravated bodily harm."[30] Thus, as a measure of the physical harm done by crime in 1986, I will assume that reported crimes led to roughly 20,000 deaths and 800,000 instances of serious bodily injury short of death. As a measure of property loss due to crime, we can use $11,583,489,000—the total value of property stolen in 1986 according to the UCR.[31] Whatever the shortcomings of these reported crime statistics, they are the statistics upon which public policy has traditionally been based. Because it is my aim to analyze the difference between public policy regarding crime and that regarding other dangers, it is appropriate to use the reported figures. Thus, I will consider any actions that lead to loss of life, physical harm, and property loss comparable to the figures in the UCR as actions that pose grave dangers to the community comparable to the threats posed by crimes. They are surely precisely the kind of harmful actions from which a criminal justice system whose purpose is to protect our persons and property ought to protect us. *They are crimes by other names.*

Work May Be Dangerous to Your Health

Since the publication of *The President's Report on Occupational Safety and Health*[32] in 1972, numerous studies have documented both the astounding incidence of disease, injury, and death due to hazards in the workplace *and* the fact that much or most of this carnage is the consequence of the refusal of management to pay for safety measures and of government to enforce safety standards.[33]

In that 1972 report, the government estimated the number of job-related illnesses at 390,000 per year and the number of annual deaths from industrial disease at 100,000. For 1986, the Bureau of Labor Statistics of the U.S. Department of Labor estimates 136,800 job-related illnesses and 3,610 work-related deaths.[34] Note that the latter figure applies only to private-sector work environments with eleven or more employees. It is not limited to death from occupational disease but includes all work-related deaths, including those resulting from accidents on the job.

Before considering the significance of these figures, it should be pointed out that there is wide agreement that occupational diseases are seriously underreported. *The Report of the President to the Congress on Occupational Safety and Health* for 1980 stated that

> *recording and reporting of illnesses continue to present measurement problems, since employers (and doctors) are often unable to recognize some illnesses as work-related. The annual survey includes data only on the visible illnesses of workers. To the extent that occupational illnesses are unrecognized and, therefore, not recorded or reported, the illness survey estimates may understate their occurrence.*[35]

Part of the difficulty is that there may be a substantial delay between contracting a fatal disease on the job and the appearance of symptoms, and from these to death. Moreover, OSHA (Occupational Safety and Health Administration) relies on employer reporting for its figures and there are many incentives for underreporting. Writing in the journal *Occupational Hazards*, Robert Reid states that

> *OSHA concedes that many factors—including insurance rates and supervisor evaluations based on safety performance—are incentives to underreport. And the agency acknowledges that recordkeeping violations have increased more than 27 percent since 1984, with most of the violations recorded for not maintaining the injuries and illnesses log examined by compliance officers and used for BLS' [Bureau of Labor Statistics'] annual survey.*[36]

A study by the National Institute for Occupational Safety and Health (NIOSH) concludes that "there may be several thousand more workplace deaths each year than employers report."[37]

For these reasons, plus the fact that BLS's figures on work-related deaths are only for private workplaces with eleven or more employees, we must supplement the BLS figures with other estimates. In 1982, then U.S. Secretary of Health and Human Services Richard Schweiker stated that "current estimates for overall workplace-associated cancer mortality vary within a range of five to fifteen percent."[38] With annual cancer deaths currently running more than 460,000, that translates into between 23,000 and 69,000 job-related cancer deaths per year. In testimony before the Senate Committee on Labor and Human Resources, Dr. Philip Landrigan, director of the Division of Environmental and Occupational Medicine at the Mount Sinai School of Medicine in New York City, stated that,

> *Recent data indicate that occupationally related exposures are responsible each year in New York State for 5,000 to 7,000 deaths and for 35,000 new cases of illness (not including work-related injuries). These deaths due to occupational disease include 3,700 deaths from cancer. . . .*
>
> *Crude national estimates of the burden of occupational disease in the United States may be developed by multiplying the New York State data by a factor of 10. New York State contains slightly less than 10 percent of the nation's workforce, and it includes a broad mix of employment in the manufacturing, service and agricultural sectors. Thus, it may be calculated that occupational disease is responsible each year in the United States for 50,000 to 70,000 deaths, and for approximately 350,000 new cases of illness.*[39]

It is some confirmation of Dr. Landrigan's estimates that they imply work-related cancer deaths of approximately 37,000 a year—a figure that is squarely in the middle of the range implied in Secretary Schweiker's statement on this issue. Thus, even if we discount OSHA's 1972 estimate of 100,000 deaths a year due to occupational disease or Dr. Landrigan's estimate of between 50,000 to 70,000, we would surely be erring in the other direction to accept the BLS figure of 3,610. We can hardly be overestimating the actual toll if we set it at 25,000 deaths a year resulting from occupational disease.

As for the BLS estimate of 136,800 job-related illnesses, here, too, there is reason to assume that the figure considerably understates the real situation. Dr. Landrigan's estimates suggest that the BLS figure represents less than half of the actual number. However, the BLS figure is less inaccurate than its figure for job-related deaths for at least two reasons: It is not limited to firms with eleven or more employees and symptoms of illness generally can be expected to appear sooner after contracting an illness than does death. To stay on the conservative side, then, I shall assume that there are annually in the United States approximately 150,000 job-related illnesses and 25,000 deaths from occupational diseases. How does this compare to the threat posed by crime? Before jumping to any conclusions, note that the risk of occupational disease and death falls only on members of the labor force, whereas the risk of crime falls on the whole population, from infants to the elderly. Because the labor force is less than half the total population (110,000,000 in 1986, out of a total population of 241,000,000), to get a true picture of the *relative* threat posed by occupational diseases compared to that posed by crime we should *halve* the crime statistics when comparing them to the figures for industrial disease and death. Using the 1986 statistics, this means that the *comparable* figures would be:

	Occupational Disease	Crime (halved)
Death	25,000	10,000
Other physical harm	150,000	400,000

If it is argued that this paints an inaccurate picture because so many crimes go unreported, my answer is this: First of all, homicides are by far the most completely reported of crimes. For obvious reasons, the general underreporting of crimes is not equal among crimes. It is much easier or tempting to avoid reporting a rape or a mugging than a corpse. Second, aggravated assaults are among the better-reported crimes, although not the best. Based on victimization studies, it is estimated that 54 percent of aggravated assaults were reported to the police in 1980, compared to 26.9 percent of thefts.[40] On the other hand, we should expect more—not less—underreporting of industrial than criminal victims because diseases and deaths are likely to cost firms money in the form of workdays lost and insurance premiums raised, occupational diseases are frequently first seen by company physicians who have every reason to diagnose complaints as either non–job-related or malingering, and many occupationally caused diseases do not show symptoms or lead to death until after the employee has left the job.

A survey conducted last year by the University of Washington reported that one in four Americans currently suffers an occupational disease. The report also disclosed that only one of the 10 workers with an occupational disease had been included in either OSHA statistics or in the state's workmen's compensation records.[41]

In sum, both occupational and criminal harms are underreported. Consequently, it is reasonable to assume that the effect of underreporting is probably balanced out, and the figures that we have give as accurate a picture of the *relative* threats of each as we need.

It should be noted further that the statistics given so far are *only* for occupational *diseases* and deaths from those diseases. They do not include death and disability from work-related injuries. Here, too, the statistics are gruesome. The National Safety Council reported that in 1986, work-related accidents caused 10,700 deaths and 1.8 million disabling work injuries, at a total cost to the economy of $34.8 billion.[42] This brings the number of occupation-related deaths to 36,700 a year. If, on the basis of these additional figures, we recalculated our chart comparing occupational to criminal dangers, it would look like this:

	Occupational Hazard	Crime (halved)
Death	36,700	10,000
Other physical harm	1,950,000	400,000

Can there be any doubt that workers are more likely to stay alive and healthy in the face of the danger from the underworld than in the face of what their employers have in store for them on the job? If any doubt lingers, consider this: Lest we falter in the struggle against crime, the FBI includes in their annual *Uniform Crime Reports* a table of "crime clocks," which graphically illustrates the extent of the criminal menace. For 1986, the crime clock shows a murder occurring every 25 minutes. If a similar clock were constructed for occupational deaths—using the conservative estimate of 36,700 cited above and remembering that this clock ticks only for that half of the population that is in the labor force—this clock would show an occupational death about every 14 minutes! In other words, in roughly the time it takes for one murder on the crime clock, two workers have died *just from trying to make a living.*

To say that some of these workers died from accidents due to their own carelessness is about as helpful as saying that some of those who died at the hands of murderers asked for it. It overlooks the fact that where workers are careless, it is not because they love to live dangerously. They have production quotas to meet, quotas that they themselves do not set. If quotas were set with an eye to keeping work at a safe pace rather than to keeping the production-to-wages ratio as high as possible, it might be more reasonable to expect workers to take the time to be careful. Beyond this, we should bear in mind that the vast majority of occupational deaths result from disease, not accident, and disease is generally a function of conditions outside a worker's control. Examples of such conditions are the level of coal dust in the air (about 10 percent of all active coal miners have black lung disease)[43] or textile dust (some 85,000 American cotton textile workers presently suffer breathing impairments caused by acute byssinosis or brown lung, and another 35,000 former mill workers are totally disabled with chronic brown lung)[44] or asbestos fibers (a study of 632 asbestos-insulation workers between 1943 and 1971 indicates that 11 percent have died of asbestosis and 38 percent of cancer; two doctors who have studied asbestos workers conclude "we can anticipate three thousand excess respiratory, cardiopulmonary deaths and cancers of the lung—three thousand excess deaths *annually* for the next twenty or thirty years"),[45] or coal tars ("workers who had been employed five or more years in the coke ovens died of lung cancer at a rate three and a half times that for all steelworkers"; coke oven workers also develop cancer of the scrotum at a rate five times that of the general population).[46] Also, some 800,000 people suffer from occupationally related skin disease each year (according to a 1968 estimate by the U.S. surgeon general),[47] and "the number of American workers experiencing noise conditions that may damage their hearing is estimated [in a 1969 Public Health Service publication of the Department of Health, Education and Welfare] to be in excess of 6 million, and may even reach 16 million."[48]

To blame the workers for occupational disease and deaths is simply to ignore the history of governmental attempts to compel industrial firms to meet safety standards that would keep dangers (such as chemicals or fibers or dust particles in the air) that are outside of the worker's control down to a safe level. This has been a continual struggle, with firms using everything from their own "independent" research institutes to more direct and often questionable forms of political pressure to influence government in the direction of loose standards and lax enforcement. So far, industry has been winning because OSHA has been given neither the personnel nor the mandate to fulfill its purpose. It is so understaffed that, in 1973, when 1,500 federal sky marshals guarded the nation's airplanes from hijackers, only 500 OSHA inspectors toured the nation's workplaces. By 1980, OSHA employed 1,581 compliance safety and health officers, but this still enabled inspection of only roughly 2 percent of the 2.5 million establishments covered by federal OSHA. The *New York Times* reports that in 1987, the number of OSHA inspectors was down to 1,044. As might be expected, the agency performs fewer inspections than it did a dozen years ago.

> When inspectors do find violations, the penalties they can assess are severely limited by the OSHA law that Congress has not updated since it established the agency. The maximum penalty for a serious OSHA violation is $1,000; an employer who acts willfully can be fined up to $10,000 for each incident. . . .
>
> Even when the agency hits employers hard, however, the sting does not often last very long. The big proposed fines that grab headlines are seldom paid in full. The two record-breaking citations of last year, against Union Carbide Corporation for $1.37 million and Chrysler for $910,000, were each settled this year for less than a third of the original amounts.[49]

According to *Occupational Hazards*,

> an October 1986 hearing of the House Governmental Operations Subcommittee of Intergovernmental Relations and Human Resources concluded that occupational disease surveillance had now fallen 72 years behind its counterpart for communicable disease data. Chaired by Rep. Ted Weiss (D.-N.Y.), this subcommittee noted that "The United States is the only large developed country without a national system for reporting occupational disease."
>
> The subcommittee report also pointed out that NIOSH's budget, rather than being increased, had continued to be cut—by as much as 47 percent since 1980, when adjusted for inflation. And that while nations such as Finland spend approximately $2 per worker each year on occupational disease surveillance, the United States spends about 2¢ per worker.[50]

An editorial in the January 1983 issue of the *American Journal of Public Health*, titled "Can Reagan Be Indicted for Betraying Public Health?" answers the question in its title affirmatively by listing the Reagan administration's attempts to cut back government support for public health programs. On the issue of occupational safety and health, the editorial states:

> The Occupational Safety and Health Administration (OSHA) has delayed the cotton and lead [safe exposure level] standards. It proposes to weaken the generic carcinogen policy, the labeling standard, the access to medical and exposure records standard. Mine fatalities are rising again, but the Mine Safety and Health Administration and OSHA enforcement have

been cut back. Research on occupational safety and health has been slashed more than any other research program in the Department of Health and Human Services. The National Institute for Occupational Safety and Health funding in real dollars is lower in 1983 than at any time in the 12-year history of the Institute. Reporting and data requirements have been devastated.[51]

The editorial ends by asking rhetorically, "How can anyone believe that the Reagan Administration wishes to prevent disease or promote health or preserve public health in America?"

And so it goes on.

Is a person who kills another in a bar brawl a greater threat to society than a business executive who refuses to cut into his profits in order to make his plant a safe place to work? By any measure of death and suffering the latter is by far a greater danger than the former. Because he wishes his workers no harm, because he is only indirectly responsible for death and disability, while pursuing legitimate economic goals, his acts are not called "crimes." Once we free our imagination from the irrational shackle of the one-on-one model of crime, can there be any doubt that the criminal justice system does *not* protect us from the gravest threats to life and limb? It seeks to protect us when danger comes from a young, lower-class male in the inner city. When a threat comes from an upper-class business executive in an office, the criminal justice system looks the other way. This is in the face of growing evidence that for every American citizen murdered by some thug, two American workers are killed by their bosses.

Health Care May Be Dangerous to Your Health

Almost twenty years ago, when the annual number of willful homicides in the nation was about 10,000, the President's Commission on Law Enforcement and Administration of Justice reported that

A recent study of emergency medical care found the quality, numbers, and distribution of ambulances and other emergency services severely deficient, and estimated that as many as 20,000 Americans die unnecessarily each year as a result of improper emergency care. The means necessary for correcting this situation are very clear and would probably yield greater immediate return in reducing death than would expenditures for reducing the incidence of crimes of violence.[52]

On July 15, 1975, Dr. Sidney Wolfe of Ralph Nader's Public Interest Health Research Group testified before the House Commerce Oversight and Investigations Subcommittee that there "were 3.2 million cases of unnecessary surgery performed each year in the United States." These unneeded operations, Dr. Wolfe added, "cost close to $5 billion a year and kill as many as 16,000 Americans."[53] Wolfe's estimates of unnecessary surgery were based on studies comparing the operations performed and surgery recommended by doctors who are paid for the operations they do with those performed and recommended by salaried doctors who receive no extra income from surgery.

The figure accepted by Dr. George A. Silver, professor of public health at the Yale University School of Medicine, is 15,000 deaths a year "attributable to unnecessary surgery."[54] Dr. Silver places the annual cost of excess surgery at $4.8 billion.[55] In an article on an experimental program by Blue Cross and Blue Shield aimed at curbing unnecessary surgery, *Newsweek* reports that

> *a Congressional committee earlier this year [1976] estimated that more than 2 million of the elective operations performed in 1974 were not only unnecessary—but also killed about 12,000 patients and cost nearly $4 billion.*[56]

Because the number of surgical operations performed in the United States rose from 16.7 million in 1975 to 20.2 million in 1985,[57] there is every reason to believe that at least somewhere between 12,000 and 16,000 people a year still die from unncessary surgery. In 1986, the FBI reported that 3,957 murders were committed by a "cutting or stabbing instrument."[58] Obviously, the FBI does not include the scalpel as a cutting or stabbing instrument. If they did, they would have had to report that between 15,957 and 19,957 persons were killed by "cutting or stabbing" in 1980—depending on whether you take *Newsweek*'s figure or Dr. Wolfe's. No matter how you slice it, the scalpel may be more dangerous than the switchblade.

While they are at it, the FBI should probably add the hypodermic needle and the prescription to their list of potential murder weapons. Professor Silver points out that these are also death-dealing instruments.

> *Of the 6 billion doses of antibiotic medicines administered each year by injection or prescription, it is estimated that 22 percent are unnecessary. Of the doses given, 10,000 result in fatal or near-fatal reactions. Some-*

where between 2,000 and 10,000 deaths probably would not have oc-curred if the drugs, meant for the patient's benefit, had not been given.[59]

The danger continues. The Public Citizen Health Research Group reports in its *Health Letter* of October 1988 that

two major U.S. drug companies—Lilly and SmithKline—have pleaded guilty to criminal charges for having withheld information from the Food and Drug Administration (FDA) about deaths and life-threatening adverse drug reactions.

The response of the Justice Department has been predictably merciful:

SmithKline, the actions of whose executives resulted in at least . . . 36 deaths, pleaded guilty to 14 criminal misdemeanor counts and was fined $34,000. Lilly and its executives, whose criminal negligence was responsible for deaths to at least 49 Americans . . . , were slapped on the wrist with a total of $45,000 in fines.[60]

In fact, if someone had the temerity to publish a *Uniform Crime Reports* that really portrayed the way Americans are murdered, the FBI's statistics on the *type of weapon used* in murder would have to be changed for 1986, from those shown in Table 2a to something like those shown in Table 2b.

The figures shown in Table 2b would give American citizens a much more honest picture of what threatens them. We are not likely to see it broadcast by the criminal justice system, however, because it would also give American citizens a more honest picture of *who* threatens them.

We should not leave this topic without noting that, aside from the other losses it imposes, unnecessary surgery was estimated to have cost between $4 and $5 billion in 1974. The price of medical care has nearly tripled between 1974 and 1986. Thus, assuming that the same number of unneeded operations were performed in 1986, the cost of unnecessary surgery would be between $12 and $15 billion. To this we should add the unnecessary 22 percent of the 6 billion administered doses of medication. Even at the extremely conservative estimate of $3 a dose, this adds about $4 billion. In short, assuming that earlier trends have continued, there is reason to believe that unnecessary surgery and medication cost the public between $16 and $19 billion annually—far outstripping the $11.6 billion taken by thieves that concern the FBI.[61] This gives us yet another way in which we are robbed of more money by practices that are not treated as criminal than by practices that are.

How Americans Are Murdered

Total	Firearms	Knife or Other Cutting Instrument	Other Weapon: Club, Arson, Poison, Strangulation, etc.	Personal Weapon: Hands, Fists, etc.
19,257[a]	11,381	3,957	2,609	1,310

[a]Note that this figure diverges somewhat from the figure of 20,613 murders and nonnegligent manslaughters used elsewhere in the FBI *Uniform Crime Reports,* 1987; see for example, p. 7.
Source: FBI *Uniform Crime Reports,* 1987: "Murder Victims: Weapons Used, 1986."

TABLE 2b

How Americans Are (Really) Murdered

Total	Occupational Hazard & Disease	Inadequate Emergency Medical Care	Knife or Other Cutting Instrument Including Scalpel	Firearms	Other Weapon: Club, Poison, Hypodermic, Prescription Drug	Personal Weapon: Hands, Fists, etc.
114,957	61,700	20,000	15,957[a]	11,381	4,609[a]	1,310

[a]These figures represent the relevant figures in Table 2a plus the most conservative figures for the relevant categories discussed in the text.

Waging Chemical Warfare Against America

One in four Americans can expect to contract cancer during their lifetimes. The American Cancer Society estimated that 420,000 Americans would die of cancer in 1981, up from 412,000 in 1980 and 404,000 in 1979. "A 1978 report issued by the President's Council on Environmental Quality (CEQ) unequivocally states that 'most researchers agree that 70 to 90 percent of cancers are caused by environmental influences and are hence theoretically preventable.' "[62] This means that a concerted national effort could result in saving 300,000 or more lives a year and reducing each individual's chances of getting cancer in his or her lifetime from one in four to one in twelve or less. If you think that this would require a massive effort in terms of money and personnel, you are right. How much of an effort, though, would the nation make to stop a foreign invader who was killing a thousand people a day and bent on capturing one-quarter of the present population?

In face of this "invasion" that is already under way, the U.S. government has allocated $1 billion to the National Cancer Institute, and NCI has allocated $124 million to the study of the physical and chemical (i.e., environmental) causes of cancer.[63] Compare this to the $164 billion spent to fight the Vietnam War, in which fewer Americans were killed than are currently killed by cancer every two months! The simple truth is that the government that strove so mightily to protect us against a guerrilla war 10,000 miles from home is doing next to nothing to protect us against the chemical war in our midst. This war is being waged against us on three fronts:

- Air pollution
- Cigarette smoking
- Food additives

Not only are we losing on all three fronts, but it looks like we do not even have the will to fight.

In April 1976, Dr. Umberto Saffioti, director of the National Cancer Institute's program of research into the chemical causes of cancer, resigned to protest three years' lack of support by NCI leaders.[64] In a letter stating his reasons for stepping down, he said:

> *I cannot accept any longer a situation which in fact deprives the regulatory agencies, industry, labor, consumers, and the scientific community of data of urgent public health value: It is people who are now exposed to*

toxic agents and who are not protected because the necessary support was not provided in time.[65]

Earlier the same year, three lawyers for the Environmental Protection Agency resigned " 'because of the continued failure of the EPA to take effective action,' to regulate possible, cancer-causing and other toxic chemicals in the air, food supply, drinking water and waterways." In a joint statement, the attorneys said:

It is clear from recent actions that the agency intends to refrain from vigorous enforcement of available toxic-substances controls and to retrench from the few legal precedents which it has set for evaluating the cancer hazards posed by the chemicals.[66]

In 1976, after extensive hearings, the Senate Subcommittee on Administrative Practices and Procedure, chaired by Senator Edward M. Kennedy, issued a report extremely critical of EPA's enforcement of regulations regarding the use of chemical pesticides.[67] In the report's introduction, Senator Kennedy states:

I find it incredible that a regulatory agency charged with safeguarding the public health and the environment would be so sluggish to recognize and react to so many warnings over the past 5 years. The EPA was warned and certainly should have known that testing data, submitted by industry as long as 25 years ago, should not be accepted at face value in the re-registration of thousands of pesticide products presently being used on our farms and in our homes. But EPA by and large ignored these warnings.[68]

In testimony before the U.S. Senate Committee on Commerce, Samuel S. Epstein, M.D., Swetland Professor of Environmental Health and Human Ecology, in the Department of Pharmacology of the Case Western Reserve University School of Medicine, said in 1973:

It is preposterous . . . that [the administration] can recommend a $100 million program for the treatment and prevention of cancer when current FDA [Food and Drug Administration] practice is deliberately allowing an increase in the total burden of carcinogenic elements in our human diet.[69]

The evidence linking *air pollution* and cancer, as well as other serious and often fatal diseases, has been rapidly accumulating in recent years. During 1975, the epidemiological branch of the National Cancer Institute did a massive county-by-county analysis of cancer in the United States, mapping the "cancer hotspots" in the nation. The result was summed up by Dr. Glenn Paulson, assistant commissioner of science in the New Jersey Department of Environmental Protection: "If you know where the chemical industry is, you know where the cancer hotspots are."[70] What distinguishes these findings from the material on occupational hazards discussed above is that NCI investigators found higher death rates for *all* those living in the cancer hotspots—not just the workers in the offending plants.

For instance, NCI researchers found that Deer Lodge County in Montana ranked ninth out of 3,021 U.S. counties in lung cancer death rates. Deer Lodge County is the home of the Anaconda Company's giant copper-smelting works. The county's death rate was twice the rate expected for a rural county. A study by the Montana Department of Health and Environmental Sciences showed that the county's death rate for emphysema, asthma, and bronchitis are also well above the national average. Another study by two NCI researchers found that in *all* U.S. counties with smelters, the incidence of lung cancer is above the national average. "The researchers found high lung cancer death rates not only in men—who are often exposed to arsenic on their jobs inside smelters—but also among women, who generally never went inside smelters and were not previously believed to have been exposed to arsenic." Explanation: "neighborhood air pollution from industrial sources of inorganic arsenic."[71]

New Jersey, however, took the prize for having the highest cancer death rate in the nation. NCI investigators found that "19 of New Jersey's 21 counties rank in the top 10 percent of all counties in the nation for cancer death rates." Salem County, home of E. I. Du Pont de Nemours and Company's Chambers Works, which has been manufacturing chemicals since 1919, "has the highest bladder cancer death rate in the nation—8.7 deaths per 100,000 persons."[72]

In 1970, Lester B. Lave and Eugene P. Seskin reviewed more than fifty scientific studies of the relationship between air pollution and morbidity and mortality rates for lung cancer, nonrespiratory tract cancers, cardiovascular disease, bronchitis, and other respiratory diseases. They found in every instance a *positive quantifiable relationship*. Using sophisticated statistical techniques, they concluded that a 50 percent reduction in air pollution in major urban areas would result in:

· A 25 percent reduction in mortality from lung cancer (using 1974 mortality rates, this represents a potential saving of 19,500 lives per year)

· A 25 percent reduction in morbidity and mortality due to respiratory disease (a potential saving of 27,000 lives per year)
· A 20 percent reduction in morbidity and mortality due to cardiovascular disease (a potential saving of 52,000 lives per year)[73]

In addition, even a 10 percent reduction in air pollution could be expected to "decrease the total death rate by 0.5 percent."[74]

A more recent study, done in 1978 by Robert Mendelsohn of the University of Washington and Guy Orcutt of Yale University, estimates that air pollution causes a total of 142,000 deaths a year.[75] A government study released in February 1981 indicates that "sulfates and other air pollutants, just from coal-fired power plants, may help cause the deaths of 8,000 people a year in Ohio."[76] This chemical war is not limited to the air. The National Cancer Institute has identified as carcinogens or suspected carcinogens twenty-three of the chemicals commonly found in our drinking water. The Great Lakes, a source of drinking water for some 24 million Americans, is known to be contaminated by toxic chemicals.[77] Moreover, American industry produces some 57 to 80 million tons of toxic wastes a year.

> *The Environmental Protection Agency estimates that only about 10 percent of the hazardous wastes . . . are disposed of in a safe, legal and acceptable manner; 90 percent are dumped illegally or disposed of in a manner that represents a potential threat to humans or the natural environment.*[78]

As with OSHA, the Reagan administration instituted a general slowing down of enforcement of EPA regulations. Reagan tried to cut EPA's enforcement budget by 45 percent in his first two years. By 1983, the EPA's regional offices were staffed at levels substantially lower than needed to enforce the law effectively, according to the agency's own studies. The president also signaled his tolerant attitude toward environmental hazards in his appointments to top-level posts at EPA of such people as Anne Burford, "who fiercely opposed any legislation regulating hazardous-waste disposal"; Rita Lavelle, former director of communications for a subsidiary of Aerojet-General Corporation, a company that according to EPA records had "the third worst pollution record in California"; and John Todhunter, chief of EPA's Division on Toxic Substances and Pesticides, who "previously served on the scientific advisory board of an industry-financed group that has continually downplayed the role of chemicals and pollution in causing cancer."[79]

So the chemical war goes on. No one can deny that we know the enemy. No one can deny that we know the toll it is taking. Indeed, we can compute the number of deaths that result from every day that we refuse to mount an offensive. Yet we still refuse. Thus, for the time being the only advice we can offer someone who values his life, is: If you must breathe our air, don't inhale.

The evidence linking *cigarette smoking* and cancer is overwhelming and need not be repeated here. It should be noted, however, that cigarettes are widely estimated to cause 30 percent of all cancers, including 85 percent of lung cancer, which is responsible for the largest number of cancer deaths—approximately 130,000 a year. To this must be added approximately 60,000 deaths a year from other forms of lung disease such as emphysema. Moreover, 30 percent of heart disease is attributed to smoking, estimated to result in 100,000 deaths a year.[80] This is enough to expose the hypocrisy of running a full-scale war against heroin (which produces no degenerative disease) while allowing cigarette sales and advertising to flourish. It also should be enough to underscore the point that once again there are threats to our lives much greater than criminal homicide. The legal order does not protect us against them. Indeed, not only does our government not protect us against this threat, it subsidizes the tobacco industry to the extent of nearly $100 million annually in the form of direct assistance programs and indirect support.[81] Moreover, the Reagan administration first supported and then, under intense lobbying pressure from the tobacco industry, withdrew its support for more and stronger warnings on cigarettes.[82]

The average American consumes *one pound* of chemical *food additives* per year.[83] Speaking on the floor of the U.S. Senate in 1972, Senator Gaylord Nelson said:

> *People are finally waking up to the fact that the average American daily diet is substantially adulterated with unnecessary and poisonous chemical and frequently filled with neutral, nonnutritious substances. We are being chemically medicated against our will and cheated of food value by low nutrition foods.*[84]

A hard look at the chemicals we eat and at the federal agency that is empowered to protect us against eating dangerous chemicals reveals the recklessness with which we are being "medicated against our will."

Beatrice Hunter has taken such a hard look and reports her findings in a book aptly titled *The Mirage of Safety*. Her book is a catalogue of the possible dangers that lurk in the foods we eat. More than this, however, it is a description of how the Food and Drug Administration, through a combination of lax enforcement and uncritical acceptance of the results of the food industry's own "scientific" research, has allowed a situation to exist in which the American food-eating public is the real guinea pig for nearly *three thousand* food additives. As a result, we are subjected to chemicals that are strongly suspected of producing cancer,[85] gallbladder ailments,[86] hyperkinesis in children,[87] and allergies;[88] to others that inhibit "mammalian cell growth" and "may adversely affect the rate of DNA, RNA, and protein synthesis";[89] and to still others that are capable of crossing the placental barrier between mother and fetus and are suspected causes of birth defects and congenital diseases.[90]

The food additives are, of course, only part of the dangerous chemicals that we eat.

Deadly synthetic chemicals are now present in our food, air, water, and even our own bodies—including mother's milk—where they remain and accumulate. By the time many of the dangerous pesticides were banned or restricted as powerful cancer-causing agents, they had contaminated virtually every American and most of our food supply. Dieldrin was being found in the flesh of 99.5 percent of all human tissue samples tested, as well as in 96 percent of all meat, fish and poultry. BHC [benzene hexachloride] had been detected in 99 percent of all Americans tested, and heptachlor in 95 percent, as well as in 70 percent of meat, poultry, fish and dairy products. DDT and PCB's [pentachlorophenols] were turning up in almost all human tissue samples, fresh water fish, meat, and dairy products.[91]

"A 1976 EPA study of cancer-causing chemicals in the milk of nursing mothers across the United States found that virtually all samples contained DDT and PCB's, 81 percent showed levels of dieldrin, and 87 percent had BHC."[92]

To call government and industry practices reckless is mild in view of the fact that "one out of every five to ten people has a major allergy of disabling proportions and consequences"[93] and that between "4 to 7.5 percent of human deliveries yield individuals that have developmental defects that will interfere with survival or result in clinical disease before the end of the first year of life."[94] According "to the March of Dimes Birth Defects Foundation, each year some 233,000 infants are born with birth defects."[95] Couple these facts with what we already know about the role of external chemicals in the causation of cancer and we have a callous policy that subjects the food-eating public to unknown but reasonably suspected risks to their lives and well-being in the name of food industry profits.

Based on the knowledge we have, there can be no doubt that air pollution, tobacco, and food additives amount to a chemical war that makes the crime wave look like a football scrimmage. Quite conservatively, I think we can estimate the death toll in this war as at least a quarter of a million lives a year—*more than ten times the number killed by criminal homicide!*

Poverty Kills

We are long past the day when we could believe that poverty was caused by forces outside human control. Poverty is "caused" by lack of money, which means that once a society reaches a level of prosperity at which many enjoy a relatively high standard of living, then poverty can be eliminated or at least significantly reduced by transferring some of what the "haves" have to the "have-nots." In other words, regardless of what caused poverty in the past, what causes it to continue in the present is the refusal of those who have more to share with those who have less. Now you may think these remarks trite or naive. They are not offered as an argument for redistribution of income, although I think such a redistribution is long overdue. These remarks are presented to make a much simpler point, which is that poverty exists in a wealthy society like our own *because we allow it to exist.* Therefore, we[96] share responsibility for poverty and for its consequences.

The poverty for which we are responsible appears to be at a higher level now than at any time in the last twenty years. Moreover, it has particularly nasty features. For example, it affects children and blacks at a rate higher than the national average. Whereas about one out of every seven Americans is poor, one out of every five children grows up in poverty. One out of every three black Americans is poor, whereas one out of every two black children is poor. A study published by the Urban Institute ranked the United States highest in child poverty among eight industrialized nations studied. The other nations were Switzerland, Sweden, Norway, West Germany, Canada, United Kingdom, and Australia. Moreover, it is estimated that there are now between 350,000 and 3 million Americans whose poverty has rendered them homeless. The fastest-growing group among the homeless "consists of families headed by single mothers who can no longer afford to feed their children *and* pay the rent."[97]

We are prone to think that the consequences of poverty are fairly straightforward: less money equals less things. So poor people have fewer clothes or cars or appliances, go to the theater less often, and live in smaller homes with less or cheaper furniture. This is true and sad, but perhaps not intolerable. I will argue that one of the things poor people have less of is *good health*. Less money means less nutritious food, less heat in winter, less fresh air in summer, less distance from other sick people, less knowledge about illness or medicine, fewer doctor visits, fewer dental visits, less preventive health care, and above all, less first-quality medical attention when all these other deprivations take their toll and a poor person finds himself seriously ill. What this means is that the poor suffer more from poor health and die earlier than do those who are well off. Poverty robs them of their days while they are alive and then kills them before their time. A prosperous society that allows poverty in its midst is guilty of murder.

William Ryan writes in his book *Blaming the Victim:*

> *Our health problems are concentrated among the poor. In New York City, the central Harlem health district reports an infant mortality rate of 49.5 per thousand while the well-to-do district of Kips Bay–Yorkville has a rate of only 14.7 per thousand. According to the American Public Health Association, poor families suffer from disabling heart disease three times more frequently than others; and from visual impairment, seven times more frequently. A study of Head Start children in Boston revealed that almost one in three had major undiscovered health problems. The statistics can be cited almost indefinitely, and they add up to a formulation that is wearingly familiar—the poor man and the black man suffer and end up with the lowest health status.*[98]

In the 1960s, a study was done in Chicago comparing health in the poor areas of the city with health in the wealthier areas.[99] The study found that

> *the overall mortality rate in poverty areas was 40 percent higher than in nonpoverty areas. With respect to infant mortality rates, the measure used worldwide as a general indicator of community health, poverty areas exceeded nonpoverty areas by 75 percent. In a measure that many students consider to be an even better and more sensitive indicator of community health, the post-neonatal mortality rate (deaths among infants who survive the first month of life) for poverty areas exceeded nonpoverty areas by 100 percent.*[100]

A review of more than thirty historical and contemporary studies of the relationship of economic class and life expectancy affirms the obvious conclusion that "class influences one's chances of staying alive. Almost without exception, the evidence shows that classes differ on mortality rates."[101] An article in the July 1976 issue of the *American Journal of Epidemiology* states that a "vast body of evidence has shown consistently that those in the lower classes have higher mortality, morbidity, and disability rates" and that these "are in part due to inadequate medical care services as well as to the impact of a toxic and hazardous physical environment."[102] Supporting this is an article in the September 1982 issue of the *New England Journal of Medicine*, titled "National Estimates of Blood Lead Levels: United States, 1976–1980." An editorial in the same issue comments on the findings:

> *The survey confirms earlier reports that black, inner-city, and poor children are at greater risk. Elevated blood lead levels were found in 2 percent of white children but 12.2 percent of black children, in 2.1 percent of rural children but 11.6 percent of inner-city children, and in 1.2 percent of children from families with an annual income of $15,000 or more but 10.9 percent of those from families with an income under $6,000.[103]*

A study of parents' ratings of their children's health status found that 69.1 percent of children in families with incomes of $15,000 or more were rated by their parents as in excellent health, compared to 41 percent of children in families with incomes under $5,000, 49.7 percent of children in families with incomes from $5,000 to $9,999, and 60.4 percent of children in families with incomes between $10,000 and $14,999. Of children in families with incomes of $15,000 or more 1.8 percent were rated by their parents as in poor health, compared to 6.7 percent in the under $5,000 group, 4.1 percent in the $5,000–$9,999 group, and 2.9 percent in the $10,000–$14,999 group.[104] Another indication of the correlation between low income and poor health is found in statistics on the number of days of reduced activity due to illness or injury suffered by members of different income groups. In 1979, persons from families earning less than $5,000 a year suffered an average of 37.5 such days, persons from families earning from $5,000 to $9,999 suffered 26.8 days, persons from families earning between $10,000 and $14,999 suffered 17.4 days, and persons from families earning $15,000 and over suffered 13.6 days of reduced activity.[105]

A 1978 article in *Public Health Reports*, surveying the research on the link between socioeconomic status and mortality rates, concludes that there is not only a strong positive correlation between socioeconomic status and life expectancy, but that this relationship "has changed little, if any, since the 1950s." Their survey of Chicago, Houston, Providence, Hartford, Phoenix, and Tucson, from 1930 to 1970, shows the average annual death rates per 1,000 white males in the lowest socioeconomic group to be from 1.3 to 1.86 times greater than the rates for those in the highest socioeconomic group.[106] A study comparing the survival rates of indigent and nonindigent cancer patients in the University of Iowa Hospital from 1940 to 1969 concludes that "The indigents had poorer survival than the private patients for every cancer type for which there was data."[107]

Here, too, things have gotten worse rather than better during the Reagan years. According to a report in the *Wall Street Journal*, the number of Americans without health insurance grew during those years to an estimated 37 million. From 1982 to 1985, the percentage of the (nonfarm) population without health insurance grew from 15.5 to 17.4. Over the past decade, the percentage of the poor covered by Medicaid has gone from 65 percent to less than 40 percent. Hardest hit have been poor women and their children, many of whom have been removed from Medicaid coverage because of income-eligibility rules that have not kept up with inflation. "In 1986, the average state income cutoff for Medicaid was 48 percent of the federal poverty level, compared to 71 percent in 1975."[108]

A comparison of the health and mortality of blacks and whites in America yields further insight into the relationship of health and mortality to economic class. In 1986, about one out of every three blacks lived below the poverty line, as compared to one out of every nine whites. When the value of in-kind benefits is added in, the figures improve to one out of every five blacks and one out of fifteen whites. In either case, blacks are about three times worse off than whites. In 1987, 13 percent of blacks were unemployed compared to 5.3 percent of whites. In 1986, the median income of black families was $17,604 compared to $30,809 for white families.[109] For these reasons it is generally a safe bet to assume that data on the lives of blacks in America are also data on the impact of low economic status in America.

In 1985, black mothers died in childbirth at a rate *four times* that of white mothers. Black infant mortality was 18.2 per 1,000 live births compared to 9.3 for whites.[110] In short, black mothers lose their babies within the first year of life nearly twice as often as white mothers. In the face of this situation, the Reagan administration reduced funding for maternal and child health programs by more than 25 percent and attempted to reduce support for immunization programs for American children.[111]

Cancer survival statistics show a similar picture. Between 1974 and 1983, 38 percent of blacks diagnosed with cancer were still alive five years after the diagnosis, compared to 50 percent of whites.[112] One important cause of this difference is that "white patients tended to have higher percentages of cancers diagnosed while localized,"[113] that is, earlier in their development. This means that the difference is not due to genetic factors, but to such things as better access to medical care, higher levels of education about the early warning signs of cancer, and so on, all of which strongly correlate with higher income levels. Berg, Ross, and Latourette, in their study of cancer survival and economic status referred to earlier, state, "We submit that economic differences could explain most, if not all, the general poor showing of Blacks."[114]

Life expectancy figures paint the most tragic picture of all. In 1986, life expectancy among blacks was 69.6 years, whereas among whites it was 75.4 years. This difference cannot be wholly attributed to genetic factors because the difference has steadily shrunk in response to advances in medicine during this century.[115]

From this, an inescapable conclusion follows. If we assume that in the absence of poverty, blacks would have about the same life expectancy as whites, then poverty robs every black person of six years of life, on the average. In short, *poverty hurts, injures, and kills—just like crime.* A society that could remedy its poverty but does not is an accomplice in crime.

Summary

Once again, our investigations lead to the same result. The criminal justice system does not protect us against the gravest threats to life, limb, or possessions. Its definitions of crime are not simply a reflection of the objective dangers that threaten us. The workplace, the medical profession, the air we breathe, and the poverty we refuse to rectify lead to far more human suffering, far more death and disability, and take far more dollars from our pockets than the murders, aggravated assaults, and thefts reported annually by the FBI. What is more, this human suffering is preventable. A government really intent on protecting our well-being could enforce work safety regulations, police the medical profession, require that clean air standards be met, and funnel sufficient money to the poor to alleviate the major disabilities of poverty— but it does not. Instead we hear a lot of cant about law and order and a lot of rant about crime in the streets. It is as if our leaders were not only refusing to protect us from the major threats to our well-being but trying to cover up this refusal by diverting our attention to crime—as if this were the only real threat. As we have seen, the criminal justice system is a carnival mirror that presents a distorted image of what threatens us. The distortions do not end with the definitions of crime. As we will see in what follows, new distortions enter at every level of the system, so that in the end, when we look in our prisons to see who really threatens us, all we see are poor people. By that time, virtually all the well-to-do people who endanger us have been discreetly weeded out of the system. As we watch this process unfold in the following chapter, we should bear in mind the conclusion of the present chapter: All the mechanisms by which the criminal justice system comes down more frequently and more harshly on the poor criminal than on the well-off criminal take place *after* most of the dangerous acts of the well-to-do have been excluded from the definition of crime itself. The bias against the poor within the criminal justice system is all the more striking when we recognize that the door to that system is shaped in a way that excludes in advance the most dangerous acts of the well-to-do. Demonstrating this has been the purpose of the present chapter.

Study Questions

1. What should be our definition of the term *crime?* Why does it matter what we call things?

2. Quickly—without thinking about it—picture to yourself a criminal. Describe what you see. Are there people in our society who pose a greater danger to you than the individual you pictured?

3. What is meant by likening the criminal justice system to a "carnival mirror"?

4. Do you think a business executive who refuses to invest in safety precautions with the result that several workers die is morally better than, equal to, or worse than a mugger who kills his victim after robbing him? Why?

5. What is meant by speaking of criminal justice as "creative art"? How does the view presented here differ from that of Quinney?

6. Give examples of social practices that are more dangerous to your well-being than common crime. How should these practices be dealt with?

3

. . . and the Poor Get Prison

*When we come to make an intelligent
study of the prison at first hand . . . we are
bound to conclude that after all it is not
so much crime in its general sense that is
penalized, but that it is poverty which
is punished.*

*Take a census of the average prison and
you will find that a large majority of
people are there not so much because of
the particular crime they are alleged to
have committed, but for the reason that
they are poor and . . . lacked the money to
engage the services of first class and
influential lawyers.*

Eugene V. Debs, *Walls and Bars*

WEEDING OUT THE WEALTHY

*The offender at the end of the road in prison is likely to be a member of the
lowest social and economic groups in the country.*[1]

This statement in the *Report of the President's Commission on
Law Enforcement and Administration of Justice* is as true today as it
was over two decades ago when it was written. Our prisons are
indeed, as Ronald Goldfarb has called them, the "national poor-

80

house."[2] To most citizens this comes as no surprise—recall the Typical Criminal and the Typical Crime. Dangerous crimes, they think, are mainly committed by poor people. Seeing that prison populations are made up primarily of the poor only makes them surer of this. They think, in other words, that the criminal justice system gives a true reflection of the dangers that threaten them.

In my view, it also comes as no surprise that our prisons and jails predominantly confine the poor. This is not because these are the individuals who most threaten us. Instead, it is because the criminal justice system effectively weeds out the well-to-do, so that at *the end of the road in prison*, the vast majority of those we find there come from the lower classes. This "weeding out" process starts before the agents of law enforcement go into action. In the last chapter, I argued that our very definition of crime *excludes* a wide variety of actions at least as dangerous as those included and often worse. Is it any accident that the kinds of dangerous actions excluded are the kinds most likely to be performed by the affluent in America? Even before we mobilize our troops in the war on crime, we have already guaranteed that large numbers of upper-class individuals will never come within their sights.

This process does not stop at the definition of crime. It continues throughout each level of the criminal justice system. At each step, from arresting to sentencing, the likelihood of being ignored or released or lightly treated by the system is greater the better off one is economically. As the late U.S. Senator Philip Hart wrote:

> *Justice has two transmission belts, one for the rich and one for the poor. The low-income transmission belt is easier to ride without falling off and it gets to prison in shorter order.*
>
> *The transmission belt for the affluent is a little slower and it passes innumerable stations where exits are temptingly convenient.*[3]

This means that the criminal justice system functions from start to finish in a way that makes certain that "the offender at the end of the road in prison is likely to be a member of the lowest social and economic groups in the country."

For the same criminal behavior, the poor are more likely to be arrested; if arrested, they are more likely to be charged; if charged, more likely to be convicted; if convicted, more likely to be sentenced to prison; and if sentenced, more likely to be given longer prison terms than members of the middle and upper classes. In other words, the image of the criminal population one sees in our nation's jails and prisons is distorted by the shape of the criminal justice system itself. It is the face of evil reflected in a carnival mirror, but it is no laughing matter.

The face in the criminal justice carnival mirror is also, as we have already noted, very frequently a black face. Although blacks do not comprise the majority of the inmates in our jails and prisons, they make up a proportion that far outstrips their proportion in the population.[5] Here, too, the image we see is distorted by the processes of the criminal justice system itself. Edwin Sutherland and Donald Cressey write, in their widely used textbook, *Criminology*, that

> *numerous studies have shown that African-Americans are more likely to be arrested, indicted, convicted, and committed to an institution than are whites who commit the same offenses, and many other studies have shown that blacks have a poorer chance than whites to receive probation, a suspended sentence, parole, commutation of a death sentence, or pardon.*[6]

Recently, William Wilbanks has attacked this conclusion in a book titled *The Myth of a Racist Criminal Justice System*.[7] This is not the place to mount a full reply to Wilbank's provocative claim; nonetheless, a comment is in order. Wilbanks uses as "perhaps the most important criticism" of the charge that there is discrimination against blacks in arrests, the work of Michael Hindelang, which compares the rate at which respondents to the National Crime Survey report being victimized by assailants perceived to be black with the rate at which blacks are arrested for the relevant crimes according to the UCR, and finds "that the racial gap in *offending* for robbery, assault, and rape (whether or not an arrest occurred) was almost equal to that found for *arrest* statistics." Wilbanks concludes that "these results indicate that police select black and white arrestees in approximately the same proportion as they are found in the pool of offenders," and thus "argue against police bias in the arrest process."[8] Recent statistics, however, suggest quite the opposite. Consider the following:

In 1986, respondents to the NCS reported that approximately 27 percent of their assailants in violent victimizations (rape, robbery, simple and aggravated assault) were perceived to be black. That same year, the UCR indicates that 38.6 percent of the individuals arrested for these crimes were black. If we drop out simple assault on the assumption that it is less often reported to the police than the other violent crimes, the figures change only slightly: 35 percent of violent victimizers are perceived to be black, whereas 46 percent of those arrested for rape, robbery, and aggravated assault are black. These figures indicate that police are arresting blacks about 30 percent more frequently than the occurrence of their perceived offenses. This understates the black-white arrest gap. For the same year, respondents to the NCS reported that approximately 58 percent of violent victimizers (rape, robbery, aggravated assault) were perceived to be white, although the UCR reports that whites made up 52 percent of those arrested for these offenses. This means that for every 100 perceived white offenders, 90 whites are arrested; and for every 100 perceived black offenders, 131 blacks are arrested. In short, per perceived offense, blacks are arrested more than 45 percent more frequently than whites.[9] Because arrest determines the pool from which charged, convicted, and imprisoned individuals are selected, this suggests that deep bias persists throughout the criminal justice system.

I am aware that there are various problems with comparing UCR and NCS statistics and various possible explanations for the divergence of black-white arrest rates from the rates at which blacks and whites are perceived offenders. Thus, I do not claim that the results just presented prove definitively the presence of racism. Nonetheless, because they come from the statistics that Wilbanks uses as "the most important criticism" of the discrimination thesis, I think they suffice to cast significant doubt on Wilbanks' claim. Thus, I shall treat Wilbanks' thesis as currently unsubstantiated and continue to follow the majority of researchers in holding that the criminal justice system is widely marked by racial discrimination as well as by economic bias.[10] Nevertheless, it does not pay to look at these as two independent forms of bias. It is my view that, at least as far as criminal justice is concerned, racism is simply one powerful form of economic bias. I use evidence on differential treatment of blacks as evidence of differential treatment of members of the lower classes. There are five reasons:

1. First and foremost, black Americans are disproportionately poor. By 1986, approximately *one-third* of all black Americans were below the poverty level, compared to about *one-ninth* of white Americans. When in-kind benefits are factored in, the figures improve but the relative position of blacks and whites remains the same: *One-fifth of blacks and one-fifteenth* of whites are below the poverty level.[11]
2. Blacks who travel the full route of the criminal justice system and end up in jail or prison are close in economic condition to whites who do. In 1978, 53 percent of black jail inmates had pre-

arrest incomes below $3000, compared to 44 percent of whites.[12] In 1983, the median pre-arrest income of black jail inmates was $4,067 and that of white jail inmates was $6,312. About half of blacks in jail were unemployed before arrest and 44 percent of whites were.[13]

3. The factors that are most likely to keep one out of trouble with the law and out of prison, such as a suburban living room instead of a tenement alley to gamble in or legal counsel able to devote time to one's case instead of an overburdened public defender, are the kinds of things that money can buy regardless of one's race, creed, or national origin.

4. Curiously enough, statistics on differential treatment of races are available in greater abundance than are statistics on differential treatment of economic classes. For instance, although the FBI tabulates arrest rates by race (as well as by sex, age, and geographical area), it omits class or income. Similarly, both the President's Crime Commission Report and Sutherland and Cressey's *Criminology* have index entries for race or racial discrimination but none for class or income of offenders. It would seem that both independent and government data gatherers are more willing to own up to America's racism than to its class bias.

5. Finally, it is my belief that the economic powers that be in America have sufficient power to end or drastically reduce racist bias in the criminal justice system. To the extent that they allow it to exist, it is not unreasonable to assume that it furthers their economic interests.

For all these reasons, racism will be treated here as either a form of economic bias or a tool that achieves the same end.

In the remainder of this chapter, I show how the criminal justice system functions to *weed out the wealthy* (meaning both middle- and upper-class offenders) at each stage of the process and thus produces a distorted image of the crime problem. Before entering into this discussion, two provisos should be noted: First, it is not my view that the poor are all innocent victims persecuted by the evil rich. The poor do commit crimes, and my own assumption is that the vast majority of the poor who are confined in our prisons are guilty of the crimes for which they were sentenced. In addition, there is good evidence that the poor do commit a greater portion of the crimes against person and property listed in the FBI Index than the middle and upper classes do, relative to their numbers in the national population. What I have already tried to prove is that the crimes in the FBI Index are not the acts that threaten us most, and what I will try to prove in what follows is that the poor are arrested and punished by the criminal justice system much more frequently than their contribution to the crime problem would warrant—thus the criminals who populate our prisons as well as the public's imagination are disproportionately poor.

The second proviso is this: The following discussion has been divided into three sections that correspond to the major criminal justice decision points and that also correspond to hypotheses two, three, and four that were stated on page 49. As always, such classifications are a bit neater than reality, and so they should not be taken as rigid compartments. Many of the distorting processes operate at all criminal justice decision points. So, for example, while I will primarily discuss the light-handed treatment of white-collar criminals in the section on sentencing, it is also true that white-collar criminals are less likely to be arrested or charged or convicted than are blue-collar criminals. The section in which a given issue will be treated is a reflection of the point in the criminal justice process at which the disparities are most striking. Suffice it to say, however, that the disparities between the treatment of the poor and the nonpoor are to be found at all points of the process.

Arrest

The problem with most official records of who commits crime is that they are really statistics on who gets arrested and convicted. If, as I will show, the police are more likely to arrest some people than others, these official statistics may tell us more about police than about criminals. In any event, they give us little reliable data about those who commit crime and do not get caught. Some social scientists, suspicious of the bias built into official records, have tried to devise other methods of determining who has committed a crime. Most often, these methods involve an interview or questionnaire in which the respondent is assured of anonymity and asked to reveal whether he has committed any offenses for which he could be arrested and convicted. Techniques to check reliability of these self-reports also have been devised; however, if their reliability is still in doubt, common sense would dictate that they would understate rather than overstate the number of individuals who have committed crimes and never come to official notice. In light of this, the conclusions of these studies are rather astounding. It would seem that crime is the national pastime.

The President's Crime Commission conducted a survey of 10,000 households and discovered that "91 percent of all Americans have violated laws that could have subjected them to a term of imprisonment at one time in their lives."[14] They also report the findings of a study of 1,690 persons (1,020 males, 670 females) mostly from the state of New York. Asked which of forty-nine felonies and misdemeanors (excluding traffic offenses) they had committed:

> *Ninety-one percent of the respondents admitted they had committed one or more offenses for which they might have received jail or prison sentences. Thirteen percent of the males admitted to grand larceny, 26 percent to auto theft, and 17 percent to burglary.* Sixty-four percent of the males and 27 percent of the females committed at least one felony for which they had not been apprehended.[15]

Keep in mind that a felony is a crime for which an individual can serve one or more years in prison and that many of the individuals now in jail are there only for misdemeanors.

A number of other studies support the conclusion that serious criminal behavior is widespread among middle- and upper-class individuals, although these individuals are rarely, if ever, arrested. Some of the studies show that there are no significant differences between economic classes in the incidence of criminal behavior.[16] Others conclude that while lower-class individuals do commit more than their share of crime, arrest records overstate their share and understate that of the middle and upper classes.[17]

Still other studies suggest that some forms of serious crime—forms usually associated with lower-class youth—show up *more frequently* among higher-class persons than among lower.[18] For instance, Empey and Erikson interviewed 180 white males aged fifteen to seventeen who were drawn from different economic strata. They found that "virtually all respondents reported having committed not one but a variety of different offenses." Although youngsters from the middle classes constituted 55 percent of the group interviewed, they admitted to 67 percent of the instances of breaking and entering, 70 percent of the instances of property destruction, and an astounding 87 percent of all the armed robberies admitted to by the entire sample.[19] Williams and Gold studied a national sample of 847 males and females between the ages of thirteen and sixteen.[20] Of these, 88 percent admitted to at least one delinquent offense. Eugene Doleschal writes of the Williams-Gold study:

> *In support of recent studies, this research found that the relationship between social status and delinquent behavior was weak except that*

higher-status white boys were more delinquent than lower-status white boys. *The greater seriousness of the higher-status boys' delinquent behavior stemmed from their committing proportionally more thefts, joy riding, and (surprisingly) assaults.*[21]

Even those who conclude "that more lower status youngsters commit delinquent acts more frequently than do higher status youngster"[22] also recognize that lower-class youth are significantly overrepresented in official records. Gold writes that "about five times more lowest than highest status boys appear in the official records; if records were complete and unselective, we estimate that the ratio would be closer to 1.5:1.[23] The simple fact is that for the same offense, *a poor person is more likely to be arrested and, if arrested charged, than a middle- or upper-class person.*[24]

This means, first of all, that poor people are more likely to come to the attention of the police. Furthermore, even when apprehended, the police are more likely to formally charge a poor person and release a higher-class person *for the same offense.* Gold writes that

> *boys who live in poorer parts of town and are apprehended by police for delinquency are four to five times more likely to appear in some official record than boys from wealthier sections who commit* the same kinds of offenses. *These same data show that, at each stage in the legal process from charging a boy with an offense to some sort of disposition in court, boys from different socio-economic backgrounds are treated differently, so that those eventually incarcerated in public institutions, that site of most of the research on delinquency, are* selectively poorer boys.[25]

Based on a study of self-reported delinquent behavior, Gold finds that when individuals were apprehended, "if the offender came from a higher status family, police were more likely to handle the matter themselves without referring it to the court."[26]

Terence Thornberry reaches a similar conclusion in a more recent study of 3,475 delinquent boys in Philadelphia. Thornberry found that among boys arrested *for equally serious offenses* and who had *similar prior offense records*, police were more likely to refer the lower-class youths than the more affluent ones to juvenile court. The police were more likely to deal with the wealthier youngsters informally, for example, by holding them in the station house until their parents came rather than instituting formal procedures. Of those referred to juvenile court, Thornberry found further that for *equally serious offenses* and with *similar prior records*, the poorer youngsters were more likely to be institutionalized than were the affluent ones. The wealthier youths were more likely to receive probation than the poorer ones. As might be expected, Thornberry found the same relationships when comparing the treatment of black and white youths apprehended for equally serious offenses.[27]

Recent studies continue to show similar effects. For example, Sampson found that, for the same crimes, juveniles in lower-class neighborhoods were more likely to have some police record than those in better-off neighborhoods. Again, for similar crimes, lower-class juveniles were more likely to be referred to court than better-off juveniles. If you think that these differences are not so important because they are only true of young offenders, remember that this group accounts for much of the crime problem. Moreover, other studies not limited to the young tend to show the same economic bias. Liska and Chamlin found that the degree of economic inequality in an urban area had a positive effect on arrest rates, independent of reported crime rates. They take this to support the notion that economic inequality increases the threat perceived by the dominant class and thus increases their tendency to use state coercion against the lower class to protect their interests.[28]

Any number of reasons can be offered to account for these differences in treatment. Some argue that they reflect the fact that the poor have less privacy.[29] What others can do in their living rooms or backyards, the poor do on the street. Others argue that a police officer's decision to book a poor youth and release a middle-class youth reflects either the officer's judgment that the higher-class youngster's family will be more likely and more able to discipline him or her than the lower-class youngster's or differences in the degree to which poor and middle-class complainants demand arrest. Others argue that police training and police work condition police officers to be suspicious of certain kinds of people, such as lower-class youth, blacks, Mexicans, and so on,[30] and thus more likely to detect their criminality. Still others hold that police mainly arrest those with the least political clout,[31] those who are least able to focus public attention on police practices or bring political influence to bear, and these happen to be the members of the lowest social and economic classes.

Regardless of which view one takes, and probably all have some truth in them, one conclusion is inescapable: One of the reasons that the offender "at the end of the road in prison is likely to be a member of the lowest social and economic groups in the country" is that the police officers who guard the access to the road to prison make sure that more poor people will make the trip than well-to-do people.

The *weeding out of the wealthy* starts at the very entrance to the criminal justice system: The decision about whom to investigate, arrest, or charge is not made simply on the basis of the offense committed or the danger posed. It is a decision that is distorted by a systematic economic bias that works to the disadvantage of the poor.

This economic bias is a two-edged sword. Not only are the poor arrested and charged out of proportion to their numbers for the kinds of crimes poor people generally commit—burglary, robbery, assault, and so forth—but when we reach the kinds of crimes poor people almost never have the opportunity to commit, such as anti-trust violations, industrial safety violations, embezzlement, serious tax evasion, the criminal justice system shows an increasingly benign and merciful face. The more likely that a crime is the type committed by middle- and upper-class people, the less likely that it will be treated as a criminal offense. When it comes to crime in the streets, where the perpetrator is apt to be poor, he or she is even more likely to be arrested and formally charged. When it comes to crime in the suites, where the offender is apt to be affluent, the system is most likely to deal with the crime noncriminally, that is, by civil litigation or informal settlement. Where it does choose to proceed criminally, as we will see in the section on sentencing, it rarely goes beyond a slap on the wrist. Not only is the main entry to the road to prison held wide open to the poor, but the access routes for the wealthy are largely sealed off. Once again, we should not be surprised at who we find in our prisons.

Many writers have commented on the extent and seriousness of "white-collar crime," so I will keep my remarks to a minimum. Nevertheless, for those of us trying to understand how the image of crime is created, four points should be noted.

1. White-collar crime is costly; it takes far more dollars from our pockets than all the FBI Index crimes combined.
2. White-collar crime is widespread, probably much more so than the crimes of the poor.
3. White-collar criminals are rarely arrested or charged; the system has developed kindlier ways of dealing with the more delicate sensibilities of its higher-class clientele.
4. When the white-collar criminals are prosecuted and convicted,

their sentences are either suspended or very light when judged by the cost their crimes have imposed on society.

The first three points will be discussed here, and the fourth will be presented in the section on sentencing below. There is considerable disagreement about the magnitude of the cost of white-collar crime, except that all experts agree that it is enormous. Speaking before the Executive Club of Chicago on November 14, 1980, Herschell Britton, executive vice president of Burns International Security Services, states, "White-collar crime . . . currently costs the country nearly $70 billion a year!"[32] "The [Senate] Judiciary Subcommittee on Antitrust and Monopoly, headed by the late Senator Philip Hart, estimated that faulty goods, monopolistic practices, and other violations annually cost consumers between $174 and $231 billion."[33] A 1979 article on white-collar crime in *Newsweek* reports that estimates "of the total cost to the nation vary widely—from $50 billion to $200 billion a year."[34] In 1985, *U.S. News and World Report* indicated that "Experts estimate that white-collar criminals rake in a minimum of $200 billion annually."[35] Tax evasion alone has been estimated to cost from 5 to 7 percent of the gross national product. For 1986, that would be between $216 and $296 billion.[36] In some areas of the economy, white-collar crime is growing dramatically. For example, the North American Securities Administrators Association (NASAA) conducted a survey of state enforcement actions and found that $400 million had been lost to investors as a result of fraud and abuse in the financial planning industry during the period from 1986 to 1988. Most striking, however, was their finding that "the number of state actions against financial planners rose 155 percent and the amount of lost investor funds climbed 340 percent" since their previous survey in 1985.[37] Then of course there is the recent news about fraud in the savings and loan industry.

Fortunately, all we need is a rough estimate of the cost of white-collar crime so that we can compare its impact with that of the crimes reported on by the FBI. For this purpose, we can use the conservative estimates in the U.S. Chamber of Commerce's *A Handbook on White-Collar Crime*.[38] Because the *Handbook* was issued in 1974, we will have to adjust its figures to take into account both inflation and growth in population so that we can compare these figures with losses reported for 1986 by the FBI. Between 1974 and 1986, the population of the United States increased 14 percent, and

TABLE 3

The Cost of White-Collar Crime (in Billions of Dollars)

Bankruptcy fraud		$0.21
Bribery, kickbacks, and payoffs		7.74
Computer-related crime		0.26
Consumer fraud, illegal competition, deceptive practices		54.18
Consumer victims	$14.2	
Business victims	9.0	
Government revenue loss	31.0	
Credit card and check fraud		2.84
Credit card	0.3	
Check	2.6	
Embezzlement and pilferage		18.06
Embezzlement (cash, goods, services)	7.7	
Pilferage	10.3	
Insurance fraud		5.16
Insurer victims	3.9	
Policyholder victims	1.3	
Receiving stolen property		9.03
Securities thefts and frauds		10.32
Total (billions)		$107.80

Source: Chamber of Commerce of the United States, *A Handbook on White-Collar Crime*, 1974 (figures adjusted for inflation and population growth through 1986; subtotals do not sum to totals due to rounding).

the consumer price index increased 126 percent. Assuming that the rate of white-collar crime relative to the population has remained constant from 1974 to 1986 and assuming that its real dollar value has remained constant as well (two conservative assumptions in light of the judgments just cited that white-collar crime has risen), we can bring the Chamber of Commerce's figures up to date by multiplying them by 2.58 (1.14 × 2.26 = 2.5764). The Chamber of Commerce estimated the total cost of white-collar crime in 1974 to be $41.78 billion. We can estimate, then, that in 1986 white-collar crime cost more than *$107 billion*. (See Table 3 for the breakdown into costs per category of white-collar crime.) This is certainly conservative in light of the estimates quoted earlier, but large enough for our purposes. For example, it is more than *6,000 times* the total amount taken in all bank robberies in the United States in 1986 and more than *nine times* the total amount stolen in all thefts reported in the FBI *Uniform Crime Reports* for that year.[39]

In addition to fraud and tax evasion by individuals, corporate crime is also rampant. Sutherland, in a study published in 1949 that has become a classic, analyzed the "behavior" of 70 of the largest 200 U.S. corporations over a period of some forty years:

> The records reveal that every one of the seventy corporations had violated one or more of the laws, with an average of about thirteen adverse decisions per corporation and a range of from one to fifty adverse decisions per corporation. The corporations had a total of 307 adverse decisions on charges of restraint of trade, 222 adverse decisions on charges of infringements [of patents, trademarks, and copyrights], 158 adverse decisions under the National Labor Relations Act, 97 adverse decisions under the laws regulating advertising, and 196 adverse decisions on charges of violating other laws. Thus, generally, the official records reveal that these corporations violated the trade regulations with great frequency. The "habitual criminal" laws of some states impose severe penalties on criminals convicted the third or fourth time. If this criterion were used here, about 90 percent of the large corporations studied would be considered habitual white-collar criminals.[40]

Nevertheless, corporate executives almost never end up in jail, where they would find themselves sharing cells with poorer persons who had stolen less from their fellow citizens.

Marshall Clinard and Peter Yeager attempted to replicate Sutherland's pioneering work by studying legal violations and enforcement actions for the 582 largest manufacturing, wholesale, retail, and service establishments during a two-year period, 1975 to 1976. They found that little had changed:

> A total of 1,553 federal cases were begun against all 582 largest manufacturing, wholesale, retail, and service establishments during 1975 and 1976, or an average of 2.7 federal cases of violation each. Of the 582 corporations, 350 (60.1 percent) had at least one federal action brought against them, and for those firms that had at least one action brought against them, the average was 4.4 cases.[41]

The vast majority of these were treated lightly, either by administrative action or civil penalty. Of the 1,553 cases, only 39 were dealt with criminally, and normally this meant a small fine.[42]

The continued prevalence of these practices is confirmed in a recent study of white-collar crime prosecutions by Susan Shapiro, titled "The Road Not Taken: The Elusive Path to Criminal Prosecution for White-Collar Offenders." Focusing on the enforcement practices of the Securities and Exchange Commission (SEC), Shapiro writes that,

*while criminal dispositions are often appropriate, they are rarely pursued
to the sentencing stage. Out of every 100 suspects investigated by the SEC,
93 have committed securities violations that carry criminal penalties.
Legal action is taken against 46 of them, but only 11 are selected for
criminal treatment. Six of these are indicted; 5 will be convicted and 3
sentenced to prison. Thus, for Securities and Exchange Commission enforcement, criminal prosecution most often represents the road not taken.
Of those found to have engaged in securities fraud, 88 percent never have
to contend with the criminal justice system at all.*[43]

With upper-class lawbreakers, the authorities prefer to sue in
civil court for damages or for an injunction rather than treat the
wealthy as common criminals. Judges have on occasion stated in
open court that they would not make criminals of reputable businessmen. One would think that it would be up to the businessmen
to make criminals of themselves by their actions, but alas, *this*
right is reserved for the lower classes. Other studies bear this out. A
1987 study of prosecutors' decisions to press charges shows a "pattern of discrimination," in which black and Hispanic male defendants are more likely to be prosecuted fully than white Anglo
males.[44] Another study of prosecutorial decisions shows that lower-
class individuals are more likely to have charges pressed against
them than upper-class individuals.[45]

Examples of reluctance to use the full force of the criminal
process for crimes not generally committed by the poor can be
multiplied ad infinitum. Let me close with one final example that
typifies this particular distortion of criminal justice policy.

Embezzlement is the crime of misappropriating money or property entrusted to one's care, custody, or control. Because the poor
are rarely entrusted with tempting sums of money or valuable
property, this is predominantly a crime of the middle and upper
classes. The U.S. Chamber of Commerce estimates the annual economic cost of embezzlement (adjusted for 1986) at $7.7 billion,
about two-thirds the total value of all property and money stolen
in all FBI Index property crimes in 1986. Thus, it is fair to conclude
that embezzlement imposes a cost on society comparable to that
imposed by the Index property crimes. Nevertheless, the FBI reports that in 1986, when there were 1,701,680 arrests for property
crimes, there were 10,500 arrests for embezzlement nationwide.[46]
Although their cost to society is comparable, the number of arrests
for property crimes was *162 times greater* than the number of arrests for embezzlement. Roughly, this means that there was one
property crime arrest for every $6,800 stolen, and one embezzle-

ment arrest for every $733,000 "misappropriated." Note that even the language becomes more delicate as we deal with a "better class" of crook.

The clientele of the criminal justice system forms an exclusive club. Entry is largely a privilege of the poor. The crimes they commit are the crimes that qualify one for admission—and they are admitted in greater proportion than their share of those crimes. Curiously enough, the crimes the affluent commit are not the kind that easily qualify one for membership in the club.

Conviction

Between arrest and imprisonment lies the crucial process that determines guilt or innocence. Studies of individuals accused of similar offenses and with similar prior records show that the poor defendant is more likely to be adjudicated guilty than is the wealthier defendant.[47] In the adjudication process the only thing that *should* count is whether the accused is guilty and whether the prosecution can prove it beyond a reasonable doubt. Unfortunately, at least two other factors that are irrelevant to the question of guilt or innocence significantly affect the outcome: One is the ability of the accused to be free on bail prior to trial, and the second is access to legal counsel able to devote adequate time and energy to the case. Because both bail and high-quality legal counsel cost money, it should come as no surprise that here as elsewhere the poor do poorly. "A defendant in a criminal court," writes Abraham Blumberg,

> is really beaten by the deprivations and limitations imposed by his social class, race and ethnicity. These in turn preclude such services as bail, legal counsel, psychiatric services, expert witnesses, and investigatory assistance. In essence the concomitants of poverty are responsible for the fact that due process sometimes produces greatly disproportionate results in an ill-matched struggle.[48]

Being released on bail is important in several respects. First and foremost, of course, is the fact that those who are not released on bail are kept in jail like individuals who have been found guilty. They are thus punished while they are still legally innocent. In 1972, 51,000 (out of a total of 142,000) inmates of local jails were confined while awaiting trial. Their average pre-trial or pre-sentence confinement was three months, and 60 percent of the nation's jails do not separate pre-trial defendants from convicted offenders. In 1978, out of 158,000 inmates of local jails, 67,000 had not yet been convicted.[49] Beyond the obvious ugliness of punishing people before they are found guilty, confined defendants suffer from other disabilities. Specifically, they cannot actively aid in their own defense by seeking out witnesses and evidence. Several studies have shown that among defendants accused of the same offenses, those who make bail are more likely to be acquitted than those who do not.[50]

Furthermore, because the time spent in jail prior to adjudication of guilt may count as part of the sentence if one is found guilty, the accused are often placed in a ticklish position. Let us say the accused believes that he or she is innocent or at least that the state cannot prove guilt, and let us say also that he or she has been in the slammer for two months awaiting trial. Along comes the prosecutor to offer a deal: If you plead guilty to such-and-such (usually a lesser offense than has been charged, e.g., possession of burglar's tools instead of burglary), the prosecutor promises to ask the judge to sentence you to two months. In other words, plead guilty and walk out of jail today—or maintain your innocence, stay in jail until trial, and then be tried for the full charge instead of the lesser offense! Plea-bargaining is an everyday occurrence in the criminal justice system. Contrary to the Perry Mason image, the vast majority of criminal convictions in the United States are reached without a trial. It is estimated that between 70 and 95 percent of convictions are the result of a negotiated plea,[51] that is, a bargain in which the accused agrees to plead guilty (usually to a lesser offense than he or she is charged with or to one offense out of many he or she is charged with) in return for an informal promise of leniency from the prosecutor with the tacit consent of the judge. If you were the jailed defendant offered a deal like this, how would you choose? Suppose you were a poor black man not likely to be able to retain F. Lee Bailey or Edward Bennett Williams for your defense.

The advantages of access to adequate legal counsel during the adjudicative process are obvious but still worthy of mention. In 1963, the U.S. Supreme Court handed down the landmark *Gideon* v. *Wainwright* decision, holding that the states must provide legal counsel to the indigent in all felony cases. As a result, no person accused of a serious crime need face their accusers without a lawyer. However, the Supreme Court has not held that the Constitution requires that individuals are entitled to lawyers able to devote equal time and resources to their cases. Even though *Gideon* represents significant progress in making good on the constitutional promise of equal treatment before the law, we still are left with two transmission belts of justice: one for the poor and one for the afflu-ent. There is, to be sure, an emerging body of case law on the right to effective assistance of counsel;[52] however, this is yet to have any serious impact on the assembly-line legal aid handed out to the poor.

Indigent defendants, those who cannot afford to retain their own lawyers, will be defended either by a public defender or by a private attorney assigned by the court. Because the public de-fender is a salaried attorney with a case load much larger than that of a private criminal lawyer,[53] and because court-assigned private attorneys are paid a fixed fee that is much lower than they charge their regular clients, neither is able or motivated to devote much time to the indigent defendant's defense. Both are strongly moti-vated to bring their cases to a close quickly by negotiating a plea of guilty. Because the public defender works in day-to-day contact with the prosecutor and the judge, the pressures on him or her to negotiate a plea as quickly as possible, instead of rocking the boat by threatening to go to trial,[54] are even greater than those that work on court-assigned counsel. In an essay, aptly titled "Did You Have a Lawyer When You Went to Court? No, I Had a Public De-fender," Jonathan Casper reports the perceptions of this process from the standpoint of the defendants:

> *Most of the men spent very little time with their public defender. In the court in which they eventually plead guilty, they typically reported spend-ing on the order of five to ten minutes with their public defender. These conversations usually took place in the bull-pen of the courthouse or in the hallway.*
>
> *The brief conversations usually did not involve much discussion of the details surrounding the alleged crime, mitigating circumstances or the defendants' motives or backgrounds. Instead, they focused on the deal, the offer the prosecution was likely to make or had made in return for a cop out. Often the defendants reported that the first words the public defender spoke (or at least the first words the defendants recalled) were, "I can get you . . ., if you plead guilty."[55]*

Abraham S. Blumberg studied 724 male felony defendants who pleaded guilty in a large metropolitan court. He found that in the majority of cases it was the defense counsel who first sug-gested a guilty plea and who most influenced the defendant's decision to plead guilty. More striking still, however, was the find-ing that public defenders and court-assigned lawyers suggested the plea of guilty *earlier* than privately retained attorneys. On this, Blumberg comments, "Legal-aid and assigned counsel are apparently more likely to suggest the plea in the initial interview, perhaps as a response to the pressures of time and, in the case of the assigned counsel, the strong possibility that there is no fee involved."[56] Privately retained counsel suggested the plea in the initial meeting in 35 percent of their cases, public defenders in 49 percent, and assigned counsel in 60 percent.[57] It should be noted that Blumberg concludes that these differences have little impact on the eventual outcome. Other findings point to a different conclusion.

As might be expected, with less time and ressources to devote to the cause, public defenders and assigned lawyers cannot devote as much time and research to preparing the crucial pretrial motions that can often lead to dismissal of charges against the accused. One study shows that public defenders got dismissals in 8 percent of their cases, assigned lawyers in 6 percent, and privately retained counsel in *29 percent of their cases.*[58] As also might be expected, the overall acquittal rate for privately retained counsel is considerably better than that for public defenders and assigned counsel. The same study shows that public defenders achieved either dismissal of charges or a finding of not guilty in 17 percent of the indictments they handled, assigned counsel did the same in 18 percent, and privately retained counsel got their clients off the hook in *36 percent of their indictments.* The picture that emerges from federal courts is not much different.[59]

The problem of adequate legal representation may be particularly acute in capital cases. According to Robert Johnson, "Most attorneys in capital cases are provided by the state. Defendants, as good capitalists, routinely assume that they will get what they pay for: next to nothing." Their perceptions, he concludes, "may not be far from right." Indeed, Stephen Gettinger maintains that an inadequate defense was "the single outstanding characteristic" of the condemned persons he studied. The result: Capital defendants appeared in court as "creatures beyond comprehension, virtually gagged and masked in preparation for the execution chamber."[60] Writes Linda Williams in the *Wall Street Journal,*

> *The popular perception is that the system guarantees a condemned person a lawyer. But most states provide counsel only for the trial and the automatic review of the sentence by the state appeals court. Indigent prisoners—a description that applies to just about everybody on death row—who seek further review must rely on the charity of a few private lawyers and on cash-starved organizations like the Southern Prisoners Defense Committee.*[61]

Needless to say, the distinct legal advantages that money can buy become even more salient when we enter the realm of corporate and other white-collar crime. Indeed, it is often precisely the time and cost involved in bringing to court a large corporation with its army of legal eagles that is offered as an excuse for the less formal and more genteel treatment accorded to corporate crooks. This excuse is, of course, not equitably distributed to all economic classes, any more than quality legal service is. What this means in simple terms is that regardless of actual innocence or guilt, one's chances of beating the rap increase as one's income increases. Regardless of what fraction of crimes are committed by the poor, the criminal justice system is distorted so that an even greater fraction of those convicted will be poor. With conviction comes sentencing.

Sentencing

He had a businessman's suit and a businessman's tan, but Jack L. Clark no longer had a business. His nursing home construction company had collapsed in a gigantic stock fraud, leaving shareholders out $200 million and leaving Clark in a federal courthouse, awaiting sentence for stock manipulation. Ten million of the swindled dollars had allegedly gone for Clark's personal use, and prosecutors accused him of stashing away 4 million unrecovered dollars in a retirement nest egg. Out of an original indictment of 65 counts, Clark had pleaded guilty to one charge. He faced a maximum penalty of a $10,000 fine and five years in prison. But the judge, before passing sentence, remembered the "marked improvement" in care for the elderly that Clark's nursing homes had provided. . . . He considered that Clark was a 46-year-old family man who coached little kids in baseball and football. Then he passed sentence. No fine. One year in prison. Eligible for parole after four months.

In another federal courtroom stood Matthew Corelli (not his real name), a 45-year-old, $125-a-week laborer who lived with his wife and kids in a $126-a-month apartment. Along with three other men, Corelli had been convicted of possessing $5,000 of stolen drugstore goods that government prosecutors identified as part of a $63,000 shipment. The judge considered Corelli's impoverished circumstances, his number of dependents, the nature of his crime, and then passed sentence: four years in prison. Or in other words, four times the punishment Clark received for a fraction of the crime.[62]

Jack Greenberg took $15 from a post office; last May in Federal Court in Manhattan he drew six months in jail. Howard Lazell "misapplied" $150,000 from a bank; in the same month in the same courthouse he drew probation.[63]

The first quotation is the opening passage of a magazine article on white-collar crime, aptly titled "America's Most Coddled Criminals." The second quotation is the opening paragraph of a *New York Times* article, more prosaically titled "Wide Disparities Mark Sentences Here." Both, however, are testimony to the fact the the criminal justice system reserves its harshest penalties for its lower-class clients and puts on kid gloves when confronted with a better class of crook.

The system is doubly biased against the poor. First, there is the class bias *between* crimes that we have just seen. The crimes that poor people are likely to commit carry harsher sentences than the "crimes in the suites" committed by well-to-do people. Second, for *all* crimes, the poor receive less probation and more years of confinement than well-off defendants *convicted of the same offense*, assuring us once again that the vast majority of those who are put behind bars are from the lowest social and economic classes in the nation.

The *New York Times* article just quoted reports the results of a study done by the *New York Times* on sentencing in state and federal courts. The *Times* states that "crimes that tend to be committed by the poor get tougher sentences than those committed by the well-to-do," that federal "defendants who could not afford private counsel were sentenced nearly twice as severely as defendants with private or no counsel," and that a "study by the Vera Institute of Justice of courts in the Bronx indicates a similar pattern in the state courts."[64]

Looking at federal and state courts, Stuart Nagel concludes that

> *not only are the indigent found guilty more often, but they are much less likely to be recommended for probation by the probation officer, or to be granted probation or suspended sentences by the judge.*

Further, that

> *the federal data show that this is true also of those with no prior record: 27 percent of the indigent with no prior record were not recommended for probation against 16 percent of the non-indigent; 23 percent indigent did not receive suspended sentences or probation against 15 percent non-indigent. Among those of both groups with "some" prior record the spread is even greater.*[65]

Eugene Doleschal and Nora Klapmuts report as "typical of American studies," Thornberry's analysis of "3,475 Philadelphia delinquents that found that blacks and members of lower socioeconomic groups were likely to receive more severe dispositions than whites and the more affluent even when the appropriate legal variables [i.e., offense, prior record, and so on] were held constant.[66] More recently, applying more sophisticated statistical techniques to the data upon which his Philadelphia study was based, Thornberry concludes, "When seriousness, prior record and SES [socioeconomic strata] were held constant, blacks were significantly more likely than whites to receive more severe dispositions." Although he finds the effect of socioeconomic status weaker than in the earlier study, Thornberry writes, "When the variable of race was suppressed . . . , SES was found to be significantly related to dispositions such that lower SES subjects were treated more severely than their high SES counterparts.[67]

Studying the experiences of 798 burglary and larceny defendants in North Carolina, Clarke and Koch find that

> *other things being equal, the low-income defendant had a greater chance than the higher-income defendant of emerging from the criminal court with an active prison sentence. . . . Our tentative conclusion is that most of the influence of income on the likelihood of imprisonment among the defendants studied is explained by the poorer opportunity of the low-income defendant for [release on] bail and his greater likelihood of having a court-assigned rather than a privately retained attorney.*[68]

Analyzing data from Chicago trial courts, Lizotte finds that, other things being equal,

> *laborers and non-whites are . . . twice as likely as proprietors to stay incarcerated between arrest and final disposition [i.e., not be released on bail]. Further, other factors being equal, laborers and non-whites are given longer prison sentences than higher SES groups.*[69]

As usual, data on racial discrimination in sentencing exist in much greater abundance than data on class discrimination, but they tell the same story of the treatment of those who cannot afford the going price of justice. Most striking perhaps is the fact that more than 45 percent of the inmates in federal and state prisons are black, whereas blacks make up only 34 percent of those arrested for serious (FBI Index) crimes. Furthermore, when we look only at federal prisons, where there is reason to believe that racial and economic discrimination is less prevalent than in state institutions, we find that the average sentence for a white inmate in 1986 was 112.4 months, compared to 149.6 months (more than three years more!) for nonwhite inmates. Nonwhite inmates are sentenced, on average, 33 more months for burglary than white inmates and 22 more months for income tax evasion.[70]

By an act of dubious mercy of which Americans ought hardly to be proud, blacks often receive lighter sentences for murder and rape than whites as long as the victim was black as well.[71] According to a recent four-state study of capital sentencing, this dubious mercy extends to the death penalty. In Florida, for example, blacks "who kill whites are nearly forty times more likely to be sentenced to death than those who kill blacks." Moreover, among "killers of whites, blacks are five times more likely than whites to be sentenced to death." This pattern of double discrimination was also evidenced, though less pronouncedly, in Texas, Ohio, and Georgia, the other states surveyed. Together, these four states "accounted for approximately 70 percent of the nation's death sentences" between 1972 and 1977.[72] More recent studies, in which alternative explanations, such as severity of crime, presence of aggravating factors, and relationship between criminal and victim have been ruled out, have shown the same pattern. Indeed, it was on the basis of such research that what may have been the last constitutional challenge to the death penalty was raised and rejected. In the 1987 case of *McCleskey* v. *Kemp*, the Justices of the Supreme Court acknowledged the systemic disparities, but a majority held that the disparities would not invalidate death penalty convictions unless discrimination could be shown in the individual case at hand.[73] Note that all these discriminatory sentences were rendered under statutes that had passed constitutional muster and were therefore presumed free of the biases that led the Supreme Court to invalidate death penalty statutes in *Furman* v. *Georgia* in 1972.

Mary Owen Cameron studied the sentencing practices of judges in the Chicago Women's Court during a three-year period. Her findings were as follows:

> *Judges found sixteen percent of the white women brought before them on charges of shoplifting to be "not guilty," but only four percent of the black women were found innocent. In addition, twenty-two percent of the black women as compared to four percent of the white women were sent to jail. Finally, of the twenty-one white women sentenced to jail, only two (ten percent) were to be jailed for thirty days or more; of the seventy-six black women sentenced to jail twenty (twenty-six percent) were to be jailed for thirty days or more.[74]*

An extensive study by the Boston Globe of 4,500 cases of armed robbery, aggravated assault, and rape found that *blacks convicted in the superior courts of Massachusetts receive harsher penalties than whites for the same crimes. . . . The median time served by blacks is nine weeks longer than that served by whites for armed robbery, 13½ months longer for rape and about equal for aggravated assault. . . . The typical minimum sentence for blacks . . . on all three crimes combined is more than a year longer than for whites.[75]*

The authors of a study of almost 1,200 males sentenced to prison for armed robbery in a southeastern state found that "in 1977 whites incarcerated for armed robbery had a greater than average chance of receiving the least severe sentence, while nonwhites had a greater than average chance of receiving a moderately severe sentence."[76] A study of 229 adjudicated cases in a Florida judicial district yielded the finding that "whites have an 18 percent greater chance in the predicted probability of receiving probation than blacks when all other things are equal."[77] A recent study of criminal justice systems in California, Michigan, and Texas by Petersilia confirms the continuation of this trend. "Controlling for the factors most likely to influence sentencing and parole decisions," she writes, "the analysis still found that blacks and Hispanics are less likely to be given probation, more likely to receive *prison* sentences, more likely to receive longer sentences, and more likely to serve a greater portion of their original time."[78] Myers found that "harsher treatment of persons with fewer resources (e.g., female, unemployed, unmarried, black) is . . . pronounced in highly unequal counties."[79] A study of the effects of implementing Minnesota's determinate sentencing program shows that socioeconomic bias is "more subtle, but no less real" than before the new program.[80]

Another study has shown that among blacks and whites on death row, whites are more likely to have their sentences commuted. Also, blacks or whites who have private counsel are more likely to have their execution commuted than condemned persons defended by court-appointed attorneys.[81]

As I have already pointed out, justice is increasingly tempered with mercy as we deal with a better class of crime. The Sherman Antitrust Act is a criminal law. It was passed in recognition of the fact that one virtue of a free enterprise economy is that competition tends to drive consumer prices down, so agreements by competing firms to refrain from price competition is the equivalent of stealing money from the consumer's pocket. Nevertheless, although such conspiracies cost consumers far more than lower-class theft, price-fixing was a misdemeanor until 1974.[82] In practice, few conspirators end up in prison, and when they do, the sentence is a mere token, well below the maximum provided in the law. Thus, based on the government's track record, there is little reason to expect things to change significantly now that price-fixing is a felony.

In the historic *Electrical Equipment* cases in the early 1960s, executives of several major firms secretly met to fix prices on electrical equipment to a degree that is estimated to have cost the buying public well over a billion dollars. The executives involved knew they were violating the law. They used plain envelopes for their communications, called their meetings "choir practice," and referred to the list of executives in attendance as the "Christmas card list." This case is rare and famous because it was one in which the criminal sanction was actually imposed. Seven executives received and served jail sentences. In light of the amount of money they had stolen from the American public, however, their sentences were more an indictment of the government than of themselves: *thirty days in jail!*

Speaking about the record of federal antitrust prosecution, Clinard and Yeager write that

> even in the most widespread and flagrant price conspiracy cases, few corporate executives are ever imprisoned; of the total 231 cases with individual defendants from 1955 to 1975, prison sentences were given in only 19 cases. Of a total of 1,027 individual defendants, only 49 were sentenced to prison.[83]

There is some (slight) indication of a toughening in the sentences since antitrust violations were made a felony in 1974, and penalties were increased. "In felony cases prosecuted under the new penalties through March 1978, 15 of 21 sentenced individuals (71 percent) were given terms averaging 192 days each."[84] Nevertheless, when the cost to society is reckoned, even such penalties as these are hardly severe.

To be sure, there has been some toughening of the treatment of white-collar offenders in recent years, particularly in the wake of the Watergate scandals, which vividly brought home to Americans the reality of crime in high places. Nonetheless, this toughening has been relatively mild, especially when compared to the treatment dealt out to lower-class offenders. Studies have shown that even though corporate and white-collar lawbreakers are being more frequently brought to justice and more frequently being sanctioned, they still receive more lenient sentences than do those who

TABLE 4

Sentences for Different Classes of Crime

	Average Sentence (in months)	Average Time Served (in months)
Crimes of the poor		
Robbery	128.5	46.5
Larceny/theft	36.9	18.3
Burglary	35.6	17.9
Crimes of the affluent		
Fraud	27.8	13.6
Embezzlement	23.8	11.4
Income tax evasion	18.3	10.3

Source: Federal Bureau of Prisons—Statistical Report, Fiscal Year 1986.

are sentenced for common property crimes.[85] A study by Hagan and Palloni, which focuses particularly on the differences between pre- and post-Watergate treatment of white-collar offenders, concludes that likelihood of prosecution after Watergate was increased, but that the effect of this was canceled out by the leniency of the sentences meted out:

> the new incarcerated white-collar offenders received relatively light sentences that counterbalanced the increased use of imprisonment. . . . Relative to less-educated common criminals, white-collar offenders were more likely to be imprisoned after Watergate than before, but for shorter periods.[86]

Even after the heightened public awareness of white-collar crime that came in the wake of Watergate, it remains the case that the crimes of the poor receive stiffer sentences than the crimes of the well-to-do (see Table 4). Keep in mind while looking at these figures that *each* of the "crimes of the affluent" costs the public more than *all* of the "crimes of the poor" put together.

A study of sentencing practices in the Southern District of New York, optimistically titled *Justice in Sentencing*, found

> plain indications that white collar defendants, predominantly white, receive more lenient treatment as a general rule, while defendants charged with common crimes, largely committed by the unemployed and undereducated, a group which embraces large numbers of blacks in today's society, are more likely to be sent to prison. If these indications are cor-

rect, then one may conclude that poor persons receive harsher treatment in the Federal Courts than do well-to-do defendants charged with more sophisticated crimes.

Specifically, the study reports that

during the six-month period covered by the Southern District of New York sentencing study, defendants convicted of white collar crimes stood a 36% chance of going to prison; defendants convicted of nonviolent common crimes stood a 53% chance of going to prison; and defendants convicted of violent crimes stood an 80% chance of going to prison.[87]

Several things are worthy of note here. First, the study carries forth the distorted conventional wisdom about crime by distinguishing between "white-collar" and "common" crime, when, as we have found, there is reason to believe that white-collar crime is just as common as the so-called common crimes of the poor. Second, the disparities reported refer only to likelihood of imprisonment *for any length of time,* and so they really understate the disparities in treatment, because the so-called common crimes also receive *longer* prison sentences than the white-collar crimes. Third, and most important, the disparities cannot be explained by the greater danger of lower-class criminals because even the perpetrators of *nonviolent "common" crimes* stand a 50 percent greater chance of going to prison than do white-collar crooks.

A graphic illustration of the way the criminal justice system treats the wealthy is provided by Fleetwood and Lubow in their article "America's Most Coddled Criminals." They put together their pick of ten convicted white-collar criminals, comparing their sentences with the crimes they committed. The chart speaks for itself (see Table 5).

Equally eloquent testimony to the merciful face that the criminal justice system turns toward upper-class crooks is found in a *New York Times* report on the fate of twenty-one business executives found guilty of making illegal campaign contributions during the Watergate scandal in the early 1970's:

Most of the 21 business executives who admitted their guilt to the Watergate Special Prosecutor in 1973 and 1974—especially those from large corporations—are still presiding over their companies. . . .

Only two went to jail. They served a few months and were freed. . . .

Furthermore, the fines of $1,000 or $2,000 that most of the contributors of illegal funds had to pay have not made much of a dent in their style of living. . . .

An investigation into the whereabouts and financial status of the 21

TABLE 5

Ten Bandits: What They Did and What They Got

This isn't the Chamber of Commerce list of brightest young businessmen, and it's not the ten best-dressed list. It's a list of ten very respectable criminals. Have any favorites you don't see here? Send them in.

Criminal	Crime	Sentence
Jack L. Clark	President and chairman of Four Seasons Nursing Centers, Clark finagled financial reports and earnings projections to inflate his stock artificially. Shareholders lost $200 million.	One year in prison.
John Peter Galanis	As portfolio manager of two mutual funds, Galanis bilked investors out of nearly $10 million.	Six months in prison and five years probation.
Virgil A. McGowen	As manager of the Bank of America branch in San Francisco, McGowen siphoned off $591,921 in clandestine loans to friends. Almost none of the money was recovered.	Six months in prison, five years probation, and a $3,600 fine.
Valdemar H. Madis	A wealthy drug manufacturer, Madis diluted an antidote for poisoned children with a worthless, look-alike substance.	One year probation and a $10,000 fine.

Name	Crime	Sentence
John Morgan	President of Jet Craft Ltd., John Morgan illegally sold about $2 million in unregistered securities.	One year in prison and a $10,000 fine.
Irving Projansky	The former chairman of the First National Bank of Lincolnwood, Ill., Projansky raised stock prices artificially and then dumped the shares, costing the public an estimated $4 million.	One year in prison and two years probation.
David Ratliff	Ratliff spent his twenty-one years as a Texas state senator embezzling state funds.	Ten years probation.
Walter J. Rauscher	An executive vice president of American Airlines, Rauscher accepted about $200,000 in kickbacks from businessmen bidding for contracts.	Six months in prison and two years probation.
Frank W. Sharp	The multimillion dollar swindles of Sharp, a Houston banker, shook the Texas state government and forced the resignation of the head of the Criminal Division of the Justice Department.	Three years probation and a $5,000 fine.
Seymour R. Thaler	Soon after his election to the New York State Supreme Court, Thaler was convicted of receiving and transporting $800,000 in stolen U.S. Treasury bills.	One year in prison and a fine of $10,000.

Source: Blake Fleetwood and Arthur Lubow, "America's Most Coddled Criminals," *New Times Magazine*, September 19, 1975.

executives involved in illegal contributions leads to a conclusion that the higher the position the more cushioned the fall—if indeed there was a fall.[88]

The *Times* report also includes a chart illustrating the fate of these upper-class criminals, who were found guilty of nothing less than participating in schemes that undermine the independence of the electoral process—guilty, that is, of contaminating the very life-blood of democratic government. Here, again, the chart speaks for itself (see Table 6). As for the government officials (and their hire-lings) who were directly responsible for the Watergate crimes, their treatment has also been relatively gentle (see Table 7).

On either side of the law, the rich get richer . . .

. . . AND THE POOR GET PRISON

At 9:05 A.M. on the morning of Thursday, September, 9, 1971, a group of inmates forced their way through a gate at the center of the prison, fatally injured a guard named William Quinn, and took fifty hostages. The Attica uprising had begun. It lasted almost exactly four days, until 9:43 A.M. on the morning of Monday, September 13, when corrections officers and state troopers stormed the prison and killed ten hostages and twenty-nine inmates.[89] During those four days the nation saw the faces of its captives on television—the hard black faces of young men who had grown up on the streets of Harlem and other urban ghettos. Theirs were the faces of crime in America. The television viewers who saw them were not surprised. Here were the faces of dangerous men who should be locked up. Nor were people outraged when the state launched its murderous attack on the prison, killing many more inmates and guards than did the prisoners themselves. Maybe they were shocked—but not outraged. Neither were they outraged when two grand juries refused to indict any of the attackers, nor when the mastermind of the attack, Gover-nor Nelson Rockefeller, was named to be vice president of the United States three years after the uprising and massacre.[90]

They were not outraged because the faces they saw on the TV screens fit and confirmed their beliefs about who is a deadly threat to American society—and a deadly threat must be met with deadly force. How did those men get to Attica? How did Americans get their beliefs about who is a dangerous person? Obviously, these questions are interwoven. People get their no-tions about who is a criminal at least in part from the occasional

TABLE 6
Convicted Watergate Campaign Contributors

Company	Name	Fine/Prison	Status as of 1975
American Ship Building	George M. Steinbrenner	$15,000	Still chairman at $50,000/year
	John H. Melcher, Jr.	$2,500	Discharged; practicing law in Cleveland
Ashland Oil	Orin E. Atkins[a]	$1,000	Still chairman at $314,000/year
Associated Milk Producers	Harold S. Nelson	4 months in prison $10,000	Resigned; now in commodities exports
	David L. Parr	4 months prison $10,000	Resigned
	Stuart H. Russell	2 years prison[b]	Resigned; now in private law practice
Braniff International	Harding L. Lawrence	$1,000	Still chairman at $335,000/year
Carnation	H. Everett Olson	$1,000	Still chairman at $212,500/year
Diamond International	Ray Dubrowin	$1,000	Still vice president for public affairs
Goodyear Tire and Rubber	Russell DeYoung	$1,000	Still chairman of two committees at $306,000/year and pension $144,000/year
Gulf Oil	Claude C. Wild, Jr.	$1,000	Consultant in Washington, D.C.

HMS Electric	Charles H. Huseman	$1,000	Still president
LBC&W Inc.	William G. Lyles, Sr.	$2,000	Still chairman
Lehigh Valley Cooperative Farmers	Richard L. Allison	$1,000 (suspended)	Discharged
3M	Harry Heltzer	$500	Retired as chairman, does special projects at $100,000/year
Northrop	Thomas V. Jones	$5,000	Still chief executive at $286,000/year
	James Allen	$1,000	Retired as vice president with pension estimated at $36,000/year
Phillips Petroleum	William W. Keeler	$1,000	Retired, with pension estimated at $201,742/year
Ratrie, Robbins and Schweitzer	Harry Ratrie	1 month probation	Still president
	Augustus Robbins III	1 month probation	Still executive vice president
Time Oil	Raymond Abendroth	$2,000	Still president

Source: Michael C. Jensen, "Watergate Donors Still Riding High," *New York Times*, August 24, 1975.
aPleaded no contest.
bUnder appeal.

TABLE 7

The Watergate Roster

Richard M. Nixon	Unindicted co-conspirator	Pardoned
Dwight L. Chapin	Convicted of lying to a grand jury	Sentenced to serve 10 to 30 months	Served 8 months
Charles W. Colson	Pleaded guilty to obstruction of justice	Sentenced to serve 1 to 3 years and fined $5,000	Served 7 months
John W. Dean III	Pleaded guilty to conspiracy to obstruct justice	Sentenced to serve 1 to 4 years	Served 4 months
John D. Ehrlichman	Convicted of conspiracy to obstruct justice, conspiracy to violate civil rights, and perjury	Sentenced to serve concurrent terms of 20 months to 8 years	Served 18 months
H.R. Haldeman	Convicted of conspiracy to obstruct justice and perjury	Sentenced to serve 30 months to 8 years	Served 18 months
E. Howard Hunt	Pleaded guilty to conspiracy, burglary, and wiretapping	Sentenced to serve 30 months to 8 years and fined $10,000	Served 33 months
Herbert W. Kalmbach	Pleaded guilty to violation of the Federal Corrupt Practices Act and promising federal employment as a reward for political activity	Sentenced to serve 6 to 18 months and fined $10,000	Served 6 months
Richard G. Kleindienst	Pleaded guilty to refusal to answer pertinent questions before a Senate committee	Sentenced to 30 days and fined $100	Sentence suspended
Egil Krogh, Jr.	Pleaded guilty to conspiracy to violate civil rights	Sentenced to serve 2 to 6 years (all but 6 months were suspended)	Served 4½ months
Frederick C. LaRue	Pleaded guilty to conspiracy to obstruct justice	Sentenced to serve 1 to 3 years (all but 6 months were suspended)	Served 5½ months

Name	Conviction/Plea	Sentence	Served
G. Gordon Liddy	Convicted of conspiracy, conspiracy to violate civil rights, burglary, and wiretapping	Sentenced to serve 6 years and 8 months to 20 years and fined $40,000	Served 52 months
Jeb S. Magruder	Pleaded guilty to conspiracy to obstruct justice, wiretapping, and fraud	Sentenced to serve 10 months to 4 years	Served 7 months
John N. Mitchell	Convicted of conspiracy to obstruct justice and perjury	Sentenced to serve 30 months to 8 years	Served 19 months
Donald H. Segretti	Pleaded guilty to campaign violations and conspiracy	Sentenced to serve 6 months	Served 4½ months
Maurice H. Stans	Pleaded guilty to five misdemeanor violations of the Federal Elections Campaign Act	Fined $5,000	
James W. McCord, Jr.	Convicted of conspiracy, burglary, wiretapping, and unlawful possession of intercepting devices	Sentenced to serve 1 to 5 years	Served 4 months
Bernard L. Barker	Pleaded guilty to conspiracy, burglary, wiretapping, and unlawful possession of intercepting devices	Sentenced to serve 18 months to 6 years	Served 12 months
Virgilio R. Gonzalez	Pleaded guilty to conspiracy, burglary, wiretapping, and unlawful possession of intercepting devices	Sentenced to serve 1 to 4 years	Served 15 months
Eugenio R. Martinez	Pleaded guilty to conspiracy, burglary, wiretapping, and unlawful possession of intercepting devices	Sentenced to serve 1 to 4 years	Served 15 months
Frank A. Sturgis	Pleaded guilty to conspiracy, burglary, wiretapping, and unlawful possession of intercepting devices	Sentenced to serve 1 to 4 years	Served 13 months

Source: Washington Post, June 17, 1982.

television or newspaper picture of who is inside our prisons. The individuals they see there have been put in prison because people believe that certain kinds of individuals are dangerous and should be locked up.

I have argued in this chapter that this is not a simple process of selecting the dangerous and the criminal from among the peace-loving and the law-abiding. It is also a process of *weeding out the wealthy* at every stage, so that the final picture—a picture like that that appeared on the TV screen on September 9, 1971—is not a true reflection of the real dangers in our society but a distorted image, the kind reflected in a carnival mirror.

It is not my view that the inmates in Attica were innocent of the crimes that sent them there. I am willing to assume that they and just about all the individuals in prisons in America are probably guilty of the crime for which they were sentenced and maybe more. My point is that people who are equally or more dangerous, equally or more criminal, are not there; that the criminal justice system works systematically, not to punish and confine the dangerous and the criminal, *but to punish and confine the poor who are dangerous and criminal.*

It is successful at all levels. In 1973, there were 204,211 individuals in state and federal prisons, or 96 prisoners for every 100,000 individuals (of all ages) in the general population. By 1979, state and federal inmates numbered 301,470, or 133 per 100,000 Americans. In 1986, there were 523,922 persons in state and federal prisons, a staggering 216 for every 100,000 individuals in the general population. Add to this the 256,615 people in jails throughout the country as of mid-year 1985, and you have over 780,000 men and women behind bars in America. For 1986, that would amount to 323 prisoners for every 100,000 persons (of all ages and both sexes) in the U.S. population. However, of the 780,000 prisoners, 735,000 are men, virtually all above the age of eighteen. *This means that nearly one out of every 100 American men aged eighteen or over is behind bars!*[91] This enormous number of prisoners is, of course, predominantly people from the bottom of society.

Of the estimated 450,416 people in state prisons in 1986, 31 percent were not employed at all (full or part time) prior to their arrests, and 42.6 percent were without full-time employment prior to arrest. More than 61 percent of these state prisoners had less than twelve years of education. These statistics represent a general worsening compared to 1979, when 29.5 percent of state inmates had no pre-arrest employment at all, 39.5 percent no full-time pre-arrest employment, and 52.7 percent had less than twelve years of education. Of those 1986 state inmates who had been free at least a year before arrest, 24.7 percent had some pre-arrest annual income but less than $3,000; and 58.4 percent had some pre-arrest annual income but not more than $10,000. To get an idea of what part of society is in prison, compare this to the general population, where (in 1985) 7.1 percent were unemployed, 13.4 percent of individuals with income earned between $1 and $3,999, and 31.9 percent of individuals with income earned between $1 and $9,999. Of the 223,552 people in jails in 1983, 47 percent were unemployed prior to arrest (compared to 9.5 percent of the general population unemployed in 1983), and the median income of those who had a pre-arrest income was $5,486 (compared to a median income of $14,631 for those in the general population who had incomes in 1983).[92]

The criminal justice system is sometimes thought of as a kind of sieve in which the innocent are progressively sifted out from the guilty, who end up behind bars. I have tried to show that the sieve works another way as well. It sifts the affluent out from the poor, so it is not merely the guilty who end up behind bars, but the *guilty poor.*

With this I think I have proven the hypotheses set forth in Chapter 2, in the section titled "Criminal Justice as Creative Art." The criminal justice system does not simply weed the peace-loving from the dangerous, the law-abiding from the criminal. At every stage, starting with the very definitions of crime and progressing through the stages of investigation, arrest, charging, conviction, and sentencing, the system *weeds out the wealthy.* It refuses to define as "crimes" or as serious crimes the dangerous and predatory acts of the well-to-do—acts that, as we have seen, result in the loss of hundreds of thousands of lives and billions of dollars. Instead, the system focuses its attention on those crimes likely to be committed by members of the lower classes. Thus, it is no surprise to find that so many of the people behind bars are from the lower classes. The people we see in our jails and prisons are no doubt dangerous to society, but they are not *the* danger to society, not *the gravest* danger to society. Individuals who pose equal or greater threats to our well-being walk the streets with impunity. The criminal justice system is a mirror that hides as much as it reveals. It is a carnival mirror that throws back a distorted image of the dangers that lurk in our midst—and conveys the impression that those dangers are the work of the poor.

Summary

In this chapter, I have mainly tried to document the fact that, *even among those dangerous acts that our criminal justice system labels as crimes*, the system works to make it more likely that those who end up in jail or prison will be from the bottom of society. Among those acts defined as "crimes," the system is more likely to investigate and detect, arrest and charge, convict and sentence a lower-class individual than a middle- or upper-class individual who has committed *the same offense, if not a worse one!* In Chapter 1, I argued that the criminal justice system was rigged to fail in the fight against crime. In the present chapter and the previous one, I have argued that the system is rigged to make crime appear to be the monopoly of the poor by restricting its use of the label crime to the dangerous acts of the poor and not those of the well off (previous chapter) and by more actively pursuing and prosecuting the poor rather than the well off for the acts labeled crime (present chapter). *The joint effect of all these riggings is to maintain a real threat of crime that the vast majority of Americans believes is a threat from the poor.* In Chapter 4, I suggest who benefits from this illusion and how.

Study Questions

1. Who is in our jails and prisons? How do the people behind bars in America compare to the general population in employment, wealth, and level of education?

2. What is meant by "white-collar crime"? How costly is it compared to the crimes on the FBI's Index?

3. What factors make it likelier that a poor person who commits a crime such as shoplifting or nonaggravated assault will get arrested than a middle-class person who commits the same crime?

4. What factors make it likelier that a middle- or upper-class person charged with a crime will get acquitted than a lower-class person charged with the same crime?

5. What happened in the "Watergate scandal"? What effect did it have on subsequent treatment of well-off offenders?

6. If killers of whites are more likely to get sentenced to death than killers of blacks, what should we do? Should we abolish the death penalty? Do you agree with the Supreme Court's decision in *McCleskey* v. *Kemp*? Why?

4

To the Vanquished Belong the Spoils: Who Is Winning the Losing War Against Crime?

> *In every case the laws are made by the ruling party in its own interest; a democracy makes democratic laws, a despot autocratic ones, and so on. By making these laws they define as "just" for their subjects whatever is for their own interest, and they call anyone who breaks them a "wrongdoer" and punish him accordingly.*
>
> **Thrasymachus**, in *Plato's* Republic

WHY IS THE CRIMINAL JUSTICE SYSTEM FAILING?

The streams of my argument flow together at this point in a question: *Why is it happening?* I have shown how it is no accident that "the offender at the end of the road in prison is likely to be a member of the lowest social and economic groups in the country."[1] I have shown that this is not an accurate group portrait of who threatens society—it is a picture of who the criminal justice system *selects* for arrest and imprisonment from among those who threaten society. It is an image distorted by the shape of the criminal justice carnival mirror. This much we have seen and now we want to know why: *Why is the criminal justice system allowed to function in a fashion that neither protects society nor achieves justice? Why is the criminal justice system failing?*

My answer to these questions will require looking at who benefits from this failure and who suffers from it. More particularly, I will argue that the rich and powerful in America, those who derive the greatest advantage from the persistence of the social and economic system as it is currently organized, reap benefits from the failure of criminal justice that has been documented in this book. However—as I cautioned early on—this should not lead the reader to think that my explanation for the current shape of the criminal justice system is a "conspiracy theory."

A conspiracy theory would argue that the rich and the powerful, seeing the benefits to be derived from the failure of criminal justice, consciously set out to use their wealth and power to make it fail. There are many problems with such a theory. First, it is virtually impossible to prove. If the conspiracy succeeds, then this is only possible to the extent that it is kept secret. Thus, evidence for a conspiracy would be as difficult to obtain as the conspiracy was successful. Second, conspiracy theories strain credibility precisely because the degree of secrecy they would require seems virtually impossible in a society as open and fractious as our own. If there is a "ruling elite" in the United States that comprises a group as small as the richest *one thousandth of 1 percent* of the population, it would still be made up of more than 2,000 people. To think that a conspiracy to make the criminal justice system fail in the way that it does could be kept secret among this number of people in a country like ours is just unbelievable. Third, conspiracy theories are not plausible because they do not correspond to the way most people act most of the time. Although there is no paucity of conscious mendacity and manipulation in our politics, most people most of the time seem sincerely to believe that what they are doing is right. Whether this is a tribute to human beings' creative capacities to rationalize what they do or just a matter of shortsightedness, it seems a fact. For all these reasons, it is not plausible that so fateful and harmful a policy as the failure of criminal justice could be purposely maintained by the rich and powerful. Rather, we need an explanation that is compatible with believing that policymakers, in general, are simply doing what they sincerely believe is right.

To understand how the Pyrrhic defeat theory explains the current shape of our failing criminal justice policy, note that this failure is really *three* failures that work together. First, there is the failure to identify as crimes the harmful acts of the rich and powerful. (This is the first of the hypotheses listed on page 49, and it is confirmed by the evidence presented in Chapter 2.) Second, there is the failure to implement policies that stand a good chance of reducing crime and the harm it causes. (This was argued in Chapter 1). Third, there is the failure to eliminate economic bias in the criminal justice system, so that the poor continue to have a substantially greater chance than better-off people of being arrested, charged, convicted, and penalized for committing the acts that are treated as crimes. (This corresponds to the second through fourth hypotheses listed on page 49 and is confirmed by the evidence presented in Chapter 3.) The effect of the first failure is that the acts that are identified as crimes are acts predominantly done by the poor. The effect of the second failure is that there remains a large amount of crime—even if crime rates occasionally dip as a result of factors outside the control of the criminal justice system, such as the decline in the number of fifteen- to twenty-four-year-olds. The effect of the third failure is that the individuals who are arrested and convicted for crimes are predominantly poor people. The effect of the three failures working together is that we are largely unprotected against the harmful acts of the well off, while at the same time we are confronted on the streets and in our homes with a real and large threat of crime and in the courts and prisons with a large and visible population of poor criminals. In short, the effect of current criminal justice policy is at once to narrow the public's conception of what is dangerous to acts of the poor *and* to present a convincing embodiment of this danger.

Note that the Pyrrhic defeat theory aims to explain the *persistence* of this failing criminal justice policy, rather than its origins. The criminal justice system we have originated as a result of complex historical factors that have to do with the development of the common law tradition in England, the particular form in which this was transplanted on American soil, and the zigzagging course of reform and reaction that has marked our history since the English colonies were transformed into an independent American nation. The study of these factors would surely require another book longer than this one—but, more important, for our purposes it would be unnecessary because it is not the origin of criminal justice policy and practices that is puzzling. The focus on one-on-one harm reflects the main ways in which people harmed each other in the days before large-scale industrialization; the refusal to implement policies that might reduce crime (such as gun control or legalization of heroin or amelioration of poverty) reflects a defensive and punitive response to crime that is natural and understandable, if not noble and farsighted; and the existence of economic bias in the criminal justice system reflects the real economic and political inequalities that characterize the society in which that system is embedded. What is puzzling, then, is not how these policies came to be what they are, but why they persist in the face of their failure to achieve either security or justice. The explanation that I shall offer for this persistence, I call "historical inertia."

Put briefly, the historical inertia explanation argues that current criminal justice policy persists because it fails in a way that does not tend to give rise to an effective demand for change, for two reasons: First, this failing system provides benefits for those with the power to make changes, while it imposes costs on those without such power. Second, because the criminal justice system shapes the public's conception of what is dangerous, it creates the impression that the harms it is fighting are the *real* threats to society—thus, even when people see that the system is less than a roaring success, they generally do no more than demand more of the same: more prisons, more prison sentences, and so on.

Consider first the benefits that the system provides for those with wealth and power. I have argued that the triple failure of criminal justice policy diverts attention from the harmful (noncriminal) acts of the well off and confronts us in our homes and on our streets with a real and substantial threat of crime and in the courts and prisons with a large and visible population of poor criminals. This in turn has the effect of conveying a vivid image to the American people, namely, that *there is a real threat to our lives and limbs, and it is a threat from the poor.* This image provides benefits to the rich and powerful in America. It carries an *ideological message* that serves to protect their wealth and privilege. Crudely put, the message is this:

- *The threat to "law-abiding middle America" comes from below them on the economic ladder, not above them.*

· *The poor are morally defective, and thus their poverty is their own fault, not a symptom of social or economic injustice.*

The effect of this message is to funnel the discontent of middle Americans into hostility toward, and fear of, the poor. It leads Americans to ignore the ways in which they are injured and robbed by the acts of the affluent (as catalogued in Chapter 2) and leads them to demand harsher doses of "law and order" aimed mainly at the lower classes. Most important, it nudges middle America toward a *conservative* defense of American society with its vast disparities of wealth, power, and opportunity—and nudges them away from a progressive demand for equality and an equitable distribution of wealth and power.

On the other hand, but equally important, is the fact that those who are mainly victimized by the "failure" to reduce crime are by and large the poor themselves. That is, those people who are most hurt by the failure of the criminal justice system are those with the least power to change the system. The Department of Justice's *Criminal Victimization in the United States, 1979* states that "in 1979, as in prior years, members of families in the lower income bracket (less than $3,000 per year) had the highest overall rates [of victimization] for crimes of violence."[2] Also, "the unemployed had an overall violent crime [victimization] rate that was about twice that for employed persons."[3] The report for 1986 indicates that individuals from families earning less than $7,500 annually were victims of crimes of violence at a rate of about 50 per 1,000 in the population, compared to a rate of about 20 per 1,000 for individuals from families earning $30,000 a year. The former were victims of robbery with injury at a rate more than two and a half times that of the latter, and victims of aggravated assault with injury at a rate about four times that of the latter. Even for burglary, where victimization rates are much closer among the different income groups, households with incomes less than $7,500 were burglarized 50 percent more frequently than households with incomes more than $50,000 and more than 60 percent more frequently than households with incomes between $25,000 and $49,999.[4]

The greater similarity of rates of property crime victimization between rich and poor understates the difference in the harms that result. The poor are far less likely than the affluent to have insurance against theft, and, because they have little to start with, what they lose to theft takes a much deeper bite into their ability to meet their basic needs. Needless to add, the various noncriminal harms documented in Chapter 2 (occupational hazards, pollution, poverty, and so on) also fall more harshly on workers and those at the bottom of society than on those at the top.

To summarize, those who suffer most from the failure to reduce crime (and the failure to treat noncriminal harms as crimes) are not in a position to change criminal justice policy. Those who are in a position to change the policy are not seriously harmed by its failure—indeed, there are actual benefits to them from that failure. Note that I do not maintain that criminal justice policy is created in order to achieve this distribution of benefits and burdens. Instead, my claim is that because current criminal justice policy happens to produce this distribution, nothing in the society generates forces with both an inclination to change the criminal justice system and the power to do so. Moreover, because the criminal justice system shapes the public's conception of what is dangerous, it effectively limits its conception of how to protect itself to more of the same. Thus, although it fails, the system persists.

My argument in the remainder of this chapter takes the following form. In the section titled "The Poverty of Criminals and the Crime of Poverty," I spell out the content of the ideological message broadcast by the failure of the criminal justice system. In the section titled "Ideology, or How to Fool Enough of the People Enough of the Time," I discuss the *nature* of ideology in general and the *need* for it in America. For those who doubt that our legal system could function in such questionable ways, I also present evidence on how the criminal justice system has been used in the past to protect the rich and powerful against those who would challenge their privileges or their policies. These sections, then, flesh out the historical inertia explanation of the failure of criminal justice by showing the ideological benefits that that failure yields and to whom.

Ultimately, the test of the argument in this chapter is whether it provides a plausible explanation of the failure of criminal justice and draws the arguments of the previous chapters together into a coherent theory of contemporary criminal justice policy and practice.

THE POVERTY OF CRIMINALS AND THE CRIME OF POVERTY

Criminal justice is a very visible part of the American scene. As fact and fiction, countless images of crime and the struggle against it assail our senses daily, even hourly. In every newspaper, in every TV or radio newscast, there is at least one criminal justice story and often more. It is as if we live in an embattled city, besieged by the forces of crime and bravely defended by the forces of the law, and as we go about our daily tasks, we are always conscious of the war raging not very far away. Newspapers bring us daily and news-casts bring us hourly reports from the "front." Between reports, we are vividly reminded of the stakes and the desperateness of the battle by fictionalized portrayals of the struggle between the forces of the law and the breakers of the law. There is scarcely an hour on television without some dramatization of the struggle against crime. (Remember that 98 percent of American homes have televisions, and it is estimated that they are on an average of six hours a day!)[5] If we add to this the news accounts, the panel discussions, and the political speeches about crime, there can be no doubt that as fact or fantasy or both, criminal justice is vividly present in the imaginations of most Americans.

This is no accident. Everyone can relate to criminal justice in personal and emotional terms. Everyone has some fear of crime, and, as we saw in Chapter 3, just about everyone has committed some. Everyone knows the primitive satisfaction of seeing justice done and the evildoers served up their just deserts. Furthermore, in reality or in fiction, criminal justice is naturally dramatic. It contains the acts of courage and cunning, the high risks and high stakes, and the life-and-death struggle between good and evil that are missing from the routine lives so many of us lead. To identify with the struggle against crime is to expand one's experience vicariously to include the danger, the suspense, the triumphs, the meaningfulness—in a word, the drama—often missing in ordinary life. How else can we explain the seemingly bottomless appetite Americans have for the endless repetition, in only slightly altered form, of the same theme: the struggle of the forces of law against the forces of crime? Criminal justice has a firm grip on the imaginations of Americans and is thus in a unique position to convey a message to Americans and to convey it with drama and with conviction.

Let us now look at this message in detail. Our task falls naturally into two parts. There is an ideological message, a message supportive of the status quo, built into *any* criminal justice system by its very nature. Even if the criminal justice system were not failing, even if it were not biased against the poor, it would still—by its very nature—broadcast a message supportive of established institutions. This is *the implicit ideology of criminal justice.* Beyond this, there is an additional ideological message conveyed by the *failure* of the system and by its *biased* concentration on the poor. I call this the *bonus of bias.*

The Implicit Ideology of Criminal Justice

Any criminal justice system like ours conveys a subtle, yet powerful message in support of established institutions. It does this for two interconnected reasons: first, because it concentrates on *individual* wrongdoers. This means that *it diverts our attention away from our institutions, away from consideration of whether our institutions themselves are wrong or unjust or indeed "criminal."*

Second, the criminal law is put forth as the *minimum neutral ground rules* for any social living. We are taught that no society can exist without rules against theft and violence, and thus the criminal law is put forth as politically neutral, as the minimum requirements for *any* society, as the minimum obligations that any individual owes his fellows to make social life of any decent sort possible. Thus, it not only diverts our attention away from the possible injustice of our social institutions, but *the criminal law bestows upon those institutions the mantle of its own neutrality.* Because the criminal law protects the established institutions (e.g., the prevailing economic arrangements are protected by laws against theft, and so on), attacks on those established institutions become equivalent to violations of the minimum requirements for any social life at all. In effect, the criminal law enshrines the established institutions as equivalent to the minimum requirements for *any* decent social existence—and it brands the individual who attacks those institutions as one who has declared war on *all* organized society and who must therefore be met with the weapons of war.

This is the powerful magic of criminal justice. By virtue of its focus on *individual* criminals, it diverts us from the evils of the *social* order. By virtue of its presumed neutrality, it transforms the established social (and economic) order from being merely *one* form of society open to critical comparison with others into *the* conditions of *any* social order and thus immune from criticism. Let us look more closely at this process.

What is the effect of focusing on individual guilt? Not only does this divert our attention from the possible evils in our institutions, but it puts forth half the problem of justice as if it were the *whole* problem. To focus on individual guilt is to ask whether the individual citizen has fulfilled his obligations to his fellow citizens. *It is to look away from the issue of whether his fellow citizens have fulfilled their obligations to him.* To look only at individual responsibility is to look away from social responsibility. To look only at individual criminality is to close one's eyes to social injustice and to close one's ears to the question of whether our social institutions have exploited or violated the individual. *Justice is a two-way street—but criminal justice is a one-way street.* Individuals owe obligations to their fellow citizens because their fellow citizens owe obligations to them. Criminal justice focuses on the first and looks away from the second. *Thus, by focusing on individual responsibility for crime, the criminal justice system literally acquits the existing social order of any charge of injustice!*

This is an extremely important bit of ideological alchemy. It stems from the fact that the same act can be criminal or not, unjust or just, depending on the conditions in which it takes place. Killing someone is ordinarily a crime, but if it is in self-defense or to stop a deadly crime, it is not. Taking property by force is usually a crime, but if the taking is just retrieving what has been stolen, then no crime has been committed. Acts of violence are ordinarily crimes, but if the violence is provoked by the threat of violence or by oppressive conditions, then, like the Boston Tea Party, what might ordinarily be called criminal is celebrated as just. This means that when we call an act a crime *we are also making an implicit judgment about the conditions in response to which it takes place.* When we call an act a crime, we are saying that the conditions in which it occurs are not themselves criminal or deadly or oppressive or so unjust as to make an extreme response reasonable or justified, that is, to make such a response noncriminal. This means that when the system holds an individual responsible for a crime, *it implicitly conveys the message that the social conditions in which the crime occurred are not responsible for the crime,* that they are not so unjust as to make a violent response to them excusable.

Judges are prone to hold that an individual's responsibility for a violent crime is diminished if it was provoked by something that might lead a "reasonable man" to respond violently and that criminal responsibility is eliminated if the act was in response to conditions so intolerable that any "reasonable man" would have been likely to respond in the same way. In this vein, the law acquits those who kill or injure in self-defense and treats lightly those who commit a crime when confronted with extreme provocation. The law treats leniently the man who kills his wife's lover and the woman who kills her brutal husband, even when neither has acted directly in self-defense. By this logic, when we hold an individual completely responsible for a crime, we are saying that the conditions in which it occurred are such that a "reasonable man" should find them tolerable. In other words, by focusing on individual responsibility for crimes, *the criminal justice system broadcasts the message that the social order itself is reasonable and not inherently unjust.*

Thus, the criminal justice system focuses moral condemnation on individuals and deflects it away from the social order that may have either violated the individual's rights or dignity or literally pushed him or her to the brink of crime. This not only serves to carry the message that our social institutions are not in need of fundamental questioning, but it further suggests that the justice of our institutions is obvious, not to be doubted. Indeed, because it is deviations from these institutions that are crimes, the established institutions become the implicit standard of justice from which criminal deviations are measured.

This leads to the second way in which a criminal justice system always conveys an implicit ideology. It arises from the presumption that the criminal law is nothing but the politically neutral minimum requirements of any decent social life. What is the consequence of this?

Obviously, as already suggested, this presumption transforms the prevailing social order into justice incarnate and all violations of the prevailing order into injustice incarnate. This process is so obvious that it may be easily missed.

Consider, for example, the law against theft. It does indeed seem to be one of the minimum requirements of social living. As long as there is scarcity, any society—capitalist or socialist—will need rules preventing individuals from taking what does not belong to them. The law against theft, however, is more: It is a law against stealing what individuals *presently* own. *Such a law has the effect of making present property relations a part of the criminal law.*

Because stealing is a violation of the law, this means that present property relations become the implicit standard of justice against which criminal deviations are measured. Because criminal law is thought of as the minimum requirements of any social life, this means that present property relations become the equivalent to the minimum requirements of *any* social life. The criminal who would alter the present property relations becomes nothing less than someone who is declaring war on all organized society. The

question of whether this "war" is provoked by the injustice or bru-
tality of the society is swept aside. Indeed, this suggests yet another
way in which the criminal justice system conveys an ideological
message in support of the established society.

Not only does the criminal justice system acquit the social order of any charge of injustice, it specifically cloaks the society's
own crime-producing tendencies. I have already observed that by
blaming the individual for a crime, the society is acquitted of the
charge of injustice. I would like to go further now and argue that by
blaming the individual for a crime, the society is acquitted of the
charge of *complicity* in that crime. This is a point worth developing, because many observers have maintained that modern competitive societies such as our own have structural features that
tend to generate crime. Thus, holding the individual responsible
for his or her crime serves the function of taking the rest of society
off the hook for their role in sustaining and benefiting from social
arrangements that produce crime. Let us take a brief detour to look
more closely at this process.

Cloward and Ohlin argue in their book *Delinquency and Opportunity*[6] that much crime is the result of the discrepancy between social
goals and the legitimate opportunities available for achieving them.
Simply put, in our society everyone is encouraged to be a success,
but the avenues to success are open only to some. The conventional
wisdom of our free enterprise democracy is that anyone can be a
success if he or she has the talent and the ambition. Thus, if one is
not a success, it is because of one's own shortcomings: laziness or
lack of ability or both. On the other hand, opportunities to achieve
success are not equally open to all. Access to the best schools and the
best jobs is effectively closed to all but a few of the poor and becomes
more available only as one goes up the economic ladder. The result is
that many are called but few are chosen. Many who have taken the
bait and accepted the belief in the importance of success and the
belief that achieving success is a result of individual ability must
cope with feelings of frustration and failure that result when they
find the avenues to success closed. Cloward and Ohlin argue that
one method of coping with these stresses is to develop alternative
avenues to success. Crime is such an alternative avenue. Crime is a
means by which people who believe in the American dream pursue
it when they find the traditional routes barred. Indeed, it is plain to
see that the goals pursued by most criminals are as American as
apple pie. I suspect that one of the reasons that American movie-
goers enjoy gangster films—movies in which gangsters such as Al

Capone, Bonnie and Clyde, or Butch Cassidy and the Sundance Kid are the heroes, as distinct from police and detective films whose heroes are defenders of the law—is that even where they deplore the hero's methods, they identify with his or her notion of success, because it is theirs as well, and respect the courage and cunning displayed in achieving that success.

It is important to note that the discrepancy between success goals and legitimate opportunities in America is not an aberration. It is a structural feature of modern competitive industrialized society, a feature from which many benefits flow. Cloward and Ohlin write that

> *a crucial problem in the industrial world . . . is to locate and train the most talented persons in every generation, irrespective of the vicissitudes of birth, to occupy technical work roles. . . . Since we cannot know in advance who can best fulfill the requirements of the various occupational roles, the matter is presumably settled through the process of competition. But how can men throughout the social order be motivated to participate in this competition? . . .*
>
> *One of the ways in which the industrial society attempts to solve this problem is by defining success-goals as potentially accessible to all, regardless of race, creed, or socioeconomic position.*[7]

Because these universal goals are urged to encourage a competition to weed out the best, there are necessarily fewer openings than seekers. Also, because those who achieve success are in a particularly good position to exploit their success to make access for their own children easier, the competition is rigged to work in favor of the middle and upper classes. As a result, "many lower-class persons . . . are the victims of a contradiction between the goals toward which they have been led to orient themselves and socially structured means of striving for these goals."[8]

> *[The poor] experience desperation born of the certainty that their position in the economic structure is relatively fixed and immutable—a desperation made all the more poignant by their exposure to a cultural ideology in which failure to orient oneself upward is regarded as a moral defect and failure to become mobile as a proof of it.*[9]

The outcome is predictable. "Under these conditions, there is an acute pressure to depart from institutional norms and to adopt illegitimate alternatives."[10]

In brief, this means that the very way in which our society is structured to draw out the talents and energies that go into producing our high standard of living has a costly side effect: It produces crime. By holding individuals responsible for this crime, those who enjoy that high standard of living can have their cake and eat it. They can reap the benefits of the competition for success and escape the responsibility of paying for the costs of the competition. By holding the poor crook legally and morally guilty, the rest of society not only passes the costs of competition on to the poor, but they effectively deny that they (the affluent) are the beneficiaries of an economic system that exacts such a high toll in frustration and suffering.

Willem Bonger, the Dutch Marxist criminologist, maintained that competitive capitalism produces egotistic motives and undermines compassion for the misfortunes of others and thus makes human beings literally *more capable of crime*—more capable of preying on their fellows without moral inhibition or remorse—than earlier cultures that emphasized cooperation rather than competition.[11] Here again, the criminal justice system relieves those who benefit from the American economic system of the costs of that system. By holding criminals morally and individually responsible for their crimes, we can forget that the motives that lead to crime—the drive for success at any cost, linked with the beliefs that success means outdoing others and that violence is an acceptable way of achieving one's goals—are the *same motives* that powered the drive across the American continent and that continue to fuel the engine of America's prosperity.

David Gordon, a contemporary political economist, maintains "that nearly all crimes in capitalist societies represent perfectly *rational* responses to the structure of institutions upon which capitalist societies are based."[12] That is, like Bonger, Gordon believes that capitalism tends to provoke crime in all economic strata. This is so because most crime is motivated by a desire for property or money and is an understandable way of coping with the pressures of inequality, competition, and insecurity, all of which are essential ingredients of capitalism. Capitalism depends, Gordon writes,

> on basically competitive forms of social and economic interaction and upon substantial inequalities in the allocation of social resources. Without inequalities, it would be much more difficult to induce workers to work in alienating environments. Without competition and a competitive ideology, workers might not be inclined to struggle to improve their relative income and status in society by working harder. Finally, although rights of property are protected, capitalist societies do not guarantee economic security to most of their individual members. Individuals must fend for themselves, finding the best available opportunities to provide for

themselves and their families. ... *Driven by the fear of economic insecurity and by a competitive desire to gain some of the goods unequally distributed throughout the society, many individuals will eventually become "criminals."*[13]

To the extent that a society makes crime a reasonable alternative for a large number of its members from all classes, that society is itself not very reasonably or humanely organized and bears some degree of responsibility for the crime it encourages. Because the criminal law is put forth as the minimum requirements that can be expected of any "reasonable man," its enforcement amounts to a denial of the real nature of the social order to which Gordon and the others point. Here again, by blaming the individual criminal, the criminal justice system serves implicitly but dramatically to acquit the society of its criminality.

The Bonus of Bias

We now consider the additional ideological bonus that is derived from the criminal justice system's bias against the poor. This bonus is a product of the association of crime and poverty in the popular mind. This association, the merging of the "criminal classes" and the "lower classes" into the "dangerous classes," was not invented in America. The word *villain* is derived from the Latin *villanus*, which means a farm servant. The term *villein* was used in feudal England to refer to a serf who farmed the land of a great lord and who was literally owned by that lord.[14] In this respect, our present criminal justice system is heir to a long tradition.

The value of this association was already seen when we explored the "average citizen's" concept of the Typical Criminal and the Typical Crime. It is quite obvious that throughout the great mass of middle America, far more fear and hostility are directed toward the predatory acts of the poor than the rich. Compare the fate of politicians in recent history who call for tax reform, income redistribution, prosecution of corporate crime, and any sort of regulation of business that would make it better serve American social goals with that of politicians who erect their platform on a call for "law and order," more police, less limits on police power, and stiffer prison sentences for criminals—and consider this in light of what we have already seen about the real dangers posed by corporate crime and "business as usual."

It seems clear that Americans have been systematically deceived as to what are the greatest dangers to their lives, limbs, and possessions. The very persistence with which the system functions to apprehend and punish poor crooks and ignore or slap on the wrist equally or more dangerous individuals is testimony to the sticking power of this deception. That Americans continue to tolerate the gentle treatment meted out to white-collar criminals, corporate price fixers, industrial polluters, and political-influence peddlers while voting in droves to lock up more poor people faster and longer indicates the degree to which they harbor illusions as to who most threatens them. It is perhaps also part of the explanation for the continued dismal failure of class-based politics in America. American workers rarely seem able to forget their differences and unite to defend their shared interests against the rich whose wealth they produce. Ethnic divisions serve this divisive function well, but undoubtedly the vivid portrayal of the poor—and, of course, the blacks—as hovering birds of prey waiting for the opportunity to snatch away the workers' meager gains serves also to deflect opposition away from the upper classes. A politician who promises to keep working-class communities free of blacks and their prisons full of them can get their votes even if the major portion of his or her policies amount to continuation of the favored treatment of the rich at their expense. The sensationalistic use, in the 1988 presidential election, of photos of Willie Horton (a convicted black criminal who committed a brutal rape while out of prison on a furlough) suggests that such tactics are still effective politics.

The most important "bonus" derived from the identification of crime and poverty is that it paints the picture that the threat to decent middle Americans comes from those below them on the economic ladder, not those above. For this to happen the system must not only identify crime and poverty, but *it must also fail to reduce crime so that it remains a real threat.* By doing this, it deflects the fear and discontent of middle Americans, and their possible opposition, away from the wealthy.

There are other bonuses as well. For instance, if the criminal justice system functions to send out a message that bestows legitimacy on present property relations, the dramatic impact is greatly enhanced if the violator of the present arrangements is without property. In other words, the crimes of the well-to-do "redistribute" property among the haves. In that sense, they do not pose a symbolic challenge to the larger system in which some have much and many have little or nothing. If the criminal threat can be portrayed as coming from the poor, then the punishment of the poor criminal becomes a morality play in which the sanctity and legitimacy of the system in which some have plenty and others have little or nothing is dramatically affirmed. It matters little who the poor criminals really victimize. What counts is that middle Americans come to fear that those poor criminals are out to steal what they own.

There is yet another bonus for the powerful in America, produced by the identification of crime and poverty. It might be thought that the identification of crime and poverty would produce sympathy for the criminals. My suspicion is that it produces or at least reinforces the reverse: *hostility toward the poor.*

Indeed, there is little evidence that Americans are very sympathetic to poor criminals. Very few Americans believe poverty to be a cause of crime (6 percent of those questioned in a 1981 survey, although 21 percent thought unemployment was a cause). Other surveys find that most Americans believe that the police should be tougher than they are now in dealing with crime (83 percent of those questioned in a 1972 survey); that courts do not deal harshly enough with criminals (79 percent of those questioned in 1987); that a majority of Americans would like to see the death penalty for convicted murderers (70 percent of those questioned in 1987); and that most would be more likely to vote for a candidate who advocated tougher sentences for lawbreakers (83 percent of those questioned in a 1972 survey).[15] Indeed, the experience of Watergate seems to suggest that sympathy for criminals begins to flower only when we approach the higher reaches of the ladder of wealth and power. For some poor ghetto youth who robs a liquor store, five years in the slammer is our idea of tempering justice with mercy. When a handful of public officials try to walk off with the U.S. Constitution, a few months in a minimum security prison will suffice. If the public official is high enough, say, president of the United States, resignation from office and public disgrace tempered with a $60,000-a-year pension is punishment enough.

My view is that, because the criminal justice system, in fact and fiction, deals with *individual legal and moral guilt,* the association of crime with poverty does not mitigate the image of individual moral responsibility for crime, the image that crime is the result of an individual's poor character. My suspicion is that it does the reverse: It generates the association of poverty and individual moral failing and thus *the belief that poverty itself is a sign of poor or weak character.* The clearest evidence that Americans hold this belief is to be found in the fact that attempts to aid the poor are regarded as acts of charity, rather than as acts of justice. Our welfare system has all the demeaning attributes of an institution designed to give handouts to the undeserving and none of the dignity of an institution designed to make good on our responsibilities to our fellow human beings. If we acknowledged the degree to which our economic and social institutions themselves breed poverty, we would have to recognize our own responsibilities toward the poor. If we can convince ourselves that the poor are poor because of their own shortcomings, particularly moral shortcomings like incontinence and indolence, then we need acknowledge no such responsibility to the poor. Indeed, we can go further and pat ourselves on the back for our generosity in handing out the little that we do, and of course, we can make our recipients go through all the indignities that mark them as the undeserving objects of our benevolence. By and large, this has been the way in which Americans have dealt with their poor.[16] It is a way that enables us to avoid asking the question of why the richest nation in the world continues to produce massive poverty. It is my view that this conception of the poor is subtly conveyed by the way our criminal justice system functions.

Obviously, no ideological message could be more supportive of the present social and economic order than this. It suggests that poverty is a sign of individual failing, not a symptom of social or economic injustice. It tells us loud and clear that massive poverty in the midst of abundance is not a sign pointing toward the need for fundamental changes in our social and economic institutions. It suggests that the poor are poor because they deserve to be poor or at least because they lack the strength of character to overcome poverty. When the poor are seen to be poor in character, then economic poverty coincides with moral poverty and the economic order coincides with the moral order. As if a divine hand guided its workings, capitalism leads to everyone getting what they morally deserve!

If this association takes root, then when the poor individual is found guilty of a crime, the criminal justice system acquits the society of its responsibility not only for crime *but for poverty as well.*

With this, the ideological message of criminal justice is complete. The poor rather than the rich are seen as the enemies of the majority of decent middle Americans. Our social and economic institutions are held to be responsible for neither crime nor poverty and thus are in need of no fundamental questioning or reform. The poor are poor because they are poor of character. The economic order and the moral order are one. To the extent that this message sinks in, the wealthy can rest easily—even if they cannot sleep the sleep of the just.

Thus, we can understand why the criminal justice system creates the image of crime as the work of the poor and fails to reduce it so that the threat of crime remains real and credible. The result is ideological alchemy of the highest order. The poor are seen as the real threat to decent society. The ultimate sanctions of criminal justice dramatically sanctify the present social and economic order, and *the poverty of criminals makes poverty itself an individual moral crime!*

Such are the ideological fruits of a losing war against crime whose distorted image is reflected in the criminal justice carnival mirror and widely broadcast to reach the minds and imaginations of America.

IDEOLOGY, OR HOW TO FOOL ENOUGH OF THE PEOPLE ENOUGH OF THE TIME

What Is Ideology?

The view that the laws of a state or nation are made to serve the interests of those with power, rather than to promote the well-being of the whole society, is not a new discovery made in the wake of Watergate. It is a doctrine with a pedigree older even than Christianity itself. Writing during the fourth century B.C., virtually at the dawn of Western thought, Plato expressed this view through the lips of Thrasymachus.[17] A more contemporary and more systematic formulation of the idea is found in the works of Karl Marx. Written during the nineteenth century, not long after the dawn of western industrialism, Marx wrote in *The Communist Manifesto* that the bourgeoisie—the class of owners of businesses and factories, the class of capitalists—has

> conquered for itself, in the modern representative State, exclusive political sway. The executive of the modern State is but a committee for managing the common affairs of the whole bourgeoisie.[18]

Anyone who thinks that this is a ridiculous idea ought to look at the backgrounds of our political leaders. The vast majority of the president's cabinet, the administrators of the federal regulatory agencies, and the members of the two houses of Congress come from the ranks of business or are lawyers who serve business. Many still maintain their business ties or law practices, with no sense of a conflict of interest with their political role.[19] If either Thrasy-machus or Marx is right, there *is* no conflict with their political role because that role is to protect and promote the interests of business.

It is clear that the most powerful criminal justice policymakers come from the have-plenties, not from the have-littles. It is no surprise that legislators and judges—those who make the laws that define criminality and those who interpret those laws—are pre-dominantly members of the upper classes, if not at birth, then surely by the time they take office. One study of justices appointed to the U.S. Supreme Court between 1933 and 1957 found that 81 percent were sons of fathers with high social status occupations and that 61 percent had been educated in schools of high standing. Richard Quinney has compiled background data on key members of criminal justice policymaking and policy-advising committees and agencies, such as the President's Commission on Law Enforce-ment and Administration of Justice, the National Advisory Com-mission on Civil Disorders, the National Commission on the Causes and Prevention of Violence, the Senate Judiciary Committee's Sub-committee on Criminal Laws and Procedures (the subcommittee had a strong hand in shaping the Omnibus Crime Control and Safe Streets Act of 1968), the Law Enforcement Assistance Administra-tion, The Federal Bureau of Investigation, and, last but not least, the U.S. Department of Justice. With few exceptions, Quinney's report reads like a *Who's Who* of the business, legal, and political elite. For instance, 63 percent of the members of the President's Crime Commission had business and corporate connections.[20]

It should be noted that there is considerable evidence that the American criminal justice system has been used throughout its history in rather unsubtle ways to protect the interests of the powerful against the lower classes and political dissenters. The use of the FBI and local police forces to repress dissent by discred-iting, harassing, and undermining dissident individuals and groups has been recently revealed. The FBI, often with active cooperation or tacit consent of local police, has engaged in literally hundreds of illegal burglaries of the offices of law-abiding left-wing political parties,[21] and in political sabotage against the Black Panthers (e.g., "a Catholic priest, the Rev. Frank Curran, became the target of FBI operations because he permitted the Black Panthers to use his church for serving breakfasts to ghetto children").[22] It con-ducted a campaign to discredit the late Martin Luther King, Jr.

("the FBI secretly categorized . . . King as a 'Communist' months before it ever started investigating him").[23] Although directors of the FBI have said that the bureau is "truly sorry" for these past abuses and that they are over, later reports indicate that they still continue.[24]

These acts of repression are only the latest in a long tradition. The first organized uniformed police force in the English-speaking world was established in London in 1829. They came to be called "bobbies" because of the role played by Sir Robert Peel in securing passage of the London Metropolitan Police Act that established the force. The first full-time uniformed police force in the United States was set up in New York City in 1845.[25] It was also in the period from the 1820s to the 1840s that the movement to build penitentiaries to house and reform criminals began in New York and Pennsylvania and spread rapidly through the states of the young nation.[26] That these are also the years that saw the beginnings of a large industrial working class in the cities of England and America is a coincidence too striking to ignore.

The police were repeatedly used to break strikes and harass strikers.[27] The penitentiaries were mainly used to house the laborers and foreigners (often one and the same) whom the middle and upper classes perceived as a threat.[28] Throughout the formative years of the American labor movement, public police forces, private police such as the Pinkertons, the National Guard, and regular army troops were repeatedly used to protect the interests of capital against the attempts of labor to organize in defense of its interests. The result was that "the United States has had the bloodiest and most violent labor history of any industrialized nation in the world"—with most of the casualties on the side of labor.[29]

Marx, of course, went further. Not only are the laws of a society made to protect the interests of the most powerful economic class, but also, Marx argued, the prevailing ways of thinking about the world—from economic theory to religion to conventional moral ideas about good and evil, guilt and responsibility—are shaped in ways that promote the belief that the existing society is the best of all possible worlds. Marx wrote that

> *the ideas of the ruling class are in every epoch the ruling ideas: i.e. the class which is the ruling* material *force of society, is at the same time its ruling* intellectual *force. The class which has the means of material production at its disposal, has control at the same time over the means of mental production.*[30]

In simple terms, because those who have economic power own the newspapers, endow the universities, finance the publication of books and journals, and (in our own time) control the television and radio industries, they have a prevailing say in what is said, heard, and thought by the millions who get their ideas—their picture of reality—from these sources. This does not mean that the controllers of the "means of mental production" consciously deceive or manipulate those who receive their message. What it means is that the picture of reality held by these controllers—held, no doubt sincerely, to be an accurate representation of reality—will be largely the picture of reality that fills the heads of the readers and viewers of the mass media. Recognizing this involves no disrespect of the so-called common person. It is simply a matter of facing reality. The average man or woman is almost wholly occupied with the personal tasks of earning a living, piloting a family, and the like. He or she lacks the time (and usually the training) necessary to seek out and evaluate alternative sources of information. They are lucky when they have the time to catch a bit of news on television or in the papers. Moreover, except when there is division of opinion among those who control the media, the average person is so surrounded by unbroken "consensus" that he or she takes it simply as the way things are, with no particular reason even to consider the possibility that there are other sides of the issue to be considered, much less to seek these out. Then, even if people do come up with alternative sources of information, there are no general forums available for the sharing of views among members of the public. What we call mass communication is communication *to* the masses, not among them.

Consequently, the vast majority of people will accept, as a true picture of reality, the picture held by those who control the media. This is likely to be a distorted picture, even if those who create it act with the best of intentions and sincerity. The point is that, for a wide variety of reasons, people will tend to view the world in ways that make their own role in it (particularly the advantages and privileges they have in it) seem morally just, indeed, part of the best of all possible worlds. Thus, without any intention to deceive at all, those who control the content of the mass media are virtually certain to convey a picture of reality that supports the existing social order.

As a result, even in a society such as ours, where freedom of expression has reached a level probably unparalleled in history, there is almost never any *fundamental* questioning of our political-economic-legal institutions in the mass media, that is, television and radio, the major newspapers, or the news weeklies such as *Time* or *Newsweek*. There is much criticism of individuals and of individual policies. How often, though, does one find the mass media questioning whether the free enterprise system is really the best choice for America or whether our political and legal arrangements systematically promote the domination of society by the owners of big business? These issues are rarely, if ever, raised. Instead, it is taken for granted that, although they need some reform tinkering from time to time, our economic institutions are the most productive, our political institutions the most free, and our legal institutions the most just that *there can be*.

In other words, even in a society as free as ours, the ideas that fill the heads of most Americans and shape their picture of reality either explicitly or implicitly convey the message that our leaders are pursuing the common good (with only occasional lapses into personal venality—note how we congratulate ourselves on how "the system is working" when we expose these "aberrations" and then return to business as usual). Thus, we are told that the interests of the powerful coincide with the common interests of us all[31]—that "what's good for General Motors is good for the country." Where this picture of reality shows up some blemishes, they will always be portrayed as localized problems that can be remedied without fundamental overhaul of the entire social order, aberrations in an otherwise well-functioning social system. Indeed, the very willingness to publicize these blemishes "proves" that there is nothing fundamentally wrong with the social system since if the media are free, willing and able to portray the blemishes, they would surely portray fundamental problems with the social system if there were any—and because they do not, there must not be any! When ideas, however unintentionally, distort reality in a way that justifies the prevailing distribution of power and wealth, hides society's injustices, and thus secures uncritical allegiance to the existing social order, we have what Marx called *ideology*.[32]

Ideology is not conscious deception. People may spout ideology simply because it is all they know or all they have been taught or because they do not see beyond the "conventional wisdom" that surrounds them. This can be just as true of scholars who fail to see beyond the conventional assumptions of their disciplines as it is of laymen who fail to see beyond the oversimplifications of what is commonly called "common sense." Such individuals do not mouth an ideology out of a willful desire to deceive and manipulate their fellows, but rather because their own view of reality is distorted by untruths and half-truths—and criminal justice is one source of such distortion. It should be noted in passing that not everyone uses the term *ideology* as I have, to point to what is necessarily deceptive. Some writers speak of ideology as if it meant any individual or group's "belief system" or "value system" or *Weltanschauung*, that is, "world view."[33] I do not intend to quibble about semantics. However, such a moral neutralization of the concept of "ideology" strikes me as unnecessarily dulling an instrument that thinkers like Marx and others have sharpened into an effective tool for cutting through the illusions that dog our political life. Such tools are few and hard to find. Once found, they should be carefully preserved, especially when concepts such as "belief system" or "world view" are available to perform a more neutral function.

The Need for Ideology

A simple and persuasive argument can be made for the claim that the rich and powerful in America have an interest in conveying an ideological message to the rest of the nation. The have-nots and have-littles far outnumber the have-plenties. This means, to put it rather crudely, the have-nots and the have-littles could have more if they decided to take it from the have-plenties. This, in turn, means that the have-plenties need the cooperation of the have-nots and the have-littles. Because the have-plenties are such a small minority that they could never *force* this cooperation on the have-nots and have-littles, this cooperation must be voluntary. For the cooperation to be voluntary, the have-nots and the have-littles must believe that it would not be right or reasonable to take away what the have-plenties have. In other words, they must believe that for all its problems the present social, political, and economic order, with its disparities of wealth and power and privilege, is about the best that human beings can do. More specifically, the have-nots and have-littles must believe that they are not being exploited by the have-plenties. Now this seems to me to add up to an extremely plausible argument that ours is a social system that requires for its continued operation a set of beliefs necessary to secure the allegiance of the less well-off majority. These beliefs must be in some considerable degree false, because the distribution of wealth and power in the United States is so evidently arbitrary and unjust. Ergo, the need for ideology.

A disquisition on the inequitable distribution of wealth and income in the United States is beyond the scope and purpose of this book. This subject, as well as the existence of a "dominant" or "ruling" class in America, has been documented extensively by others.[34] I will only make two points here. First, there are indeed wide disparities in the distribution of wealth and income in the United States. Second, these disparities are so obviously unjust that it is reasonable to assume that the vast majority of people who must struggle to make ends meet only put up with them because they have been sold a bill of goods, that is, an ideology.

In 1986, the richest 20 percent of American families received 43.7 percent of the income received by all families, whereas the poorest 60 percent of American families received 32.2 percent of the total income. In crude terms, this means that although the wealthiest 50 million Americans had two-fifths of the money pie to themselves, the least wealthy 150 million Americans had to share a third of that pie among them. At the outer edges the figures are more extreme: The richest 5 percent of families received 17 percent of the total income, more than the poorest 40 percent of families who receive 15.4 percent. This means that the richest 5 percent—maybe 12 million people—had more money to divide among themselves than the nearly 100 million persons who make up the bottom 40 percent.[35]

The distribution of *wealth* (property such as stocks and land that generate income and tend to give one a say in major economic decisions) is even worse than the distribution of income.[36] An article in the November 1974 issue of *Survey of Current Business* reports that, in 1971,

> *the* 1 percent of U.S. families *(including single individuals) with the largest personal income accounted for* 47 percent *of dividend income received and* 51 percent *of the market value of stock owned by all families, while the* 10 percent of families *with the largest income accounted for* 71 percent *of dividend income and* 74 percent *of market value.*[37]

I offer no complicated philosophical argument to prove that these disparities are unjust, although such arguments abound for those who are interested.[38] It is a scandal that in a nation as rich as ours, some 32 million people (21 million reckoned with the most generous valuation of in-kind benefits) should live below what the government conservatively defines as the poverty level and that many millions more must scramble to make ends meet.[39] It is tragic that in our wealthy nation so many millions cannot afford a proper diet, a college education, a decent place to live, and good health care. We know too much about the causes of wealth and poverty to believe that the rich become rich because of their talent or contribution to society or that the poor are poor because they are lazy or incapable. Because we are nowhere near offering all Americans a good education and an equal opportunity to get ahead, we have no right even to suggest that the distribution of income reflects what people have truly earned. The distribution of income in America is so fundamentally shaped by factors such as race, educational opportunity, and the economic class of one's parents,[40] that few people who are well off can honestly claim that they deserve *all* that they have. Those who think they do should ask themselves where they would be today if they had been born to migrant laborers in California or to a poor black family in the Harlem ghetto.

Enough said. I take it, then, as established that the disparities of wealth and income in America are wide and unjustified. For the vast majority, the many millions struggling hard to satisfy basic needs, to acquiesce to the vast wealth of a small minority, it is necessary that the majority come to believe that these disparities are justified, that the present order is the best that human beings can accomplish, and that they are not being exploited by the have-plenties. In other words, the system requires an effective ideology to fool enough of the people enough of the time.

This account of the nature and need for ideology, coupled with the historical inertia explanation of the persistence of criminal justice in its current form and the analysis of the ideological benefits produced by the criminal justice system, adds up to an explanation of the continued failure of criminal justice in America.

Summary

In this chapter, the "historical inertia explanation" has been presented as a way of understanding the triple failure of criminal justice in America to institute policies that are likely to reduce the incidence of crime, to treat as crime the dangerous acts of the well off, and to eliminate the bias against the poor in the treatment of those acts that are labeled crimes. It was argued that these failures most harm those who lack the power to change things and benefit those who have that power. They benefit the latter by broadcasting the message that the threat to Americans' well-being comes from below them on the economic ladder, not from above them; and that poverty results not from social causes but from the moral depravity of the poor. It was also argued that aside from these "bonuses of bias," there is an inherent ideological message of any criminal justice system, insofar as such systems, by focusing on individual guilt, implicitly broadcast the message that the social system itself is a just one.

Study Questions

1. What is a conspiracy theory? What are the shortcomings of such a theory? Is the Pyrrhic defeat theory a conspiracy theory?

2. What is meant by ideology? What is the difference between ideology and propaganda? Is ideology needed in the United States?

3. How does any criminal justice broadcast an ideological message supportive of the prevailing social and economic arrangements?

4. What additional ideological benefits result from the bias against the poor in the definition and treatment of crime?

5. Why do you think that poor people in America are poor?

6. Now that you have seen the historical inertia explanation of criminal justice in America, do you think that the Pyrrhic defeat theory has been proven?

Conclusion: *Criminal Justice or Criminal Justice*

> *What are states without justice but robber-bands enlarged?*
>
> **St. Augustine,** *Confessions*

> *. . . unjust social arrangements are themselves a kind of extortion, even violence. . . .*
>
> **John Rawls,** *A Theory of Justice*

> *. . . the policeman . . . moves through Harlem, therefore, like an occupying soldier in a bitterly hostile country; which is precisely what, and where he is, and the reason he walks in twos and threes.*
>
> **James Baldwin,** *Nobody Knows My Name*

THE CRIME OF JUSTICE

Robbers, extortionists, occupying soldiers are terms used to characterize those who enforce an unjust law and an unjust order. It would be a mistake to think that this is merely a matter of rhetoric. There is a very real and very important sense in which those who use force unjustly or who use force to protect an unjust social order

143

are no different from a band of criminals or an occupying army. If this isn't understood, you are likely to think that what has been described in the first three chapters and accounted for in the fourth amounts to no more than another call for reform of the criminal justice system to make it more effective and more fair, when in fact it is much more. A criminal justice system that functions like ours—that imposes its penalties on the poor and not equally on all who threaten society, that does not protect us against threats to our lives and possessions equal to or graver than those presently defined as "crimes," and that fails even to do those things that could better protect us against the crimes of the poor—*is morally no better than the criminality it claims to fight.*

At the end of this chapter, I propose some reforms of the system. However, these should not be taken as proposals aimed merely at improving the effectiveness or fairness of American criminal justice. If the argument of this chapter is correct, then these proposals represent the necessary conditions for establishing the moral superiority of criminal justice to criminality. They are the conditions that must be fulfilled if the criminal justice system is to be acquitted of the indictment implicit in the above statements of Baldwin, Rawls, and St. Augustine. Bear in mind that, by the criminal justice system, I do not mean only police, courts, and prisons. I include the entire legal system, from lawmakers to law-enforcers.

What is common to the charge implicit in the statements of Baldwin, Rawls, and St. Augustine is the idea that *injustice transforms a legal system into its opposite.* What is common to the robber, the extortionist, and the occupying soldier is that each uses force (or the threat of force) to coerce other people to do things against their own interests. The robber and the extortionist use force to make other people hand over things of value. The occupying soldier uses force to subject one people to domination by another.

A legal system, of course, also uses force. Its defenders, however, maintain that it uses force to protect people's control over the things they value and over their own destinies. That is, they claim that the legal system protects what people possess against robbers and extortionists and protects their autonomy against anyone who would try to impose their will on them by force. In short, although both a legal system and its opposite, either criminality or military domination, use force, the moral superiority of the legal system lies in the fact that it uses force to secure the interests of the people subject to its force, whereas criminals and occupation troops use force to subject some people to the interests of others.

The moral legitimacy of a legal system and the lack of legitimacy of crime and military domination hinge, then, on the question of whether coercion is being used to enhance people's own interests. Ordinarily, when anyone is forced to serve as an instrument for the purposes of others, we call this tyranny or exploitation—or, in a word, *injustice*. In the absence of some compelling moral reason, force used to coerce people into serving the interests of others at the expense of their own is *morally no better than criminal force*. Because a legal system purports to do the reverse—to use force to protect *everyone's* interest in freedom and security by preventing and rectifying violations of those interests—legal systems call themselves *systems of justice*.[1] With this, they assert that the force used under color of law is morally opposite from, and morally superior to, the force used by criminals or conquerors.

This adds up to something that should be obvious but is not. *A criminal justice system is criminal to the extent that it is not a system of justice.* The requirements of justice are the familiar ones. A criminal justice system serves justice to the extent that it protects equally the interests and rights of all and to the extent that it punishes equally all who endanger these interests or violate these rights. To the extent that it veers from these goals, the criminal justice system is guilty of the same sacrificing of the interests of some for the benefit of others that it exists to combat. It is, therefore, morally speaking, guilty of crime.

The experience of the twentieth century has taught us that we should not take for granted that every legal system is a system of justice. Hitler's Germany and Stalin's Russia, as well as contemporary South Africa, are testimony to the fact that what is put forth as law may well be outrageously unjust. We have come to recognize that truth implicit in the statements of Baldwin, Rawls, and St. Augustine: What is put forth under color of law may be morally no better than crime or tyranny. Therefore, we can no longer uncritically take for granted that our own legal order is just merely because it is legal. We must subject it to the moral test of whether it serves and protects the interests of all to make sure that it is not injustice disguised as justice, criminality wearing the mask of law.

It is, of course, not my aim to place the American legal system on par with that of Hitler's Germany or Stalin's Russia. As I have acknowledged, there is much in the system that is legitimate and many are caught by the system who should be. Rather my claim is this:

- *To the extent that* the American criminal justice system *fails* to implement policies that could significantly reduce crime and the suffering it produces (as argued in Chapter 1)
- *To the extent that* the American criminal justice system *fails* to protect Americans against the gravest dangers to their lives and property (as argued in Chapter 2)
- *To the extent that* the American criminal justice system apprehends and punishes individuals, not because they are dangerous, but because they are *dangerous and poor* (as argued in Chapter 3)
- *Then, to that same extent,* the American criminal justice system fails to give all Americans either protection or justice, aids and abets those who pose the greatest dangers to Americans, and uses force in ways that do not serve equally the interests of all who are subject to that force, and *thus its use of force is morally no better than crime itself.*

REHABILITATING CRIMINAL JUSTICE IN AMERICA

The criminal justice system in America is morally indistinguishable from criminality because it exercises force and imposes suffering on human beings *while violating its own morally justifying ideals: protection and justice.* Once this is understood, the requirements for rehabilitating the system follow rather directly. The system must institute policies that make good on its claim to protect society and to do justice. In the remainder of this chapter I will briefly suggest the outlines of a "treatment strategy" for *helping the system go straight.* It cannot be reiterated too frequently that these proposals are not offered as a means of *improving* the system. Nor am I under any illusion that these proposals will be easily adopted or implemented. They are presented as the necessary requirements for establishing the criminal justice system's moral difference from, and moral superiority to, *crime;* and, even if not implemented or not likely to be implemented, they stand as a measure against which this moral difference and superiority can be judged. The proposals fall under the headings of the two ideals that justify the existence of a criminal justice system. These ideals are that the criminal justice system protect us against the real dangers that threaten us and that it not be an accomplice to injustice in the larger society. In order to realize these ideals, it is necessary that the harms and injustices done by the criminal justice system itself be eliminated.

Protecting Society

First, it must be acknowledged that every day that we refuse to implement those strategies that have a good chance of cutting down on the crimes people fear—the crimes on the FBI Index—the system is an accomplice to those crimes and bears responsibility for the suffering they impose.

We must enact and vigorously enforce stringent gun controls.

Americans are armed to the teeth. The handgun is the most easily concealed, the most effective, and the deadliest weapon there is. Its ubiquity is a constant temptation to would-be crooks who lack the courage or skill to commit crime without weapons or to chance hand-to-hand combat. Its ubiquity also means that any dispute may be transformed into a fatal conflict beyond the desires or expectations of the disputants. And the handgun is only part of the story. In recent years, it has become relatively easy to obtain rapid-firing assault rifles. Trying to fight crime while allowing such easy access to guns is like trying to teach a child to walk and tripping him each time he stands up. In its most charitable light, it is hypocrisy. Less charitably, it is complicity in murder.[2]

We must legalize the production and sale of "illicit drugs" and treat addiction as a medical problem.

Although most observers seem to agree that the British system of dispensing heroin to registered addicts is superior to our own punitive system, a number of experts have gone even further. Norval Morris and Gordon Hawkins urge that narcotics use be decriminalized and the drugs be sold in pharmacies by prescription. Arnold Trebach urges that doctors be permitted to prescribe heroin for the treatment of addicts and as a powerful painkiller. Philip Baridon recommends that pure heroin—clearly labled as to contents, recommended dosage, and addictive potential—be sold at a low fixed price in pharmacies, without prescription, to anyone aged eighteen or over.[3] I will not enter into debate about the various ways in which heroin can be decriminalized. I make the simple point that when heroin addicts cannot obtain heroin legally, they will obtain it illegally. Because those who sell it illegally have a captive market, they will charge high prices to make their own risks worthwhile. To pay the high prices, addicts must, will, and do resort to crime. Thus, every day in which we keep the acquisition of heroin a crime, we are using the law to protect the high profits of heroin black marketeers, *and* we are creating a situation in which large numbers of individuals are virtually physically compelled to commit theft. Because there is little evidence that heroin is dangerous beyond the fact of addiction itself, there can be little doubt that our present "cure" for narcotics use is more criminal (and criminogenic) than the narcotics themselves. The same goes for marijuana and cocaine. There may be some drugs that are so addictive or so likely to stimulate people to violence that we must keep them illegal. This may be the case with "crack" and with PCP, also known as "angel dust." If this turns out to be true (and the government has so exaggerated the dangers of illicit drugs over the years that healthy skepticism is warranted about these recent claims), it may be necessary to exclude these from the general program of decriminalization. With other less dangerous drugs decriminalized, however, many users might switch to the less dangerous ones, and, in any event, already overstretched law enforcement resources would be freed up to concentrate on the really serious drugs and on the crucial problem of keeping illicit drugs away from youngsters.

We must develop correctional programs that promote rather than undermine personal responsibility, and we must offer ex-offenders real preparation and a real opportunity to make it as law-abiding citizens.

The scandal of our prisons has been amply documented. Like our attitudes toward guns and heroin, they seem more calculated to produce than reduce crime. The enforced childhood of imprisonment may be the painful penalty offenders deserve, but if it undermines their capacity to go straight after release, we are cutting off our noses to spite our faces. People cannot learn to control themselves responsibly if they have spent years having every aspect of their lives—the hour they wake, the number of minutes they wash, the time and content of eating and working and exercising, the hour at which lights go out—regulated by someone else. Add to this the fact that convicts usually emerge with no marketable skill and little chance of getting a decent job with the stigma of a prison sentence hanging over them. The result is a system in which we never let criminals finish paying their debt to society and give them every incentive to return to crime.

If we are going to continue to punish people by depriving them of their liberty, we must do it in a way that prepares them for the life they will lead when their liberty is returned. Anything less than this is a violation of the Constitution's Eighth Amendment guarantee against "cruel and unusual punishment." Depriving a person of his or her liberty may be an acceptable punishment, but *depriving people of their dignity and a chance to live a law-abiding life when their punishment is supposed to be over is cruel and* (should be but sadly is not) *unusual!*

Pursuant to the guarantee of the Eighth Amendment, every imprisoned person should have a right to training at a marketable skill as well as a right to compete equally with non–ex-convicts for a job once the punishment is over. This would require that it be illegal to discriminate against ex-convicts in hiring and illegal to require job applicants to state whether they had ever been arrested, convicted, and/or imprisoned for a crime. This requirement might have to be modified for particularly sensitive occupations, although on the whole I think it would be fairer and more effective in rehabilitating ex-cons to enact it across the board and to have the government finance or subsidize a fund to ensure against losses incurred as a result of ex-convicts. My hunch is that this would be much less costly than paying to support ex-cons in prison and their families on welfare when they return to crime for lack of a job. Beyond this, prison industries should pay inmates at prevailing wages; this money then could be used for restitution to victims and to purchase privileges and possibly increased privacy or freedom for the prisoners—all of which might tend to give them greater practice at controlling their own lives so that they will be prepared to do so after release.

None of this will give us a criminal justice system worthy of the name, until we:

Let the crime fit the harm and the punishment fit the crime.

For the criminal justice system to justify its methods, it must make good on its claim to protect society. This requires that the criminal law be redrawn so that the list of crimes reflects the real dangers that individuals pose to society. Avoidable acts where the actor had reason to know that his or her acts were likely to lead to someone's death should be counted as forms of murder. Avoidable acts where the actor had reason to believe that his or her acts were likely to lead to someone's injury should be counted as forms of assault and battery. Acts that illegitimately deprive people of their money or possessions should be treated as forms of theft regardless of the color of the thief's collar. Crime in the suites should be prosecuted and punished as vigorously as crime in the streets.

The law must be drawn carefully so that individuals are not punished for harm they could not foresee or could not have avoided, or that others have freely consented to risk. The pursuit of security must not swamp the legitimate claims of liberty. However, within these guidelines, we must rid the law of the distinction between *one-on-one* harm and *indirect* harm *and treat all harm-producing acts in proportion to the actual harm they produce.*[4] *We must enact and implement punishments that fit the harmfulness of the crime without respect to the class of the criminal.* There is, for instance, general agreement that incarceration functions as an effective deterrent to corporate crime where the threat of imprisonment is believed.[5] To be believed, it must be used.

The other side of the coin is the decriminalization of "victimless crimes," acts such as prostitution, homosexuality, gambling, vagrancy, drunkenness, and of course, drug use. As long as these acts only involve persons who have freely chosen to participate, they represent no threat to the liberty of any citizen. This also means that there is generally no complainant for these crimes, no person who feels harmed by these acts and who is ready and able to press charges and testify against the wrongdoers. Therefore, police have to use a variety of shady tactics involving deception and bordering on entrapment, which undermine the public's respect for the police and the police officers' respect for themselves. In any event, the use of such low-visibility tactics increases the likelihood of corruption and arbitrariness in the enforcement of the law. Beyond this, since these acts produce no palpable, undeniable, tangible harm to others, laws against them appear to be no more than the imposition of some people's ideas of virtue on others, rather than laws that really protect society. To make good on its claim to protect society, the criminal justice system must not only treat the dangerous acts of business executives as crimes, but it must also decriminalize those acts that are not clearly dangerous.[6]

More than 100 years ago, John Stuart Mill formulated a guiding principle, still relevant to our time, for the design of legislation in a society committed to personal liberty:

> *That principle is, that the sole end for which mankind are warranted, individually or collectively, in interfering with the liberty of action of any of their number, is self-protection. That the only purpose for which power*

can be rightfully exercised over any member of a civilized community, against his will, is to prevent harm to others.[7]

Although the principle has had to be modified in recognition of the ways in which individuals can cause future harm to themselves because of present injudicious choices, particularly in a complex modern society where people must deal with machines and chemicals beyond their understanding,[8] the heart of the principle is still widely accepted. This is the notion that a necessary condition of any justifiable legal prohibition is that it prohibit an act that does harm to someone other than the actor himself. Since priority should be given to freedom of action, this harm should be *demonstrable* (i.e., detectable by some widely agreed upon means, say, those used by medical science), and it should be of sufficient gravity to outweigh the value of the freedom that is to be legally prohibited.[9]

This principle should not only guide legislators and those engaged in revising and codifying criminal law, but it should be raised to the level of an implicit constitutional principle. The U.S. Supreme Court recognized certain traditional principles of legality as constitutional requirements even though they are not explicitly written into the Constitution. For instance, some laws have been held unconstitutional because of their vagueness[10] and others because they penalized a condition (like being a drunk or an addict), rather than an action (like drinking or using drugs).[11] It strikes me that the entire tenor of the Bill of Rights is to enshrine and protect individual liberty from the encroachment of the state.

Whether as a legislative or a judicial criterion, however, Mill's principle would undoubtedly rid our law of the excrescences of our puritan moralism. It would bring our law more in line with a realistic view of what is harmful, and it would eliminate the forced induction into criminality of the individuals, mainly those of the lower class, who get arrested for "victimless crimes."

These changes, taken together, would be likely to reduce dangerous crime and to bring us a legal order that actually punished (and, it is hoped, deterred) all and only those acts that really threaten our lives, limbs, and possessions, and punished them in proportion to the harm they really produce. Such a legal system could be truly said to protect society.

Promoting Justice

The changes recommended above would, in part, make the criminal justice system more just, because people would be punished in proportion to the seriousness of their antisocial acts, and the number of innocent persons victimized by those acts would be reduced. Much would still remain to be done to eliminate the disabilities of the poor caught up in the system. A criminal justice system should arrest, charge, convict, and sentence individuals with an eye only to their crime, not to their class. Any evidence of more frequent arrest or harsher penalties for poor persons than for others accused of the same crime is a grave injustice that tends to undermine the legitimacy of the criminal justice system. Because many of the decisions that work to the disadvantage of the poor—police decisions to arrest, prosecutors' decisions to charge, and judges' decisions on how long to sentence—are exercises of discretion often out of public view, they are particularly resistant to control. Because, unlike prosecutors' or judges' decisions, the police officer's decision *not* to arrest is *not* a matter of record, it is the least visible exercise of discretion and the most difficult to control. Our best hope to make arrests by police more just lies in increased citizen awareness and education of police officers so that they at least become aware of the operation and impact of their own biases and are held more directly accountable to, and by, the public they serve and sometimes arrest.

As for prosecutorial and judicial discretion, two approaches seem potentially fruitful. First, lawmakers ought to spell out the acceptable criteria that prosecutors may use in deciding whether or what to charge and the criteria that judges may use in deciding whether or what to sentence. The practice of multiple charging (e.g., charging an accused burglar with "the lesser included crimes" of breaking and entering, possession of burglar's tools, and so on) should be eliminated. It is used by prosecutors to "coax" accused persons into pleading guilty to one charge by threatening to press *all* charges. Of all the dubious features of our system of bargain justice, this seems most clearly without justification because it works to coerce a plea of guilty that should be uncoerced if it is to be legally valid.[12] The law should also set out more specific sentencing ranges because the present system leads to individuals receiving wildly different sentences for the same crimes—a practice that can only be viewed as arbitrary and capricious, that violates the principle that citizens should know in advance what is in store for them if they break a law, and that produces in convicts disrespect for the law rather than remorse for their violations. In addition to, and in conjunction with, these legislative changes, we ought to require prosecutors and judges to put in writing the reasons they have charged or sentenced in one way rather than another. They should be required to give an account of their policies and practices to some truly representative body to show that they are fair and reasonable. The recently developed federal sentencing guidelines are an important step in this direction.[13] However we achieve it, it is clear that to must make the criminal justice system function justly:

We must narrow the range in which police officers, prosecutors, and judges exercise discretion, and we must develop procedures to hold them accountable to the public for the fairness and reasonableness of their decisions.

All these changes still leave standing what is probably the largest source of injustice to the poor in the system: *unequal access to quality legal counsel.* We know that, by and large, privately retained counsel will have more incentive to put in the time and effort to get their clients off the hook, and we know that this results in a situation in which *for equal crimes* those who can retain their own counsel are more likely to be acquitted than those who cannot. The present system of allocating assigned counsel or public defenders to the poor and privately retained lawyers to the affluent is little more than a parody of the constitutional guarantee of *equal protection under the law.*

There are simply no two ways about this. In our system, even though lawyers are assigned to the poor, justice has a price. Those who pay get the choicest cut—those who cannot, get the scraps. About a hundred years ago, before there were public police forces in every town and city, people got "police protection" by hiring private police officers or bodyguards if they could afford it. Protection was available for a price, and so those who had more money were better protected under the law. Today, we regard it as every citizen's right to have police protection, and we would find it outrageous if police protection were allocated to citizens on a fee-for-service basis. *This is precisely where we stand with respect to the legal protection provided by lawyers!*

Legal protection is not only provided by the police. Attorneys are necessary to protect individuals from losing their freedom at the hands of the law before they have exhausted the legal defenses that are theirs by right. Both police officers and lawyers are essential to the individual's legal protection. It is sheer hypocrisy to acknowledge everyone's right to equal protection under the law by the police and then to allocate protection under the law by lawyers on the basis of what individuals can pay. As long as this continues, we cannot claim that there is anything like equal treatment before the law in the criminal justice system.

We must transform the equal right to counsel into the right to equal counsel as far as it is possible.

Although this would appear to be a clear requirement of the "equal protection" and "due process" clauses of the Constitution, the Supreme Court has avoided it, perhaps because it poses massive practical problems—and surely it does. However, the creation of public police forces to protect everyone posed many practical problems in its time as well.

Certainly it would not be appropriate to use the police as a model for resolving the problem of equal counsel. To establish a governmental legal service for all—in effect, to nationalize the legal profession—might make equal legal representation available to all. It would, however, undermine the adversary system by undercutting the independence of defense attorneys from the state. Some form of national legal insurance to enable all individuals to hire private attorneys of their own choice, however, could bring us closer to equal legal protection without compromising the adversarial relationship.

Such insurance would undoubtedly have to be subsidized by the government, as are the police, the courts, and prisons; but it would not necessarily have to be totally paid for out of taxes. People might rightly be expected to pay their legal bills up to some fraction of their income, if they have one. The rest would be paid for by a government subsidy that would pay the difference between what the accused could afford and the going rate for high-quality legal counsel. Nothing in the system need interfere with the freedom of the accused to select the lawyer of his or her choice (an option closer to the hearts of free enterprisers than the present public defender system allows) or interfere with the independence of the lawyer.

Undoubtedly, such a system would be costly. Our commitment to equal justice, however, remains a sham until we are willing to pay this price. Americans have paid dearly to protect the value of liberty enshrined in the Constitution. Is it too much to ask that they pay to realize the ideal of justice enshrined there too?

One final recommendation remains to be made. I have already argued that the criminal justice system, by its very nature, embodies the prevailing economic relations in its laws. This means that it is an error to think of the criminal justice system as an entity that can be reformed in isolation from the larger social order. A criminal justice system is a means to protect that social order, and it can be no more just than the order it protects. A law against theft may be enforced with an even and just hand. If it protects an unjust distribution of wealth and property, the result is *injustice evenly enforced*. A criminal justice system cannot hold individuals guilty of the injustice of breaking the law if the law itself supports and defends an unjust social order.

We must establish a more just distribution of wealth and income and make equal opportunity a reality for all Americans.

Without economic and social justice, the police officer in the ghetto is indeed an occupying soldier with no more legitimacy than his or her gun provides. Without economic and social justice, the criminal justice system is the defender of injustice and is thus morally indistinguishable from the criminal. *A criminal justice system can be no more just than the society its laws protect.* Along with the other recommendations I have made in this chapter, the achievement of economic and social justice is a necessary condition for establishing the criminal justice system's moral superiority to crime.

Summary

Every step toward domestic disarmament, toward decriminalization of "illicit drugs" and "victimless crimes," toward criminalization of the dangerous acts of the affluent and vigorous prosecution of "white-collar" crimes; every step toward creating a correctional system that promotes human dignity, toward giving ex-offenders a real opportunity to go straight, toward making the exercise of power by police officers, prosecutors, and judges more reasonable and more just, toward giving all individuals accused of crime equal access to high-quality legal expertise in their defense; every step toward establishing economic and social justice is a step that moves us from a system of *criminal* justice to a system of criminal *justice*. The refusal to take those steps is a move in the opposite direction.

Study Questions

1. What is meant by the three quotations at the beginning of this chapter? Do they apply to the American criminal justice system? How?

2. Do you support gun control legislation?

3. What is meant by "victimless crimes"? Do you think they should be kept criminal?

4. Would you be willing to have your taxes go to pay for equal quality legal counsel for the poor?

5. Do you think the distribution of wealth and income in America is just? How is this related to the justice of the criminal justice system?

6. Do you think that the recommendations made in this chapter are likely to be instituted? What does your answer imply about your view of the American legal system?

Appendix: The Marxian Critique of Criminal Justice[1]

Here in the Appendix I shall try to present the reader with an overview of Marxian theory that goes from Marxism's theory of capitalism to its theory of law and from there to criminal justice. This addresses some of the same aspects of criminal justice we discussed in the main text of this book, but it sets them in a theoretical framework different from (although not incompatible with) the Pyrrhic defeat theory, with its historical inertia explanation of the failure of criminal justice. I shall close with comments on the ethical implications of the Marxian analysis.

Criminal justice has a concrete reality comprising police, prisons, courts, guns, and the rest. What is most important for our purposes, however, is the particular shape that this concrete reality takes in capitalism. This shape is governed according to certain principles that spell out what shall count as violations, what shall be done to violators, and so on. (For simplicity's sake, I shall use the term *criminal justice* as shorthand for the principles that normally govern criminal justice practices and practitioners in capitalism and use the term *criminal justice system* as shorthand for the concrete reality of the practices and practitioners so governed.) Marxian analysis is in the first instance directed toward these governing principles. It aims to show that these principles are "economic reflexes," that is, they reflect and thus support the existing economic arrangements—in our case, the capitalist mode of production. Criminal justice plays an ideological role in support of capitalism because people do not recognize that the principles governing criminal justice are reflections of capitalism. The principles of criminal justice appear instead to be the result of pure reason, and thus a system that supports capitalism is (mistakenly) seen as an expression of rationality itself! Engels—Marx's life-long collaborator—

writes that "the jurist imagines he is operating with *a priori* [i.e., purely rational] principles, whereas they are really only economic reflexes; so everything is upside-down. . . . And it seems to me obvious that this inversion . . . , so long as it remains unrecognized, forms what we call *ideological conception.*"² As a consequence of this "inversion," criminal justice embodies and conveys a misleading and partisan view of the reality of the whole capitalist system. In particular, it obscures features of that system that undermine the normal ethical claims of criminal justice. Thus, the Marxian critique sets the stage for critical moral judgments about the ethical status of criminal justice.

Before proceeding, a word about the nature of Marxian theory is in order. In presenting his theory of capitalism, Marx portrays capitalism in perfect form. He does so, not to claim that that is how it actually exists anywhere, but rather to show the shape to which it tends everywhere. Actual systems will be a product of the force of that tendency versus the force of all those factors that block the perfect development of capitalism. Likewise, a Marxian analysis of criminal justice will indicate the perfect form toward which criminal justice systems tend insofar as they support the functioning of capitalism. Actual criminal justice systems will be approximations of this tendency. Actual criminal justice systems will clearly be shaped by human actions—often substantially so. No Marxist need deny that criminal justice in the capitalist United States is quite a different thing from criminal justice in, say, capitalist Chile. What he must claim, rather, is that as capitalism develops in both, their criminal justice systems will increasingly tend to take on the shape that the theory implies.

I shall try to show how Marxism leads to a theory of the structure that criminal justice systems tend to have under capitalism, while at the same time recognizing that any existing criminal justice system is only an approximation of this structure. In order to give the reader as complete a picture as possible (in this short space) of the whole of Marxian theory—from general theory of capitalism to particular theory of criminal justice, and from there to ethical evaluation—I shall necessarily sacrifice much detail. I shall largely ignore the differences that individual actions may make in the determining the shape of actual systems. I hope I have said enough to suggest that this in no way implies that human actions are irrelevant to historical outcomes.

I proceed in the following way. In the first section, "Marxism and Capitalism," I shall sketch out enough of Marx's theory of the capitalist mode of production as is necessary to lay the foundation for a Marxian theory of law. Because law is, for Marxism, a form of ideology, we shall have to see how ideology works in capitalism. I take this up in the next section, "Capitalism and Ideology." In "Ideology and Law," I try to construct the Marxian theory of law and from it the Marxian theory of criminal justice. Then in the final section, "Law and Ethics," I consider the characteristic Marxian moral judgments about criminal justice—particularly about guilt and punishment—that are appropriate in light of the Marxian account.

MARXISM AND CAPITALISM

Marx says that capitalism is a system of "forced labour—no matter how much it may seem to result from free contractual agreement."[3] Here is both the truth that Marx asserts about capitalism and the legal ideology that shrouds that truth. To understand precisely how this works, we must consider the nature of the coercion that Marx discovered in capitalism.

For Marx, the value of any commodity is equivalent to the average amount of labor-time necessary to produce it.[4] Under capitalism, the worker's ability to labor—Marx calls this *labor-power*—is sold to the capitalist in return for a wage. Since labor-power is also a commodity, its value is also equivalent to the average amount of labor-time necessary to produce it. Producing labor-power means maintaining a functioning worker. The value of labor-power then is equivalent to the labor-time that on the average goes into producing the goods (food, clothing, shelter, and so on) necessary to maintain a functioning worker at the prevailing standard of living, which Marx understood to differ among countries depending on their respective histories (*Capital*, vol. 1, p. 171). The worker receives this in the form of a wage, that is, in the form of the money necessary to purchase these goods.

The capitalist obtains the money he pays as a wage by selling what the worker produces during the time for which he is employed. If the worker produced an amount of value equivalent only to his wage, there would be nothing left over for the capitalist and no reason for him to hire the worker in the first place. Labor-power, however, has the unique capacity to produce more value than its own value (*Capital*, vol. 1, pp. 193–194). That is, the worker can work longer than the labor-time equivalent of the value of the wage he receives. The amount of labor-time that the worker works to produce value equivalent to his wage, Marx calls *necessary labor*. The additional labor-time that the worker works beyond this Marx calls *surplus labor*, and the value it produces, he calls *surplus value*. The surplus value, of course, belongs to the capitalist and is the source of his profit (*Capital*, vol. 1, pp. 184–186).

Profit, then, rests on the extraction of unpaid surplus labor from the worker. To see this, one need only recall that although all products in the economy are produced by labor, only a portion of those products are wage-goods that the workers get paid with (they get them for the money they receive as wages). The remainder belongs to their bosses and is effectively uncompensated. The wage-goods are not compensation because the workers produce these goods themselves. What they produce beyond this goes to the capitalist gratis. Thus, writes Marx, "The secret of the self-expansion of capital [that is, the secret of profit] resolves itself into having the disposal of a definite quality of other people's unpaid labour" (*Capital*, vol. 1, p. 534).

For Marx, however, capitalism is not only a system in which unpaid labor is extracted from workers, it is a system in which workers are *forced* to provide this unpaid labor. Workers are not merely shortchanged, they are enslaved. Capitalism is "a coercive relation" (*Capital*, vol. 1, p. 309). The coercion, however, is not of the direct sort that characterized slavery or feudal serfdom. It is, rather, an indirect force built into the very fact that capitalists own the means of production and laborers do not. Lacking ownership of means of production, workers lack their own access to the means of acquiring a livelihood. *By this very fact* workers are compelled to sell their labor to capitalists for a wage because the alternative is (depending on conditions) either painful or fatal: relative pauperization or absolute starvation.

This compulsion is not in conflict with the fact that the terms upon which the worker works for the capitalist are the result of free contractual agreements. Indeed, the compulsion works *through* free agreements. Because the agreements are free, each side must offer the other a reason for agreeing. If workers offered capitalists only as much labor as went into the wage-goods they will get back in return from the capitalists, the capitalists would have no reason to purchase their labor. It follows that, no matter how free the wage contract is, as long as it occurs in a context in which a few own all the means of production, those who do not own means of production will be compelled to give up some of their labor without compensation to those who do. Thus, Marx describes the wage-worker as a "man who is compelled to sell himself of his own free will" (*Capital*, vol. 1, p. 766). The compulsion of the worker operates through the structure of property relations: "The dull compulsion of economic relations completes the subjection of the labourer to the capitalist. Direct force, outside economic conditions, is of course still used, but only exceptionally" (*Capital*, vol. 1, p. 737).

The very existence of the social roles of capitalist and worker—defined by ownership and nonownership of means of production, respectively—is what coerces the worker to work without compensation. It coerces in the same way that a social structure that allotted to one group ownership and thus control of all the available oxygen would coerce. Beyond what was necessary to defend this group against challenges to its ownership of the oxygen, no additional force would be necessary for the coercion to operate. Indeed, it would operate quite effectively by means of bargains freely struck in which the non-oxygen-owners had to offer something to the owners to get the chance to breathe. They, too, would be compelled to sell themselves of their own free will. The same can be said of capitalism. Once its structure of social roles is in place, all that is necessary is that individuals choose, from among the alternatives available to them in their roles, the course of action that best serves their self-interest, and the extraction of unpaid surplus labor is enforced without further need for overt force except in unusual circumstances.

As with the oxygen-owning society, so too with capitalism: Overt force is used or threatened to defend owners against challenges to their ownership. That is just another way of saying that, in capitalism, the state uses overt force to protect private property. This differs crucially from the way in which overt force is exercised in social relations like slavery. In slavery, the use of overt force is part of the normal exercise of the master's power. In capitalism, overt force is used to defend everyone against forceful interference with their right to dispose of whatever property they happen to own, be it means of production or labor-power. Accordingly, such force is not part of the capitalist's power, but left to a third party that is neutral toward all owners—the state.

With both capitalists and workers protected in their capacity to dispose of what they own, the process by which workers are forced to work gratis can proceed apace. Note that this effect can be achieved with the state functioning neutrally. Although the state normally favors the interests of capitalists over workers,[5] it can serve the process of forced extraction of unpaid labor by protecting both capitalists and workers alike in their freedom to dispose of what they happen to own. It just turns out that what capitalists happen to own is means of production, and what workers happen to own is the muscles in their arms. Capitalism, then, naturally appears as a system of free exchanges between people of equal rights. This brings us to the phenomenon of ideology.

CAPITALISM AND IDEOLOGY

Of the study of social revolutions, Marx writes:

> In considering such transformations a distinction should always be made between the material transformation of the economic conditions of production, which can be determined with the precision of natural science, and the legal, political, religious, aesthetic or philosophic—in short, ideological forms in which men become conscious of this conflict and fight it out.[6]

The legal, then, is an ideological form. This is not to say that it is merely mental. It has a material reality in the form of police and prisons and guns and courts and legislators and lawbooks and the rest. What is crucial is how this material reality is shaped, and for that we must understand how ideology is shaped.

As its etymology suggests, "ideology" means the science of ideas, where science can be taken in the ordinary sense as the study of causal connections. (Recall the discussion of ideology in Chapter 4.) In the context of Marxian theory, ideology comes to mean the ideas caused by the mode of production, and, equally important for Marxism, the caused ideas are in some important way false. Thus understood, for Marxism, the study of ideology denotes the study of how the mode of production gives rise to people's false beliefs about society. In *The German Ideology*, Marx writes,

> If in all ideology men and their circumstances appear upside down as in a camera obscura, *this phenomenon arises just as much from their historical life-process as the inversion of objects on the retina does from their physical life-process.*
> . . . The phantoms formed in the human brain are also, necessarily, sublimates of their material life-process, which is empirically verifiable and bound to material premises.[7]

As this statement makes clear, the study of ideology requires that both the existence and the falsity of ideological beliefs must be given a *materialist* explanation. To understand this requirement, consider that Marxian materialism is the conjunction of two distinct claims, an ontological claim and a social scientific one. The *ontological* claim is that what exists is material, that is, physical objects in space. Mind or spirit in any immaterial sense are chimera. ("From the start the 'spirit' is afflicted with the curse of being 'burdened' with matter, which here makes its appearance in the form of agitated layers of air, sounds, in short, of language" [*German Ideology*, p. 19]). The *social scientific* claim is that the way in which a society is organized for the production of the material conditions of its existence and reproduction ("the mode of production") plays the chief (though by no means the only) causal role in determining the nature and occurrence of social events. ("The mode of production of material life conditions the social, political and intellectual life process in general."[8]) The notion that societies are shaped primarily by their members' attitudes or, likewise, that history is shaped by the progressive development of knowledge or ideals, is rejected as a misapprehension. Rather, it is primarily the organization of production that shapes people's attitudes, and the progressive development of modes of production that shapes history. ("That is to say, we do not set out from what men say, imagine, conceive, nor from men as narrated, thought of, conceived, in order to arrive at men in the flesh. We set out from real, active men, and on the basis of their real life-process we demonstrate the development of the ideological reflexes and echoes of this life-process" [*German Ideology*, p. 14]; "it is not the consciousness of men that determines their being, but, on the contrary, their social being that determines their consciousness."[9])

Of these two claims, the social scientific is more restrictive than the ontological. The ontological claim requires only that we attribute ideology to material realities, be they brains or agitated layers of air or modes of production. The social scientific claim requires that among these material realities, pride of place be given to the mode of production as the primary cause of ideological beliefs. This means that the *main* source of false ideology is to be looked for not in the perceiving subject but in the perceived objects. It is not a "subjective illusion," the result of erroneous perception by individuals of their material conditions, but an "objective illusion," the result of more or less accurate perception of those conditions.[10] Viewing ideology this way has the added benefit of leaving the door open just wide enough so that the theory of ideology does not exclude the possibility of all true beliefs—and thus of the very science upon which it is based. A materialist theory of ideology, then, must show that false ideology is an *objective illusion* arising primarily from more or less accurate perception of the organization of material production, rather than from some subjective error.[11] Bear in mind that this is a matter of placing primary emphasis on objective factors, not of absolutely excluding subjective ones.

We can fix the idea of an objective illusion by considering a very common example of one, namely, the illusion that the sun goes around the earth. Any illusion, any erroneous belief that an individual holds, can be *stated* as a subjective error—but not every erroneous belief arises primarily *because* of a subjective error. A person who believes that the sun rises above a stationary horizon in the morning makes a mistake. However, this sort of mistake differs crucially from, say, the mistake that a colorblind person might make of believing that the light is green when it is red, or the mistake a person balancing his checkbook might make of believing that a number is 4 when it is 2. In these latter cases, the mistaken beliefs are not merely held by the individuals, they arise in the individuals primarily as the result of a defective perceptual faculty or misuse of a sound one. These are subjective illusions. In these cases, correcting the defect in or the use of the perceptual faculty should undo the mistake. The mistaken belief that the sun goes around the earth, by contrast, arises as a result of a sound perceptual faculty properly exercised. This is an objective illusion. Neither healthier vision nor looking more carefully is likely to enable an individual to correct this mistake and see that what occurs at dawn is not the sun rising above the horizon, but the horizon tipping down before the sun.

The ideology of capitalism is the illusion that capitalism is uncoercive. This illusion is a mistake of the same type as the illusion that the sun goes around the earth. What corresponds in capitalism to the movement of the sun seen from the earth is the free exchange of wages and labor-power between capitalists and workers. That the sphere of exchange is the objective basis of ideology is recognized in effect by Marx, when he writes that this sphere,

> *within whose boundaries the sale and purchase of labour-power goes on, is in fact a very Eden of the innate rights of man. There alone rule Freedom, Equality, Property. . . . Freedom, because both buyer and seller of a commodity, say of labour-power, are constrained only by their free will* [Capital, *vol. 1, 176*].

The normal perception of what goes on in exchange gives rise to the ideological illusion that capitalism is uncoercive. This is not because the freedom in exchange is an illusion. The fact is that, for Marx, capitalism only works because the moment of exchange, through which the circuit of capital continually passes, is truly free.

For the conversion of his money into capital, therefore, the owner of money must meet in the market with the free labourer, free in the double sense, that as a free man he can dispose of his labour-power as his own commodity, and that on the other hand, he has no other commodity for sale, is short of everything necessary for the realization of his labourpower [Capital, vol. 1, p. 169].

That the second of these senses of freedom is the worker's "freedom from" ownership of means of production does not deny the reality of the first sense, without which we would have slavery or serfdom rather than capitalism.

In exchange, the power that capitalists have over workers recedes from view. If we distinguish two sorts of power—the power to withhold one's commodity until offered something preferable and the power to command obedience and back this up with violent force—then it is clear that, in the sphere of exchange, the latter power is suspended and all that remains is the former power. This former power is a power that all parties to the exchange have equally. Thus, the unequal power of capitalist and worker appears as their equal power to withhold from exchange what they happen to own, and their social inequality appears as the difference between the things that they happen to own. To use the celebrated words of Marx's analysis of the fetishism of commodities, a "social relation between men . . . assumes, in their eyes, the fantastic form of a relation between things" (*Capital*, vol. 1, p. 72).

If this accurate perception of what goes on in exchange is to explain how capitalism appears uncoercive, we need to understand how the sphere of exchange—which is only part of capitalism—should be the source of beliefs about the whole of capitalism. Why should the experience of freedom in exchange, rather than, say, the experience of taking orders on the production line, determine the beliefs that members of capitalist societies come naturally to have? How is the representation of exchange *generalized* into a view of capitalism as a whole?

Marx offers a clue to the answer to this question when he says that the fetishism of commodities results because "the producers do not come into contact with each other until they exchange" (*Capital*, vol. 1, p. 73). Exchange transactions are the salient points of social contact for economic actors in capitalism. They literally punctuate capitalist social relations. Every social interaction between individuals playing roles in the capitalist mode of production begins with such a transaction (say, the signing of a wage contract, exchanging labor-power for money) and can be ended with such a transaction (say, the dissolution of the wage contract). Each of these beginnings and endings is characterized by the absence of either party's having the power to command the other's obedience and use violence to get it. Each party knows that he can enter or withdraw from any capitalist social interaction without being subject to the command or the overt force of the other. What constraint either feels seems to be only a matter of what he happens to own, which naturally appears as a feature of his own good or bad fortune rather than a condition coercively imposed by the other. Thus, *all* capitalist social interactions, *not just the exchanges themselves*, appear as voluntary undertakings between equal people who happen to own different things.

Exchange accurately perceived and then generalized is what leads workers in capitalist societies to believe that they are free although they take orders most of their waking lives. Thus, partisan ideological beliefs result from accurate perception of exchange when its local nature is not seen and the rest of capitalism is, by default, assumed to be more of the same. The law follows suit.

IDEOLOGY AND LAW

"Law," wrote Marx, in *The Poverty of Philosophy*, "is only the official recognition of fact."[12] For capitalist law, the decisive fact is exchange. Law in capitalism is the official recognition of the fact of the economic relations in which the exchangers stand to one another. This insight—which will guide the materialist explanation of criminal law that I shall develop in this section—must be credited to the work of the Soviet legal theorist, Evgeny Pashukanis, whose *General Theory of Law and Marxism* was published in Russian in 1924.[13] Among the things for which Pashukanis argued was the notion that law was a product of capitalism and consequently had no legitimate place in socialism. As Stalin took firm control of the Soviet Union and saw fit to use the law to shore up that control, Pashukanis came eventually into disfavor. He recanted his views to some extent, but it was too late. By 1937, he had been declared an enemy of the people, and shortly thereafter "disappeared." Recently rediscovered by western Marxists, Pashukanis's work was first the object of lavish praise and subsequently the target of harsh criticism. I do not intend to endorse or defend the whole of Pashukanis's theory. He aimed at a general theory of law and made only a few observations about criminal law, which is my main concern here. I shall try to show that his basic insight about the relation between law and exchange can be developed into an explanation of the content of the criminal law and of the constitutional protections relevant to criminal justice.

Marx writes that parties to an exchange

must behave in such a way that each does not appropriate the commodity of the other, and part with his own, except by means of an act done by mutual consent. They must, therefore, mutually recognize in each other the rights of private proprietors. This juridical relation, which thus expresses itself in a contract, whether such contract be part of a developed legal system or not, is a relation between two wills, and is but the reflex of the real economic relation between the two [Capital, vol. 1, pp. 88–89].

Exchangers must in fact refrain from forcing those with whom they would trade to part with their goods or services or money. Official recognition of this fact takes the form of granting to exchangers "the rights of private proprietors." Because this recognition is related to the ideological failure to perceive the coerciveness reproduced in exchanges between proprietors of capital and proprietors of labor, exchanges are understood legally as acts of the free will of the parties as long as no overt violence is used or threatened. Consequently, exchangers treat one another as *free subjects* whose freedom is expressed in their *right to dispose of their property without interference from others.*

It is the difference between what capitalists own and what workers own that, for Marx, makes it possible to reproduce a coercive relation through free exchange. If the law follows ideology in representing the relation between exchangers as noncoercive, then the law must abstract from this difference in what is owned and treat each party as having the same right to dispose of his property irrespective of what that property is. The law reflects this in its formality. The legal right of property is an empty form to be filled in with different content, depending on what an individual owns. Capitalists and workers have the same right of property, they just happen to own different things. It just happens that what some people own are factories and what others own are their bodies, but their property rights in these things are the same. Their freedom to dispose of their property also is the same.[14] Thus, exchangers treat each other as *equal* free subjects with equal property rights—that is to say, as legal *persons*.[15]

We saw in the previous section that ideology is not to be understood as merely an illusion. Ideology reflects the real way in which capitalism appears to its participants. By the same token, the ideological nature of law reflects the real relations in which exchangers stand to one another. The written law, even the institutions of law (from lawmakers to law enforcers), are not the source of law. They reflect real, objective, "legal" relations between members of a capitalist society, relations that exist, so to speak, on the ground first and only later on the page or in the courts for that matter. It is here that the "inversion" of which Engels wrote does its ideological work. Although the law is a reflection of the relations of exchangers on the ground, it appears that the law is an expression of rationality itself, with the consequence that the relations among exchangers seem so as well. Here, however, a problem arises for the Marxian materialist: If law is the reflection of the actual practice of economic exchange, how does law come to function as a norm? A simple reflection would represent whatever occurs, and thus could not identify some actions as infractions. How can the materialist account for the normative dimension of law that arises as a reflection of economic relations?

The answer to this is that law is not a simple reflection of economic relations, but an *idealized* reflection. As exchanges occur over and over, people naturally tend to average out the peculiarities of individual cases and discern an "essential core." In time, when individual cases diverge enough from this essential core, they are seen as deviant and thus as violations. The legal reflex of economic relations, then, is not an exact replica but the result of a natural sifting out of arbitrariness and idiosyncrasy such that what emerges is an idealized "average" that stands in a normative relation to particular instances. This tendency to go from what happens "on average" to what is normative is a common feature of human social existence. The tendency of the statistical norm (what people can generally be expected to do) to become the moral norm (what is expected of people) is visible in early civilization (where, for example, natural and moral law are not distinguished from one another) and in advanced civilization (where, for example, existing business practice is often taken by courts as creating legally enforceable obligations).

This brings us to a second question. It would seem that law that reflects (even the idealized "average" core of) exchanges would include not only the criminal law but also what we currently understand as contract or civil law. How can the theory that traces law to exchange account for the nature of the criminal law per se, with its special content and its unique remedies?

To answer this, note first that there is considerable overlap in the content of criminal and civil law; criminal acts, such as theft or battery, also can be causes of civil action. This overlap, however, is largely asymmetrical: Virtually any criminal act can be a cause of civil action, but only some civil causes are subject to criminal prosecution. What this suggests is that the criminal law is more distinctive in its remedies than in its content. In general, criminal prosecution seeks punishment of the guilty, and civil action seeks recovery of damages from the one responsible for a loss. Now on the materialist theory, both sorts of law—criminal and civil—represent the "essential core" of normal exchange and aim to rectify violations of or deviations from that core. Thus, to explain the nature of the criminal law per se, we must show why some class of deviations from normal exchange are singled out for the distinctive "criminal" remedy, namely, punishment. Because punishment is generally a graver matter than recovery of damages, we should expect the criminal law to be addressed to the most serious violations of normal exchange, whereas the civil law can be addressed to all violations.

Violations of normal exchange can be distinguished in the following way: Some threaten the very possibility of free exchange by depriving people of the ability to dispose of their property. Other violations threaten not the possibility of free exchange but its success in meeting the wishes of the exchangers. What threatens the very possibility of exchange are acts of violence that overtly block the capacity of individuals to exercise their wills, acts of theft that overtly bypass the capacity of individuals to choose how their property is disposed of, and acts of deception that have the same effect, so to speak, behind the backs of their victims. These are so serious that they must be presented in advance—and that requires a standing threat of punishment. Accordingly, the criminal law is primarily aimed at acts of violence, theft, and fraud.[16]

Less serious violations are compatible with the existence of exchange but cause exchanges in some way to fall short of the wishes of the exchangers. These violations are mainly failures to live up to the terms of explicit or implied contracts. They can be remedied by requiring performance or payment from the one responsible. These are suitable targets for the civil law, although nothing is lost by allowing the civil law to apply to recovery of losses due to the more serious violations as well.

Actual exchanges will be characterized by the full range of violations and deviations, from failure to meet agreed-upon deadlines to gross expropriation with the threat or use of violence. All such violations undermine the likelihood of the same parties exchanging again. Because it is generally in people's long-term interest that stable trading relationships be maintained, it will generally be in people's interest to eliminate such violations. Accordingly, over time the vast majority of exchanges, particularly those between people in continuing exchange relationships, will tend to be free of violations. Thus, an average core of exchange, characterized by absence of violence and fraud as well as by dependable fulfillment of agreements, will emerge as the norm. The law in general will represent this norm. However, of the violations, there is a class that stands out in the extremity of the threat it poses to the possibility of exchange. This is the class of threats and acts of violence, theft, and fraud because all of these directly attack the ability of people to dispose of what they own according to their own free will. Consequently, the maintenance of stable exchange relations will require establishing a secure peace, free of violence, theft, and fraud.[17] Because these violations are so serious as to threaten the very possibility of ongoing exchange relations, they must be prevented in advance by the standing threat of punishment, rather than remedying them afterward. They are appropriately the subject of the criminal law.

On the whole, then, although the entire law in capitalism reflects the conditions of normal exchange, the content of the criminal law—the acts it identifies as "crimes"—are those that threaten the very possibility of normal exchange. Moreover, because the normal relations of exchange are not only idealized but (as we saw in the previous section) generalized to the whole of capitalism, they will shape people's normative expectations beyond exchange. Thus, they determine the limits that will be imposed on officials taxed with the job of finding and prosecuting criminals, the shape of court proceedings, the relation of punishment to offense, and the emphasis on the free will of the offender. Accordingly, by tracing law to its source in exchange, we can account for at least the general content of criminal law and the general shape of the criminal justice system and of the constitutional limits within which that system operates. Here, briefly sketched and numbered for ease of identification, are the main ways in which this works:

1. Normal exchange presupposes that people are treated as having property rights in whatever they are to trade, and that must mean not only goods but their bodies as well, because bodily actions are what workers trade with capitalists for their wage. Crime, then, is any violation by one individual of the property rights of another in whatever he owns, including his body. This explains why the criminal law is primarily directed against acts of violence, theft, and fraud. Moreover, because criminal law protects an individual's body because he owns it (and not, say, because it is the earthly vessel of his immortal soul), the law will be primarily concerned with injuries done to people's bodies against their will—otherwise such injuries do not violate the individual's ownership of his body. This accounts for the liberal principle, *volenti non fit injuria* (no injury to one who has consented) and thus, via generalization, for the tendency in capitalism to decriminalize (or reduce in importance) "victimless crimes" or "morals offenses."

2. This account also tells us what we are not likely to see as crime in capitalist society, namely, exercises of the power inherent in the ownership of property itself. Thus, we will not generally find that death due to preventable dangers in the workplace will be taken as murder because that would assume that the worker was somehow forced into the workplace by the power inherent in his boss's private ownership of the means of production. Because that is just the power that is invisible in capitalism, the worker is taken as freely consenting to his job and thus freely accepting its risks. Accordingly, when the criminal law is used against employers to get them to eliminate occupational hazards, it is never with the understanding that employers who do not eliminate such hazards are violent criminals. If the criminal law is used in these cases at all, it is as a regulatory mechanism applied to employers because this is the most efficient way to reduce the social costs of occupational injury and disease. The treatment of guilty employers is generally light-handed, even though far more people lose their lives due to preventable occupational hazards than as a result of what the law currently treats as murder. In capitalism, subjection to one person is seen as arbitrary and thus unlawful coercion, but subjection to the capitalist class is not seen at all. (Here is how the Marxian theory understands the phenomena we discussed in the main text of this book and accounted for with the historical inertia explanation.)

3. The other side of criminal law—the limits placed on legal officials in their pursuit of suspected criminals (for example, in the
Bill of Rights)—likewise reflects the generalized conception of
people as owners of their bodies and other property. Accordingly,
we find protections against official invasions of suspects' property (for example, the Fourth Amendment protections against
unreasonable search and seizure) and against penetration of suspects' bodies or minds (for example, the Fifth Amendment protection against self-incrimination). Moreover, this explains why corporal punishment, which was the norm in feudalism and slavery,
tends to be eliminated in capitalism. The bodies of slaves are
literally owned by their masters, and lords have natural (that is,
parent-like) authority over their serfs. In these cases corporal
punishment fits the existing social relations. In capitalism, employer and employee meet as owners of their respective bodies,
and thus corporal punishment looks increasingly out of place.
  The existence of these various limitations on what can be
done to enforce the law is evidence that the Marxian view of law
includes recognition of the way law functions not only to control
the working class but as a limit on the behavior of the ruling
class. Indeed, the Marxian view can be taken as claiming that it is
precisely as a system that protects everyone alike in his property
(including his body) by limiting both what citizens and law enforcers can do to the bodies (and other property) of other citizens,
that the law most effectively serves the purpose of keeping the
working class selling its labor-power to owners of means of
production—both classes safe in the knowledge that no one can
interfere with their right to dispose of what they happen to own.

4. As crime is a violation of normal exchange, so punishment is
thought of on the same model of equivalence as exists in exchange. "Punishment emerges as an equivalent which compen-
sates the damage sustained by the injured party."[18] The commer-
cial model doesn't end here. The adversary system reproduces it
in court. "The public prosecutor demands . . . a 'high' price, that
is to say a severe sentence. The offender pleads for leniency, a
'discount,' and the court passes sentence in equity."[19] Crime de-
forms exchange by taking with force rather than payment. Punishment restores exchange by using force to pay the criminal
back for his force. This is the tribute in retribution. The court is
the extraordinary market where this extraordinary exchange is
negotiated. The scales in Justice's hands are the same as those
used by the merchant.

5. Because exchange normally brings payment to an individual only when he freely chooses to offer up his goods or services for it, so then the payment of punishment comes due only when the offender has freely chosen to commit the offense for which the punishment is payment. Accordingly, liability for punishment is subject to conditions of the same sort as apply to liability to contractual obligations. One is not bound by a contract that he has not signed freely, or that he signed while insane, or in ignorance of its contents, and so on. Likewise, the offender is liable to punishment, and thus is truly a criminal, only if he has committed his violation freely, sanely, and with knowledge of what he was doing. By the same logic, the law generally prohibits *ex post facto* attribution of criminal liability because a person cannot choose freely to violate a law before it has been passed.

Here, then, we read off the face of exchange, albeit idealized and generalized, the main contours of criminal justice as it develops in capitalism. As I suggested at the outset, this is no more than a skeleton. It does not aim to account for the full rich detail of any particular criminal justice system. Actual criminal justice systems exist in societies with other modes of production present alongside capitalism and are affected by the complex interplay of human actions, and so on, so that each actual system—like each actual face—will have a distinct physiognomy while sharing in the basic structure. Some criminal justice systems will be slower in eliminating "morals offenses," some will be stricter on occupational hazards, some will abolish the death penalty while others will retain it, and so on.[20] These specific outcomes will be a function of the strength of various social groupings (such as religious organizations, labor unions, academia, the press, and the like) come to have in the specific history of specific countries, and of all the largely unpredictable features that determine the outcome of particular battles over the content of the law and the funding of the legal apparatus. This notwithstanding, the Marxian claim is that criminal justice will tend toward the shape sketched out above.

LAW AND ETHICS

We reach now the question of the moral stance toward capitalist criminal justice that is appropriate if the Marxian account is correct. Marxism describes capitalism as an exploitative system, meaning one in which workers are forced to work for capitalists without compensation. Marxists characteristically regard exploitation, and consequently capitalism, as unjust or immoral. Broadly speaking, they reach this condemnation by one of three routes. One is to view capitalist exploitation as wrong because it promotes antagonistic or alienated relations between human beings.[21] The second way is to view capitalist exploitation as wrong because it is a form of forced servitude or slavery.[22] The third way is to view capitalist exploitation as wrong because it is based on an unjust distribution of wealth, namely, the unjustifiable exclusive ownership by a few of the means of production.[23] I shall call these three views, respectively, "the alienation charge," "the slavery charge," and "the maldistribution charge." Each of these has moral implications for capitalist criminal justice. The task of identifying these implications is simplified by the fact that the second and third charges incorporate each other. The slavery charge accepts that private ownership of means of production is a case of unjust maldistribution (because it is a means of forcing servitude), and the maldistribution charge accepts that private ownership of means of production is a means of enslavement (because it is a power wrongly monopolized by a few). For our purposes, then, the charges against capitalism can be reduced to two: the alienation charge and the slavery-maldistribution charge.

Those who raise the alienation charge point out that capitalism is a system in which each person's well-being is in conflict with that of others. Capitalism pits class against class (competing over the division of the economic product into wages versus profit), worker against worker (competing for jobs), and capitalist against capitalist (competing for market shares). Moreover, proponents of this charge hold that antagonism of interests is neither a necessary feature of human life nor a desirable condition. It is caused by capitalism, and overcome only by socialism (at least largely, and then completely by communism). Criminal justice as it emerges in capitalism is understood as a means to regulate this antagonism of interests. Because it assumes that this antagonism is inevitable, criminal justice serves to confer permanent validity on capitalism. Moreover, criminal justice promotes this antagonism by teaching people that the rights of each are in conflict with the rights of others rather than mutually supportive, that freedom is *freedom from* invasion by others rather than freedom to develop with others, that what people owe each other is noninterference rather than a helping hand.

Also important is the fact that a society based on antagonism of interests is one in which people earn their daily bread only as long as someone else can profit as a result. When that changes, workers may find themselves in need and with little in the way of help from the rest of society. On this view, then, the large crime rates characteristic of capitalism are due to the fact that people in capitalism are taught to see their interests as in conflict with others' and thus they are trained to have limited altruism and fellow feeling, and to the fact that a society based on antagonism of interests is one in which economic need and insecurity are endemic. When limited fellow feeling meets economic need and insecurity, the result is crime. (Recall the views of Bonger and Gordon, discussed in Chapter 4.) The same system that calls criminals individually guilty, then, is responsible for the antagonism of interests that breeds crime in the first place. The upshot of this charge is that criminals are not—or at least not wholly—guilty of the crimes they commit. On this charge, criminals are in large measure unjustly punished for actions caused by the very system that punishes them.

On the slavery-maldistribution charge, the emphasis is on the wrongness and coerciveness of private ownership of means of production. Capitalism promotes a system of criminal justice based on protecting the freedom of individuals to dispose of what they rightly own; but the system itself is based on the wrongful appropriation of means of production, and with it the power to coerce others to labor without compensation. On this view, socialism cures capitalism not so much by replacing antagonism of interest with harmony but by replacing private ownership of means of production by a few with social ownership by everyone.

To understand the moral implications for criminal justice of this charge, imagine for a moment that we see someone take a sheep from the field owned by another. In response, suppose that we make the normal judgment that a theft, an unjust expropriation, has occurred. Now suppose further that we learn that the field-owner had himself stolen the sheep from the sheep-taker some time before. Based on these new facts, we shall change our views about the moral status of the sheep-taking. Now we are likely to say that the one we saw take the sheep was not, morally speaking, a criminal, but the opposite, a victim responding justifiably (or less unjustifiably than it seemed at first) to an earlier crime. Likewise, if we come to see ownership of means of production as itself a violation of justice (because it is unjustly maldistributive or unjustifiably coercive), we will see the things that people do in response to it as more just (or less unjust) than they appeared when we didn't question the justice of ownership of means of production. (Recall the discussion in Chapter 4 of how a judgment that an individual is guilty of a crime presupposes that the social context in which his act occurred was just.)

On the slavery-maldistribution view, then, the individuals normally labeled "criminal" are seen as the victims of a prior "crime" to which they are responding. That criminals may not (and usually do not) see themselves as doing this only reflects the fact that they are taken in by capitalist ideology no less than law-abiding folks are. The "criminal" then is not a doer of injustice but the reverse. He is a victim of injustice trying to improve his situation by means that have been made necessary by the fact that capitalism leaves him few alternatives. The upshot of this charge is that criminals are not really morally guilty. They are in large measure unjustly punished for *re*acting against crimes perpetrated by the very system that punishes them.

In sum, the Marxist critique of criminal justice does lead to a moral condemnation of criminal justice under capitalism. This moral condemnation comes in two forms, both of which share the claim that capitalist criminal justice wrongly punishes people who do not deserve to be punished. In the first form, the alienation charge, criminals are thought not to deserve punishment because their acts are caused by socially conditioned antagonism to their fellows in conjunction with limited and unstable opportunities to satisfy their needs and desires. In the second form, the slavery-maldistribution charge, criminals are thought not to deserve punishment because their apparent crimes are themselves reactions against conditions that are themselves, morally speaking, criminal. Needless to say, it is possible for the same person to endorse both forms of condemnation.

Several things that apply to both charges are worth noting. First of all, in both cases, the features of capitalist criminal justice that come in for ethical condemnation reflect the failure to see the way criminal justice reflects the mode of production—mentioned at the outset. In the case of the alienation charge, the failure is that of not seeing that capitalist criminal justice emerges to regulate the antagonistic relations between human beings that capitalism produces. Seeing capitalist criminal justice as the product of independent reason, it seems that those antagonistic relations are a natural feature of human life, that always must be so regulated. Then, capitalist criminal justice, rather than protecting the interests of capitalists, appears merely to be the necessary condition of any peaceful social coexistence. In the case of the slavery-maldistribution charge, the failure is of not seeing how property in capitalism is an expression of a particular and morally questionable constellation of social forces. Seeing capitalist criminal justice as the product of independent reason, it seems that the property criminal justice protects is a natural feature of human life, which is always in need of such protection. Then, capitalist criminal justice, rather than protecting the interests of capitalists, appears merely to be protecting everyone's interest. What's more, it follows that the continued and heavily publicized activities of criminal justice serve to reinforce ideological blindness, in the first view, to capitalism's role in causing the attitudes and conditions that lead to crime and, in the second view, to the moral dubiousness of capitalist property relations.

It also must be borne in mind that the ethical implications of both charges are general propositions that will fit actual criminal cases in varying degrees. For example, while the alienation charge suggests that criminals are not culpable because shaped by an antagonistic society, in actual cases, the degree to which individual law-breakers have been so shaped will vary. There may be some who have largely escaped the deleterious influences and yet, out of selfishness or greed, commit crimes. Marxism naturally claims that the number of criminals of this sort is small compared with the number of criminals all told. Marxism, however, need not deny that there are some criminals like this and thus that they deserve punishment. Likewise, on the slavery-maldistribution charge, whereas criminals are generally taken to be victims of the prior injustice of private ownership of means of production, actual criminals will differ in the degree to which they are so victimized and in the degree to which their actual crimes can be thought of as reactions thereto. Relatively privileged persons, or others whose crimes bear little relation to their class position (some rapists, for example), may well be more culpable than the general run of criminals. It seems to me appropriate for Marxists to view responsibility—and thus guilt—as existing in varying degrees, relative to the actual impact of the social structure on a given individual's criminal act.

Finally, note that on neither of the two views we have discussed does the criminal emerge as any kind of "proto-revolutionary," as is sometimes asserted of Marxism. On the alienation charge, the criminal is at best relieved of responsibility because he has been shaped by the social system to have antisocial attitudes and fated by that system to experience need and insecurity that, together with those attitudes, lead to crime. On the slavery-maldistribution charge, the criminal is at best a victim because he is the object of the unjust coercion or expropriation characteristic of private ownership of means of production. His crime, rather than being a kind of rebellion against what victimizes him, is most often a narrowly self-interested striking out against whatever he can get his hands on. On both charges, Marxism does imply reduced or no blame for (most) criminals; but it does not imply any celebration of their acts. This is particularly so in light of the fact that most victims of crime are other exploited people, members or would-be members of the working class. Crime and criminality must on the whole be placed by Marxism among the costs of capitalism, lined up alongside poverty, unemployment, pollution, and the rest.

Notes

ABBREVIATIONS USED IN THE NOTES

Challenge

The Challenge of Crime in a Free Society: A Report by the President's Commission on Law Enforcement and Administration of Justice (Washington, D.C.: U.S. Government Printing Office, February 1967).

Sourcebook-1981

T. J. Flanagan, D. J. van Alstyne, and M. R. Gottfredson, eds., *Sourcebook of Criminal Justice Statistics—1981*. U.S. Department of Justice, Bureau of Justice Statistics (Washington, D.C.: U.S. Government Printing Office, 1982).

Sourcebook-1987

T. J. Flanagan and K. M. Jamieson, eds., *Sourcebook of Criminal Justice Statistics— 1987*. U.S. Department of Justice Statistics (Washington, D.C.: U.S. Government Printing Office, 1988).

StatAbst-1988

U.S. Bureau of the Census, *Statistical Abstract of the United States: 1988*, 108th ed. (Washington, D.C., 1988). References to other editions of this annual publication will be indicated by StatAbst, followed by the year for which the statistics are reported.

UCR-1986

Federal Bureau of Investigation, *Uniform Crime Reports for the United States: 1986* (Washington, D.C.: U.S. Government Printing Office, 1987). References to other editions of this annual report will be indicated by *UCR* followed by the year for which the statistics are reported. In general, these reports are published in the fall of the year following the year they cover.

NOTE TO THE INTRODUCTION

1. See, especially, Louis Althusser, "Ideology and Ideological State Apparatuses," in *Lenin and Philosophy and Other Essays* (London: New Left Books, 1971), pp. 121–173; and Nicos Poulantzas, *Fascism and Dictatorship* (London: New Left Books, 1974), pp. 299–309. These writers refer back to the pioneering insights of Antonio Gramsci into the ideological functions of state institutions. See Quintin Hoare and Geoffrey Nowell-Smith, eds., *Selections from the Prison Notebooks of Antonio Gramsci* (London: Lawrence and Wishart, 1971); and Carl Boggs, *Gramsci's Marxism* (London: Pluto Press, 1976). For other contemporary analyses of the relationship between the state and ideology, see Ralph Miliband, *The State in Capitalist Society* (New York: Basic Books, 1969), pp. 179–264; and Jürgen Habermas, *Legitimation Crisis* (Boston: Beacon Press, 1975). The Frankfurt School of social theory, of which Jürgen Habermas and Herbert Marcuse are probably the best-known representatives, is distinguished by the application of Marxism as well as Freudian theory to the analysis of ideology. See Martin Jay, *The Dialectical Imagination: The Frankfurt School of Social Theory, 1930–1950* (Boston: Little Brown, 1973).

NOTES TO CHAPTER 1

1. Speech of the president to the International Association of Chiefs of Police, New Orleans, Louisiana, September 28, 1981, reported in *Weekly Compilation of Presidential Documents* (July–September 1981), pp. 1039ff.
2. UCR-1986, p. 41; Sourcebook-1987, p. 240.
3. *Challenge*, p. 35.
4. UCR-1986, p. 41.
5. Sourcebook-1987, pp. 2, 26; also, StatAbst-1988, p. 168, Table no. 288.
6. Louise I. Shelley, *Crime and Modernization* (Carbondale: Southern Illinois University Press, 1981), p. 76.
7. Figures from the International Criminal Police Organization (INTERPOL), cited in Peter Jones, "Comparing Crime Here and Abroad," *Scholastic Update*, March 21, 1986, p. 21.
8. UCR-1986, p. 41.
9. UCR-1986, pp. 44–51.
10. Quoted in *Violence: An Element of American Life*, eds. K. Taylor and F. Soady (Boston: Holbrook Press, 1972), p. 49.
11. UCR-1986, pp. 44–51, 335–63.
12. UCR-1986, pp. 335–363.
13. UCR-1986, p. 41; Sourcebook-1987, p. 246; StatAbst-1988, p. 32.
14. UCR-1986, pp. 335–363; StatAbst-1988, pp. 32–34.
15. *Challenge*, p. 56.

16. *Time*, June 30, 1975, p. 11.
17. I have calculated the population of sixteen- to twenty-four-year-olds from *Economic Report of the President* (Washington, D.C.: U.S. Government Printing Office, 1988), p. 283, Table B-31; the victimization figures are from Sourcebook-1987, p. 240; and the FBI crime totals are from UCR-1980, p. 41, and UCR-1986, p. 41.
18. Preliminary figures released by the FBI show that crime rates decreased by 4 percent in 1982 compared with 1981. The *Washington Post*, April 20, 1983, p. A3. Serious crime decreased in the Washington, D.C. area in the first three months of 1983 compared with the same period in 1982. "Dr. Charles Wellford, director of the University of Maryland Institute of Criminal Justice and Criminology . . . attributed the decline to demographic changes. 'We are shifting from a very young to an older population,' he said. 'In particular, 15- to 29-year-olds have very high rates of crime. As fewer people are in those categories, there will be lower rates of crime.' " *Washington Post*, April 29, 1983, p. C1. See also "A Battle That Must Be Fought on Many Fronts," *Scholastic Update*, March 21, 1986, p. 3.
19. "Serious Crime Rises Again in New York," *New York Times*, March 22, 1988, pp. B1, B6.
20. Quoted in "Forum," *Harper's*, May 1985, p. 41.
21. Morton O. Schapiro and Dennis A. Ahlberg, "Why Crime Is Down," *American Demographics*, October 1986, p. 56.
22. *Washington Post*, August 4, 1975, p. A2.
23. Ibid., August 17, 1975, pp. A1, A4.
24. Jeffrie G. Murphy, "Marxism and Retribution," *Philosophy & Public Affairs*, 2, no. 3 (Spring 1973), p. 237.
25. Lawrence Mishel and Jacqueline Simon, *The State of Working America* (Washington, D.C.: Economic Policy Institute, 1988), p. iii.
26. Ibid., p. 8.
27. StatAbst-1988, p. 428, Table no. 701.
28. *Washington Post*, September 6, 1982, p. 2; the report was issued by the Full Employment Action Council (a coalition of religious, civil rights, and union groups) and the National Policy Exchange (an economic research and educational organization).
29. *Washington Post*, September 14, 1982, pp. 1, 4.
30. Figures from Bureau of Labor Statistics and National Center for Health Statistics, cited in "Racial Gulf: Blacks' Hopes, Raised by '68 Kerner Report, Are Mainly Unfulfilled," *Wall Street Journal*, February 26, 1988, pp. 1, 9. See also "Today's Native Sons," *Time*, December 1, 1986, pp. 26–29; and StatAbst-1988, p. 75, Table no. 113.
31. Robert Johnson and Hans Toch, "Introduction," in Johnson and Toch, eds., *The Pains of Imprisonment* (Beverly Hills, Calif.: Sage Publications, 1982), pp. 19–20.
32. Franklin Zimring, *Firearms and Violence in American Life* (Washington,

D.C.: U.S. Government Printing Office, 1968), pp. 6–7 (emphasis added).

33. Address by the Honorable Edward H. Levi, attorney general of the United States, before the Law Enforcement Executives Conference, April 6, 1975.
34. *Challenge*, p. 239 (emphasis added).
35. UCR-1986, pp. 7, 10.
36. Presidential News Conference, June 16, 1981; see also "Reagan Denounces Gun Control Laws," *Washington Post*, May 7, 1983, p. A8.
37. Zimring, *Firearms and Violence in American Life*, Chapter 11.
38. Arnold S. Trebach, *The Heroin Solution* (New Haven, Conn.: Yale University Press, 1982), pp. 3–4, 246.
39. U.S. Department of Health, Education and Welfare, Public Health Services, National Institute on Alcohol Abuse and Alcoholism, Special Action Office for Drug Abuse Prevention, *Social Cost of Drug Abuse* (Washington, D.C., 1974), pp. 20–21.
40. "The largest study ever made of drug abuse in this country shows that two widely available legal drugs—alcohol and the tranquilizer Valium—are responsible for the greatest amount of drug-related illness, the government reported yesterday." Stuart Auerbach, "2 Drugs Widely Abused," *Washington Post*, July 9, 1976, p. A1. See also Jeffrey H. Reiman, "Prostitution, Addiction, and the Ideology of Liberalism," in *Contemporary Crises* 3 (1979), pp. 53–68.
41. U.S. Department of Health, Education and Welfare, *Social Cost of Drug Abuse*, p. 25.
42. Robert L. DuPont, "Operation Trip-Wire: A New Proposal Focused on Criminal Heroin Addicts," speech, Federal Bar Association Convention, Washington, D.C., October 1, 1977, p. 11; quoted in Trebach, *The Heroin Solution*, p. 247.
43. Trebach, *The Heroin Solution*, p. 248.
44. Sourcebook-1981, pp. 464, 485.
45. Trebach, *The Heroin Solution*, p. 246.
46. Troy Duster, *The Legislation of Morality: Law, Drugs, and Moral Judgment* (New York: Free Press, 1970), pp. 3, 7, inter alia.
47. Cf. Philip C. Baridon, *Addiction, Crime, and Social Policy* (Lexington, Mass.: Lexington Books, 1976), pp. 4–5.
48. Arnold S. Trebach, Testimony at the Hearings on Proposals to Legalize Drugs held by the House Select Committee on Narcotics Abuse and Control, September 29, 1988, p. 2.
49. "Enemy Within: Drug Money Is Corrupting the Enforcers," *New York Times*, April 11, 1988, p. A12.
50. "U.S. Anti-Drug Effort Criticized," *Washington Post*, November 12, 1988, p. A15.
51. "Cocaine Downs: Signs Indicate That America's Cocaine Habit is Easing," *Wall Street Journal*, July 20, 1987, p. 21.

52. "Prosecutors Admit: No Victory in Sight," *The National Law Journal*, August 8, 1988, p. S-2.
53. "The Unspeakable Is Debated: Should Drugs Be Legalized?" *New York Times*, March 15, 1988, p. 21.
54. "Drug Wars Push D.C. to Brink of Homicide Record: Police Efforts Futile as Turf Disputes Raise 1988 Slaying Total to 285," *Washington Post*, October 26, 1988, p. A1. By year's end, the record was soundly broken with the number of murders reaching 372!
55. "Enemy Within: Drug Money Is Corrupting the Enforcers," pp. A1, A12.
56. Ibid.
57. Marvin D. Miller, National Organization for the Reform of Marijuana Laws, Testimony at the Hearings on Proposals to Legalize Drugs held by the House Select Committee on Narcotics Abuse and Control, September 29, 1988, p. 12–3; UCR-1986, p. 163.
58. Miller, testimony, p. 19.
59. Ibid., p. 18.
60. Trebach, testimony, pp. 11–12.
61. Ibid., p. 31.
62. *Time*, June 30, 1975, p. 17 (emphasis added).
63. Kai T. Erikson, *Wayward Puritans* (New York: John Wiley, copyright © 1966), p. 4. Reprinted by permission of John Wiley & Sons, Inc.
64. Ibid., p. 11.
65. Ibid., pp. 13–15 (emphasis added).

NOTES TO CHAPTER 2

1. *Washington Star*, March 14, 1976, pp. A1, A9.
2. Ibid., p. A9.
3. Gerald R. Ford, "To Insure Domestic Tranquility: Mandatory Sentence for Convicted Felons," speech delivered at the Yale Law School Sesquicentennial Convocation, New Haven, Connecticut, April 25, 1975, in *Vital Speeches of the Day* 41, no. 15 (May 15, 1975), p. 451.
4. "Arrest Data Reveal Profile of Suspect," *Washington Post*, September 16, 1975, p. C1.
5. Ibid.; see also Maryland-National Capital Parks and Planning Commission, *Crime Analysis 1975: Prince George's County* (August 1975), p. 86.
6. UCR-1974, p. 186.
7. UCR-1980, p. 200.
8. "Arrest Data Reveal Profile of Suspect," p. C1; and Maryland-National Capital Parks and Planning Commission, *Crime Analysis 1975*, p. 86.
9. UCR-1974, p. 191.
10. UCR-1986, p. 182; StatAbst-1988, p. 16, Table no. 17.

11. Speech to International Association of Chiefs of Police, September 28, 1981.
12. Out of 1,289,524 persons arrested for FBI Index crimes in 1974, 1,043,155, or more than 80 percent were males. See *UCR-1974*, p. 190. In Prince George's County, males "represented three of every four serious crime defendants." Maryland—National Capital Parks and Planning Commission, *Crime Analysis 1975*, p. 3.
13. Out of 1,474,427 persons arrested for FBI Index Crimes in 1974, 1,267,955 were "city arrests" and 420,682 were "suburban" (suburban arrest figures include arrests in suburban cities, and thus overlap with statistics for city arrests). UCR-1974, p. 180.
14. Jeffrie G. Murphy, "Marxism and Retribution," *Philosophy & Public Affairs* 2, no. 3 (Spring 1973), p. 237. Cf. Samuel Jordan, "Prison Reform: In Whose Interest?" *Criminal Law Bulletin* 7, no. 9 (November 1971), pp. 779–797: "Of the 1.2 million criminal offenders handled each day by some part of the United States correctional system, 80 percent are members of the lowest 12 percent income group—or black and poor," quoted in Jessica Mitford, *Kind and Usual Punishment* (New York: Alfred A. Knopf, 1973), p. 289.
15. *Challenge*, p. 44; see also p. 160.
16. John N. Mitchell, "Crime Prevention: Citizen Participation," speech delivered before the Conference on Crime and the Urban Crisis in the National Emergency Committee of the National Council on Crime and Delinquency, San Francisco, California, February 3, 1969, in *Vital Speeches of the Day* 35, no. 10 (March 1, 1969), p. 290.
17. See note 11.
18. See note 15.
19. This transformation has been noted by Erving Goffman in his sensitive description of total institutions, *Asylums* (Garden City, N.Y.: Doubleday, 1961).

> *The interpretative scheme of the total institution automatically begins to operate as soon as the inmate enters, the staff having the notion that entrance is* prima facie *evidence that one must be the kind of person the institution was set up to handle. A man in a political prison must be traitorous; a man in a prison must be a lawbreaker; a man in a mental hospital must be sick. If not traitorous, criminal, or sick, why else would he be here? [p. 84]*

So, too, a person who calls forth the society's most drastic weapons of defense must pose the gravest danger to its well-being. Why else the reaction? The point is put well and tersely by D. Chapman: "There is a circular pattern in thinking: we are hostile to wicked people, wicked people are punished, punished people are wicked, we are hostile to punished people because they are wicked." "The Stereotype of the

Criminal and the Social Consequences," *International Journal of Criminology and Penology* 1 (1973), p. 16.

20. Richard Quinney, *The Social Reality of Crime* (Boston: Little, Brown, 1970). In his later work, for example, *Critique of Legal Order: Crime Control in Capitalist Society* (Boston: Little, Brown, 1973), and *Class, State & Crime* (New York: McKay, 1977), Quinney moves clearly into a Marxist problematic and his conclusions dovetail with many in this book. In my own view, however, Quinney has not yet accomplished a satisfactory synthesis between the "social reality" theory and his later Marxism. Elsewhere, I have examined Quinney's theory from the standpoint of moral philosophy. See Jeffrey H. Reiman, "Doing Justice to Criminology: Reflections on the Implications for Criminology of Recent Developments in the Philosophy of Justice," in *Issues in Criminal Justice: Planning and Evaluation*, eds., Marc Riedel and Duncan Chappell (New York: Praeger, 1976), pp. 134–142.

21. Quinney, *Social Reality of Crime*, p. 15.

22. *Washington Post*, January 11, 1983, p. C10.

23. Barbara Matusow, "If It Bleeds, It Leads," *The Washingtonian*, January 1988, p. 102.

24. "Titillating Channels: TV Is Going Tabloid As Shows Seek Sleaze and Find Profits, Too," *Wall Street Journal*, May 18, 1988, p. 1.

25. "Crime in America: The Shocking Truth," *McCall's*, March 1987, p. 144.

26. Sir James Fitzjames Stephen, from his *History of the Criminal Law of England* 2 (1883), excerpted in *Crime, Law and Society*, eds., Abraham S. Goldstein and Joseph Goldstein (New York: Free Press, 1971), p. 21.

27. Troy Duster, *The Legislation of Morality: Law, Drugs and Moral Judgment* (New York: Free Press, 1970), pp. 3–76.

28. Norval Morris and Gordon Hawkins, *The Honest Politician's Guide to Crime Control* (Chicago: University of Chicago Press, 1970), p. 2.

29. *Challenge*, p. 7.

30. UCR-1986, pp. 7, 21, 331.

31. UCR-1986, p. 153.

32. *The President's Report on Occupational Safety and Health* (Washington, D.C.: U.S. Government Printing Office, 1972).

33. See, for instance, Joseph A. Page and Mary-Win O'Brien, *Bitter Wages: Ralph Nader's Study Group Report on Disease and Injury on the Job* (New York: Grossman, 1973); Rachel Scott, *Muscle and Blood* (New York: E. P. Dutton, 1974); and Jeanne M. Stellman and Susan M. Daum, *Work Is Dangerous to Your Health* (New York: Vintage Books, 1973). See also Fran Lynn "The Dust in Willie's Lungs," *The Nation* 222, no. 7 (February 21, 1976), pp. 209–212; and Joel Swartz, "Silent Killers at Work," *Crime and Social Justice* 3 (Summer 1975), pp. 15–20.

34. *President's Report on Occupational Safety and Health*, p. 111; U.S. Department of Labor, Bureau of Labor Statistics, *Occupational Injuries*

and Illnesses in the United States by Industry, 1986 (Washington, D.C.: U.S. Government Printing Office, May 1988), pp. 8, 50.

35. *Report of the President to the Congress on Occupational Safety and Health, 1980* (August 4, 1981), p. 86; reporting on deaths and illnesses for 1979. Robert Johnson, who has conducted extensive interviews with present and former textile workers suffering from brown lung, indicates that another reason for the underreporting of occupational disease is that workers are often hesitant to admit symptoms for fear of being seen as "defective" or "worn out" and therefore losing their jobs (personal communication).

36. Robert Reid, "How Accurate Are Safety and Health Statistics?" *Occupational Hazards*, March 1987, p. 49.

37. "Is OSHA Falling Down on the Job?" *New York Times*, August 2, 1987, pp. 1, 6.

38. Letter from Schweiker to B. J. Pigg, Executive Director of the Asbestos Information Association, dated April 29, 1982.

39. Philip Landrigan, Testimony before the Senate Committee on Labor and Human Resources, April 18, 1988, p. 2. For cancer deaths, see StatAbst-1988, p. 77, Table no. 117, and p. 80, Table no. 120.

40. U.S. Department of Justice, *Bureau of Justice Statistics Technical Report: Criminal Victimization in the U.S.* (July 1982), p. 3.

41. Susan Q. Stranahan, "Why 115,000 Workers Will Die This Year," *Boston Sunday Globe*, March 21, 1976, p. A4.

42. National Safety Council, *Accident Facts*, 1981 edition, pp. 23–24.

43. Page and O'Brien, *Bitter Wages*, p. 16.

44. Testimony of Peter Henle, deputy assistant secretary for policy evaluation and research, given before the Labor Standards Subcommittee of the House Committee on Education and Labor, 96th Cong., 1st Sess., May 26, 1979. Chronic brown lung is a severely disabling occupational respiratory disease. For a description of its impact on its victims, see Robert Johnson, "Labored Breathing: Living with Brown Lung," paper presented at the Annual Meeting of the American Society of Criminology, Fall 1982, Toronto, Canada. See also Page and O'Brien, *Bitter Wages*, p. 18.

45. Page and O'Brien, *Bitter Wages*, p. 23; and Scott, *Muscle and Blood*, p. 196.

46. Scott, *Muscle and Blood*, pp. 45–46; cf. Page and O'Brien, *Bitter Wages*, p. 25.

47. Page and O'Brien, *Bitter Wages*, p. 37.

48. Ibid., p. 45.

49. "Is OSHA Falling Down on the Job?" pp. 1, 6.

50. Reid, "How Accurate Are Safety and Health Statistics?" p. 51.

51. Anthony Robbins, "Can Reagan Be Indicted for Betraying Public Health?" *American Journal of Public Health* 73, no. 1 (January 1983), p. 13.

52. *Challenge,* p. 52 (emphasis added). See also p. 3 for then-prevailing homicide rates.

53. *Washington Post,* July 16, 1975, p. A3.

54. George A. Silver, "The Medical Insurance Disease," *The Nation,* 222, no. 12 (March 27, 1976), p. 369.

55. Ibid., p. 371.

56. *Newsweek,* March 29, 1976, p. 67. Lest anyone think this is a new problem, compare this passage written in a popular magazine over thirty-five years ago:

> *In an editorial on medical abuses, the* Journal of the Medical Association of Georgia *referred to "surgeons who paradoxically are often cast in the role of the supreme hero by the patient and family and at the same time may be doing the greatest amount of harm to the individual."*
>
> *Unnecessary operations on women, stemming from the combination of a trusting patient and a split fee, have been so deplored by honest doctors that the phrase "rape of the pelvis" has been used to describe them. The American College of Surgeons, impassioned foe of fee-splitting, has denounced unnecessary hysterectomies, uterine suspensions, Caesarian sections. [Howard Whitman, "Why Some Doctors Should Be in Jail," Colliers, October 30, 1953, p. 24.]*

57. StatAbst-1988, p. 97, Table no. 153.

58. UCR-1986, p. 10.

59. Silver, "The Medical Insurance Disease," p. 369. Silver's estimates are extremely conservative. Some studies suggest that between 30,000 and 160,000 individuals die as a result of drugs prescribed by their doctors. See Boyce Rensberger, "Thousands a Year Killed by Faulty Prescriptions," *New York Times,* January 28, 1976, pp. 1, 17. If we assume with Silver that at least 20 percent are unnecessary, then this puts the annual death toll from unnecessary prescriptions at between 6,000 and 32,000 persons. For an in-depth look at the recklessness with which prescription drugs are put on the market and the laxness with which the Food and Drug Administration exercises its mandate to protect the public, see the series of eight articles by Morton Mintz, "The Medicine Business," *Washington Post,* June 27–30, July 1–4, 1976.

60. "More Crime in the Drug and Device Industry," *Health Letter,* October 1988, p. 12.

61. Rate of increase of medical costs is calculated from StatAbst-1988, p. 91, Table no. 138. Note that the assumption that the *number* of unnecessary operations and prescriptions has remained the same between 1974 and 1986 is a conservative assumption in that it effectively assumes that the rate of these practices relative to the population has declined because population has increased about 14 percent in the period.

62. Lewis Regenstein, *America the Poisoned* (Washington, D.C.: Acropolis Books, 1982), pp. 246–247.

63. National Institutes of Health, *1980 NCI Fact Book*, pp. 12, 24.

64. Morton Mintz, "Cancer Scientist Quits in Policy Split," *Washington Post*, April 30, 1976, p. A2.

65. "The New War on Cancer, Part I," *Washington Star*, May 23, 1976, p. A10.

66. Morton Mintz, "3 Lawyers Leave EPA in Protest," *Washington Post*, February 6, 1976, p. A1. The three lawyers are Jeffrey H. Howard, Frank J. Sizemore III, and William E. Reukauf. All were assigned to regulation of pesticides and toxic substances.

67. "The Environmental Protection Agency and the Regulation of Pesticides," Staff Report to the Senate Subcommittee on Administrative Practice and Procedure, Washington, D.C., December 1976; cited in Regenstein, *America the Poisoned*, pp. 119–120.

68. Ibid.

69. Quoted in Beatrice Hunter, *The Mirage of Safety* (New York: Charles Scribner's Sons, 1975), p. 147.

70. Quoted in Stuart Auerbach, "N.J.'s Chemical Belt Takes Its Toll: $4 Billion Industry Tied to Nation's Highest Cancer Death Rate," *Washington Post*, February 8, 1976, p. A1.

71. Bill Richards, "Arsenic: A Dark Cloud Over 'Big Sky Country,' " *Washington Post*, February 3, 1976, pp. A1, A5.

72. Quotations in this paragraph are from Auerbach, "N.J.'s Chemical Belt Takes Its Toll," p. A1.

73. Lester B. Lave and Eugene P. Seskin, "Air Pollution and Human Health," *Science* 169, no. 3947 (August 21, 1970), pp. 723–733, especially p. 730. The source for the 1974 mortality rates for lung cancer, respiratory disease (excluding cancer), and cardiovascular disease is the Department of Health, Education and Welfare.

74. Ibid., p. 728.

75. Robert Mendelsohn and Guy Orcutt, "An Empirical Analysis of Air Pollution Dose-Responsive Curves," *Journal of Environmental Economics and Management* (June 1979), pp. 85–106; cited in Regenstein, *America the Poisoned*, p. 194.

76. Regenstein, *America the Poisoned*, p. 195.

77. "Toxic Chemicals and Public protection," A Report to the President by the Toxic Substances Strategy Committee, Council on Environmental Quality, Washington, D.C. (May 1980), p. 6; quoted by Regenstein, *America the Poisoned*, p. 184. See also p. 170 in Regenstein.

78. Regenstein, *America the Poisoned*, pp. 136–137.

79. Joan Claybrook et al., *Retreat from Safety: Reagan's Attack on America's Health* (New York: Pantheon, 1984), pp. 117–129.

80. "More Crime in the Drug and Device Industry," p. 2.

81. Samuel Epstein, *The Politics of Cancer* (San Francisco: Sierra Club Books, 1978), p. 165.

82. Robbins, "Can Reagan Be Indicted?" p. 12.
83. Hunter, *The Mirage of Safety*, p. 4.
84. Quoted in ibid., p. 2.
85. Ibid., pp. 40–41, 64–65, 85, 148–151, *inter alia.*
86. Ibid., p. 119.
87. Ibid., pp. 123–124.
88. Ibid., pp. 127–140.
89. Ibid., pp. 102–103.
90. Ibid., pp. 162–176.
91. Regenstein, *America the Poisoned*, p. 246.
92. Ibid., p. 251.
93. Ibid., p. 128. The National Institute of Allergy and Infectious Diseases reports that 17 out of every 100 persons suffer from a major allergy.
94. Hunter, *The Mirage of Safety*, p. 162.
95. Regenstein, *America the Poisoned*, p. 253.
96. At the very least, "we" includes all those who earn considerably above the median income for the nation (around $29,000 for a family in 1986) and who resist, or vote for candidates who resist, moves to redistribute income significantly.
97. "Poverty in America," *Scholastic Update*, March 23, 1987, pp. 4–8; "Family Income Up Slightly; Poverty Rate Unchanged," *Washington Post*, September 1, 1988; and "8-Nation Study Ranks U.S. Highest in Child Poverty," *Washington Post*, October 27, 1988, p. A1.
98. William Ryan, *Blaming the Victim* (New York: Random House, 1971), p. 162.
99. Monroe Lerner, "Social Differences in Physical Health," in *Poverty and Health: A Sociological Analysis*, eds., John Kosa et al. (Cambridge: Harvard University Press, 1969); cited in Edward S. Greenberg, *Serving the Few: Corporate Capitalism and the Bias of Government Policy* (New York: John Wiley & Sons, 1974), p. 156.
100. Greenberg, *Serving the Few*, p. 156.
101. Aaron Antonovsky, "Class and the Chance for Life," in *Inequality and Justice*, ed., Lee Rainwater (Chicago: Aldine Publishing Co., 1974), p. 177.
102. S. Leonard Syme and Lisa F. Berkman, "Social Class, Susceptibility and Sickness," *American Journal of Epidemiology* 104, no. 1 (July 1976), pp. 1, 4.
103. K. Mahaffey, et al., "National Estimates of Blood Lead Levels: United States, 1976–1980," *The New England Journal of Medicine* 307, no. 10 (September 2, 1982), pp. 573–579. The editorial is on p. 615.
104. Mary Grace Kovar, "Health Status of U.S. Children and Use of Medical Care," *Public Health Reports* 97, no. 1 (January–February 1982), pp. 3–15, esp. p. 8.
105. StatAbst-1981, p. 118, Table no. 189.
106. E. Stockwell, J. Wicks, and D. Adamchak, "Research Needed on Socio-

economic Differentials in U.S. Mortality," *Public Health Reports* 93, no. 6 (November–December 1978), pp. 666–672, esp. p. 668.

107. J Berg, R. Ross, and H. Latourette, "Economic Status and Survival of Cancer Patients," *Cancer* 39, no. 2 (February 1977), pp. 467–477, esp. p. 468. See also the similar findings in L. Lipworth, T. Abelin, and R. Connelly, "Socioeconomic Factors in the Prognosis of Cancer Patients," *Journal of Chronic Diseases* 23 (1970), pp. 105–116.

108. David Stipp, "The Tattered Safety Net," *Wall Street Journal*, April 22, 1988, p. 27R.

109. StatAbst-1988, p. 437, Table no. 721, p. 427, Table no. 700; *Economic Report of the President-1988* (Washington, D.C.: U.S. Government Printing Office, 1988), p. 293, Table B-40.

110. StatAbst-1988, p. 75, Table no. 113.

111. Robbins, "Can Reagan Be Indicted?" pp. 12–13.

112. StatAbst-1988, p. 110, Table no. 176.

113. National Institutes of Health, *Cancer Patient Survival Experience* (June 1980), pp. 4–5.

114. Berg, Ross, and Latourette, "Economic Status and Survival of Cancer Patients," pp. 467–477.

115. Richard Allen Williams reports that "there is no reason why the life span of the White should differ from that of the Black," in his *Textbook of Black-Related Diseases* (New York: McGraw-Hill, 1975), p. 2.

NOTES TO CHAPTER 3

1. *Challenge*, p. 44.

2. Ronald Goldfarb, "Prisons: The National Poorhouse," *The New Republic*, November 1, 1969, pp. 15–17.

3. Philip A. Hart, "Swindling and Knavery, Inc.," *Playboy*, August 1972, p. 158.

4. Compare the statement of Professor Edwin H. Sutherland, one of the major luminaries of twentieth-century criminology:

   First, the administrative processes are more favorable to persons in economic comfort than to those in poverty, so that if two persons on different economic levels are equally guilty of the same offense, the one on the lower level is more likely to be arrested, convicted, and committed to an institution. Second, the laws are written, administered, and implemented primarily with reference to the types of crimes committed by people of lower economic levels. [E. H. Sutherland, Principles of Criminology *(Philadelphia: Lippincott, 1939), p. 179.]*

5. For example, in 1972 when blacks made up 11.3 percent of the national population, they accounted for 42.5 percent of the population of the nation's jails. U.S. Bureau of the Census, Current Population Re-

ports, Special Studies, Series P-23, no. 54, *The Social and Economic Status of the Black Population in the United States, 1974* (Washington, D.C.: U.S. Government Printing Office, 1975), pp. 11, 173.
6. Edwin H. Sutherland and Donald R. Cressey, *Criminology*, 9th ed. (Philadelphia: Lippincott, 1974), p. 133. The following studies are cited in support of this point (p. 133, note 4): Edwin M. Lemert and Judy Roseberg, "The Administration of Justice to Minority Groups in Los Angeles County," *University of California Publications in Culture and Society* 2, no. 1 (1948), pp. 1–28; Thorsten Sellin, "Race Prejudice in the Administration of Justice," *American Journal of Sociology* 41 (September 1935), pp. 212–217; Sidney Alexrad, "Negro and White Male Institutionalized Delinquents," *American Journal of Sociology* 57 (May 1952), pp. 569–574; Marvin E. Wolfgang, Arlene Kelly, and Hans C. Nolde, "Comparisons of the Executed and the Commuted Among Admissions to Death Row," *Journal of Criminal Law, Criminology, and Police Science* 53 (September 1962), pp. 301–311; Nathan Goldman, *The Differential Selection of Juvenile Offenders for Court Appearance* (New York: National Council on Crime and Delinquency, 1963); Irving Piliavin and Scott Briar, "Police Encounters with Juveniles," *American Journal of Sociology* 70 (September 1964), pp. 206–214; Robert M. Terry, "The Screening of Juvenile Offenders," *Journal of Criminal Law, Criminology, and Police Science* 58 (June 1967), pp. 173–181. See also Ramsey Clark, *Crime in America* (New York: Simon and Schuster, 1970), p. 51: "Negroes are arrested more frequently and on less evidence than whites and are more often victims of mass or sweep arrests"; and Donald Taft, *Criminology*, 3d ed. (New York: Macmillan, 1956), p. 134:

> Negroes are more likely to be suspected of crime than are whites. They are also more likely to be arrested. If the perpetrator of a crime is known to be a Negro the police may arrest all Negroes who were near the scene—a procedure they would rarely dare to follow with whites. After arrest Negroes are less likely to secure bail, and so are more liable to be counted in jail statistics. They are more liable than whites to be indicted and less likely to have their case nol prossed or otherwise dismissed. If tried, Negroes are more likely to be convicted. If convicted they are less likely to be given probation. For this reason they are more likely to be included in the count of prisoners. Negroes are also more likely than whites to be kept in prison for the full terms of their commitments and correspondingly less likely to be paroled.

7. William Wilbanks, *The Myth of a Racist Criminal Justice System* (Monterey, Calif.: Brooks/Cole, 1987).
8. Ibid., pp. 64–65.
9. Perceived race of offender percentages are calculated from Sourcebook-1987, p. 229, Table no. 3.20, and p. 231, Table no. 3.25.

Table no. 3.20 shows the number of NCS-reported victimizations by lone offenders and the percentages of these in which the offender is perceived as white or black. Table no. 3.25 shows the number of NCS-reported victimizations by groups of offenders and the percentages of these victimizations in which the whole group was perceived to be white, black, or of mixed races. I have combined these tables by adding the numbers of lone and group victimizations and then (via the percentages) adding the numbers of these perceived to be black (plus half the number in groups perceived to be of mixed races) and then arriving at percentages. This works out to 922,869 perceived blacks in (or 35 percent of) 2,621,040 reported victimizations for rape, robbery, and aggravated assault; 1,479,804 perceived blacks in (or 27 percent of) 5,422,530 reported victimizations for rape, robbery, and all assaults. Arrest percentages are calculated from UCR-1986, p. 182, Table no. 38, which shows a total of 447,547 arrests for forcible rape, robbery, and aggravated assault. The total rises to 1,038,919 when arrests for other assaults are added. The number of blacks arrested for forcible rape, robbery, and aggravated assault is 207,735—or 46 percent of 447,547. The number of blacks arrested for these offenses plus other assaults is 401,121—or 38.6 percent of 1,038,919. Similar methods were used to tally the percentage of victimizations in which the offender was perceived to be white and the percentage of whites arrested for the offenses.

10. For an overview of this double distortion, see Thomas J. Dolan, "The Case for Double Jeopardy: Black and Poor," *International Journal of Criminology and Penology* 1 (1973), pp. 129–150.

11. Center on Budget and Policy Priorities, *Analysis of Poverty in 1987*, September 1, 1988, pp. 2–3; also StatAbst-1988, p. 437, Table no. 721.

12. Sourcebook-1981, p. 463.

13. StatAbst-1988, p. 175, Table no. 304.

14. Isidore Silver, "Introduction" to the Avon edition of *The Challenge of Crime in a Free Society* (New York: Avon Books, 1968), p. 31.

15. *Challenge*, p. 43 (emphasis added). The study referred to is James S. Wallerstein and C. J. Wyle, "Our Law-abiding Lawbreakers," *Probation* 25 (April 1947), pp. 107–112.

16. This is the conclusion of Austin L. Porterfield, *Youth in Trouble* (Fort Worth: Leo Potishman Foundation, 1946); Fred J. Murphy, M. Shirley, and H. L. Witmer, "The Incidence of Hidden Delinquency," *American Journal of Orthopsychiatry* 16 (October 1946), pp. 686–696; James F. Short, Jr., "A Report on the Incidence of Criminal Behavior, Arrests, and Convictions in Selected Groups," *Proceedings of the Pacific Sociological Society*, 1954, pp. 110–118, published as vol. 22, no. 2 of *Research Studies of the State College of Washington* (Pullman: State College of Washington, 1954)]; F. Ivan Nye, James F. Short, Jr., and Virgil J. Olson, "Socioeconomic Status and Delinquent Behavior," *American*

Journal of Sociology 63 (January 1958), pp. 381–389; Maynard L. Erikson and Lamar T. Empey, "Class Position, Peers and Delinquency," *Sociology and Social Research* 49 (April 1965), pp. 268–282; William J. Chambliss and Richard H. Nagasawa, "On the Validity of Official Statistics—A Comparative Study of White, Black, and Japanese High-School Boys," *Journal of Research in Crime and Delinquency* 6 (January 1969), pp. 71–77; Eugene Doleschal, "Hidden Crime," *Crime and Delinquency Literature* 2, no. 5 (October 1970), pp. 546–572; Nanci Koser Wilson, *Risk Ratios in Juvenile Delinquency* (Ann Arbor, Mich.: University Microfilms, 1972); and Maynard L. Erikson, "Group Violations, Socioeconomic Status, and Official Delinquency," *Social Forces* 52, no. 1 (September 1973), pp. 41–52.

17. This is the conclusion of Martin Gold, "Undetected Delinquent Behavior," *Journal of Research in Crime and Delinquency* 3, no. 1 (1966), pp. 27–46; and of Sutherland and Cressey, *Criminology*, pp. 137, 220.

18. Cf. Larry Karacki and Jackson Toby, "The Uncommitted Adolescent: Candidate for Gang Socialization," *Sociological Inquiry* 32 (1962), pp. 203–215; William R. Arnold, "Continuities in Research—Scaling Delinquent Behavior," *Social Problems* 13, no. 1 (1965), pp. 59–66; Harwin L. Voss, "Socio-economic Status and Reported Delinquent Behavior," *Social Problems*, 13, no. 3 (1966), pp. 314–324; LaMar Empey and Maynard L. Erikson, "Hidden Delinquency and Social Status," *Social Forces* 44, no. 4 (1966), pp. 546–554; Fred J. Shanley, "Middle-class Delinquency As a Social Problem," *Sociology and Social Research* 51 (1967), pp. 185–198; Jay R. Williams and Martin Gold, "From Delinquent Behavior to Official Delinquency," *Social Problems* 20, no. 2 (1972), pp. 209–229.

19. Empey and Erikson, "Hidden Delinquency and Social Status," pp. 549, 551. Nye, Short, and Olson also found destruction of property to be committed most frequently by upper-class boys and girls. "Socioeconomic Status and Delinquent Behavior," p. 385.

20. Op. cit., footnote 18.

21. Eugene Doleschal and Nora Klapmuts, "Toward a New Criminology," *Crime and Delinquency Literature* 5 (December 1973), p. 611.

22. Gold, "Undetected Delinquent Behavior," p. 37.

23. Ibid., p. 44. Doleschal, reviewing a later work of Martin Gold [*Delinquent Behavior in an American City* (Belmont, Calif.: Brooks-Cole, 1970)], reports that "while the official figures on delinquency in Flint [Michigan] set the ratio of lower-class to middle-class delinquents at 8 to 1, Gold found that among the 20 percent most delinquent, there were about two lower-class boys for every two middle-class boys." Doleschal, "Hidden Crime," p. 556.

24. Comparing socioeconomic status categories "scant evidence is found that would support the contention that group delinquency is more characteristic of the lower-status levels than other socioeconomic sta-

tus levels. . . . In fact, *only arrests seem to be more characteristic of the low-status category* than the other categories." Erikson, "Group Violations, Socioeconomic Status and Official Delinquency," p. 15 (emphasis added).

25. Gold, "Undetected Delinquent Behavior," p. 28 (emphasis added).

26. Ibid., p. 38.

27. Terence P. Thornberry, "Race, Socioeconomic Status and Sentencing in the Juvenile Justice System," *The Journal of Criminal Law and Criminology* 64, no. 1 (1973), pp. 90–98.

28. Robert Sampson, "Effects of Socioeconomic Context on Official Reaction to Juvenile Delinquency," *American Sociological Review* 51 (December 1986), pp. 876–885; Allen Liska and Mitchell Chamlin, "Social Structure and Crime Control among Macrosocial Units," *American Journal of Sociology* 90, no. 2 (1984), pp. 383–395.

29. See, for example, D. Chapman, "The Stereotype of the Criminal and the Social Consequences," *International Journal of Criminology and Penology* 1 (1973), p. 24.

30. This view is widely held, although the degree to which it functions as a self-fulfilling prophecy is less widely recognized. Versions of this view can be seen in *Challenge*, p. 79; Jerome Skolnick, *Justice without Trial* (New York: John Wiley, 1966), pp. 45–48, 217–218; and Jessica Mitford, *Kind and Usual Punishment*, p. 53. Piliavin and Briar write in "Police Encounters with Juveniles":

> *Compared to other youths, Negroes and boys whose appearance matched the delinquent stereotype were more frequently stopped and interrogated by patrolmen—often even in the absence of evidence that an offense had been committed—usually were given more severe dispositions for the same violations. Our data suggest, however, that these selective apprehension and disposition practices resulted not only from the intrusion of long-held prejudices of individual police officers but also from certain job-related experiences of law-enforcement personnel. First, the tendency of police to give more severe dispositions to Negroes and to youths whose appearance correspond to that which police associated with delinquents partly reflected the fact, observed in this study, that these youths also were much more likely than were other types of boys to exhibit the sort of recalcitrant demeanor which police construed as a sign of the confirmed delinquent. Further, officers assumed, partly on the basis of departmental statistics, that Negroes and juveniles who "look tough" (e.g. who wear chinos, leather jackets, boots, etc.) commit crimes more frequently than do other types of youths. [p. 212]*

Cf. Albert Reiss, *The Police and the Public* (New Haven, Conn.: Yale University Press, 1971). Reiss attributes the differences to the differences in the actions of complainants.

31. Richard J. Lundman, for example, found higher arrest rates to be associated with "offender powerlessness." "Routine Police Arrest Practices: A Commonweal Perspective," *Social Problems* 22, no. 1 (October 1974), pp. 127–141.

32. *Vital Speeches of the Day* (July 1, 1981), pp. 485–487.

33. Marshall Clinard and Peter Yeager, *Corporate Crime* (New York: Free Press, 1980), p. 8.

34. "Crime in the Suites: On the Rise," *Newsweek*, December 3, 1979, pp. 117–121, esp. p. 117.

35. "Stealing $200 Billion the Respectable Way," *U.S. News and World Report*, May 20, 1985, p. 83.

36. Michael Levi, *Regulating Fraud: White-Collar Crime and the Criminal Process* (London: Tavistock, 1987), p. 33; *Economic Report of the President, 1988*, p. 248, Table no. B–1.

37. North American Securities Administrators Administration, *The NASAA Survey of Fraud and Abuse in the Financial Planning Industry— Report to the U.S. Senate Subcommittee on Consumer Affairs, Committee on Banking, Housing and Urban Affairs* (Washington, D.C., July 1988), pp. 1–2.

38. Chamber of Commerce of the United States, *A Handbook on White Collar Crime* (Washington, D.C., 1974), p. 6. Copyright © 1974 by the Chamber of Commerce of the United States. Table reprinted by permission of the Chamber of Commerce of the United States.

39. UCR-1986, p. 153.

40. Sutherland and Cressey, *Criminology*, p. 41 (emphasis added).

41. Clinard and Yeager, *Corporate Crime*, p. 113.

42. Ibid., pp. 124–125.

43. Susan Shapiro, "The Road Not Taken: The Elusive Path to Criminal Prosecution for White-Collar Offenders," *Law and Society Review* 19, no. 2 (1985), p. 182.

44. C. Spohn, J. Gruhl, and S. Welch, "The Impact of the Ethnicity and Gender of Defendants on the Decision to Reject or Dismiss Felony Charges," *Criminology* 25, no. 1 (1987), pp. 175–191.

45. William Bales, "Race and Class Effects on Criminal Justice Prosecution and Punishment Decisions," (unpublished doctoral dissertation, Florida State University, 1987).

46. UCR-1986, p. 165.

47. See, for example, Theodore G. Chiricos, Phillip D. Jackson, and Gordon P. Waldo, "Inequality in the Imposition of a Criminal Label," *Social Problems* 19, no. 4 (Spring 1972), pp. 553–572.

48. Abraham S. Blumberg, *Criminal Justice* (Chicago: Quadrangle, 1967), p. 33. Even for the middle-class defendant, the state with its greater financial, investigatory, and legal personnel resources holds the advantage over the accused—so the poor person is doubly disadvantaged. Cf. Abraham S. Goldstein, "The State and the Accused: Balance of Advan-

tage in Criminal Procedure," in *Crime, Law and Society,* eds., Goldstein and Goldstein, pp. 173–206.

49. Sourcebook-1981, p. 462.
50. See, for example, C. E. Ares, A. Rankin, and J. H. Sturz, "The Manhattan Bail Project: An Interim Report on the Use of Pre-trial Parole," *NYU Law Review* 38 (1963), p. 67; C. Foote, "Compelling Appearances in Court-Administration of Bail in Philadelphia," *University of Pennsylvania Law Review* 102 (1954), pp. 1031–1079; and C. Foote, "A Study of the Administration of Bail in New York City," *University of Pennsylvania Law Review* 106 (1958), p. 693. For statistics on persons held in jail awaiting trial, see *Black Population in the U.S.* (see note 5) p. 171; and USLEAA *Survey of Inmates in Local Jails 1972—Advance Report* (Washington, D.C.: U.S. Government Printing Office, 1974), pp. 5, 8.
51. Blumberg, *Criminal Justice,* pp. 28–29; *Challenge,* p. 134; and Donald J. Newman, *Conviction: The Determination of Guilt or Innocence without Trial* (Boston: Little, Brown, 1966), p. 3.
52. A good summary of these developments can be found in Joel Jay Finer, "Ineffective Assistance of Counsel," *Cornell Law Review* 58, no. 6 (July 1973), pp. 1077–1120.
53. See, for example, Dallin H. Oaks and Warren Lehman, "Lawyers for the Poor," in *Law and Order: The Scales of Justice,* ed., A. Blumberg, pp. 92–93; also Jerome H. Skolnick, "Social Control in the Adversary System," in *Criminal Justice: Law and Politics,* ed., George Cole (Belmont, Calif.: Duxbury, 1972), p. 266. "The National Legal Aid and Defender Association has suggested that experienced attorneys handle no more than 150 felony cases per year, rather than . . . the case load of over 500 felony cases per attorney with which some public defender offices in major cities are burdened." Finer, "Ineffective Assistance of Counsel," p. 1120.
54. In several essays, Abraham S. Blumberg has described the role of the public defender as an officer of the court bureaucracy rather than as a defender of the accused. See his "Lawyers with Convictions," in *Law and Order: The Scales of Justice,* pp. 51–67; "The Practice of Law as Confidence Game: Organizational Cooptation of a Profession," in *Criminal Law in Action,* ed., William J. Chambliss (Santa Barbara, Calif.: Hamilton Publishing Co., 1975), pp. 262–275; and his book *Criminal Justice* (Chicago: Quadrangle, 1967), esp. pp. 13–115.
55. Jonathan D. Casper, "Did You Have a Lawyer When You Went to Court? No, I Had a Public Defender," in *Criminal Justice: Law and Politics,* ed., Cole, pp. 239–240.
56. Blumberg, "Lawyers with Convictions," pp. 62–65; and his *Criminal Justice,* pp. 92–93.
57. Ibid.; percentages are rounded to the nearest whole number.
58. Oaks and Lehman, "Lawyers for the Poor," p. 95.
59. Of those defendants who were convicted in U.S. District Courts in

1971, 46 percent had assigned lawyers (including public defenders); of those *acquitted,* 37.5 percent had assigned counsel; and of those *dismissed,* only 33.3 percent had assigned counsel. Sourcebook-1974, p. 388.

60. Robert Johnson, *Condemned to Die: Life Under Sentence of Death* (New York: Elsevier, 1981), p. 138; Stephen Gettinger, *Sentenced to Die: The People, the Crimes, and the Controversy* (New York: Macmillan, 1979), p. 261.

61. "Death-Row Inmates Often Lack Help for Appeals, But Few Lawyers Want to Do Distasteful Work," *The Wall Street Journal,* August 27, 1987, p. 48.

62. Blake Fleetwood and Arthur Lubow, "America's Most Coddled Criminals," *New Times* (September 19, 1975), pp. 26–29. *New Times Magazine, copyright* © 1975. Reprinted by permission of *New Times Magazine.*

63. Lesley Oelsner, "Wide Disparities Mark Sentences Here," *New York Times,* September 27, 1972, p. 1. Stuart Nagel writes, "The reasons for the economic class sentencing disparities, holding crime and prior record constant, are due possibly to the quality of legal representation that the indigent receive and probably to the appearance that an indigent defendant presents before a middle-class judge or probation officer." "Disparities in Sentencing Procedure," *UCLA Law Review* 14 (August, 1967), p. 1283.

64. Oelsner, "Wide Disparities Mark Sentences Here," p. 1.

65. Nagel, "The Tipped Scales of American Justice," p. 39.

66. Doleschal and Klapmuts, "Toward a New Criminology," p. 613; reporting the findings of Terence Patrick Thornberry, *Punishment and Crime: The Effect of Legal Dispositions on Subsequent Criminal Behavior* (Ann Arbor, Mich.: University Microfilms, 1972); see note 23.

67. Terence P. Thornberry, "Sentencing Disparities in the Juvenile Justice System," *Journal of Criminal Law and Criminology* 70, no. 2 (Summer 1979), pp. 164–171, esp. p. 170.

68. Steven H. Clarke and Gary G. Koch, "The Influence of Income and Other Factors on Whether Criminal Defendants Go to Prison," *Law and Society Review* (Fall 1976), pp. 57–92, esp. pp. 81, 83–84.

69. Alan J. Lizotte, "Testing the Conflict Model of Criminal Justice," *Social Problems* 25, no. 5 (1978), pp. 564–580, esp. p. 564.

70. Sourcebook-1987, pp. 376, 491, 518.

71. Henry Allen Bullock, "Significance of the Racial Factor in the Length of Prison Sentences," in *Crime and Justice in Society,* ed. R. Quinney (Boston: Little, Brown, 1969), p. 425; also Marvin E. Wolfgang and Marc Riedel, "Race, Judicial Discretion and the Death Penalty," in *Criminal Law in Action,* ed., Chambliss, p. 375.

72. William J. Bowers and Glenn L. Pierce, "Racial Discrimination and Criminal Homicide Under Post-*Furman* Capital Statutes," in *The*

Death Penalty in America, ed., H. A. Bedau (New York: Oxford University Press, 1982), pp. 206–224.

73. *McCleskey* v. *Kemp,*107 S.Ct. 1756 (1987). The research most central to this case was that of David Baldus, reported in D. Baldus, C. Pulaski, and G. Woodworth, "Comparative Review of Death Sentences: An Empirical Study of the Georgia Experience," *Journal of Criminal Law and Criminology* 74 (1983), pp. 661–725. Other studies that support the notion of discrimination in capital sentencing based on race of victim are R. Paternoster, "Race of Victim and Location of Crime: The Decision to Seek the Death Penalty in South Carolina," *Journal of Criminal Law and Criminology* 74, no. 3 (1983), pp. 754–788; R. Paternoster, "Prosecutorial Discretion in Requesting the Death Penalty: A Case of Victim Based Racial Discrimination," *Law and Society Review* 18 (1984), pp. 437–478; S. Gross and R. Mauro, "Patterns of Death: An Analysis of Racial Disparities in Capital Sentencing and Homicide Victimization," *Stanford Law Review* 37 (1984), pp. 27–120.

74. William J. Chambliss and Robert B. Seidman, "Sentencing and Sentences," in *Criminal Law in Action*, ed., Chambliss, p. 339; reporting the findings of Mary Owen Cameron, *The Booster and the Snitch: Department Store Shoplifting* (New York: Free Press, 1964).

75. "Blacks Receive Stiffer Sentences," *Boston Globe*, April 4, 1979, pp. 1, 50f.

76. Randall Thomson and Matthew Zingraff, "Detecting Sentencing Disparity: Some Problems and Evidence," *American Journal of Sociology* 86, no. 4 (1981), pp. 869–880, esp. p. 875.

77. J. Unnever, C. Frazier, and J. Henretta, "Race Differences in Criminal Sentencing," *The Sociological Quarterly* 21 (Spring 1980), pp. 197–205, esp. p. 204.

78. J. Petersilia, "Racial Disparities in the Criminal Justice System: A Summary," *Crime & Delinquency* 31, no. 1 (1985), p. 28. See also G. Bridges and R. Crutchfield, "Law, Social Standing and Racial Disparities in Imprisonment," *Social Forces* 66, no. 3 (1988), pp. 699–724.

79. M. Myers, "Economic Inequality and Discrimination in Sentencing," *Social Forces*, 65, no. 3 (1987), p. 761.

80. T. Miethe and C. Moore, "Socioeconomic Disparities Under Determinate Sentencing Systems: A Comparison of Preguideline and Postguideline Practices in Minnesota," *Criminology* 23, no. 2 (1985), p. 358.

81. Marvin E. Wolfgang, Arlene Kelly, and Hans C. Nolde, "Comparison of the Executed and the Commuted Among Admissions to Death Row," in *Crime and Justice in Society*, ed., Quinney, pp. 508, 513.

82. "Antitrust: Kauper's Last Stand," *Newsweek*, June 21, 1976, p. 70. On December 21, 1974, the "Antitrust Procedures and Penalty Act" was passed, striking out the language of the Sherman Antitrust Act, which made price-fixing a misdemeanor punishable by a maximum sentence

of one year in prison. According to the new law, price-fixing is a felony punishable by up to three years in prison. Because prison sentences were a rarity under the old law and usually involved only thirty days in jail when actually imposed, there is little reason to believe that the new law will strike fear in the hearts of corporate crooks.

83. Clinard and Yeager, *Corporate Crime*, pp. 291–292.

84. Ibid., p. 153.

85. K. Johnson, "Federal Court Processing of Corporate, White Collar, and Common Crime Economic Offenders over the Past Three Decades," *Mid-American Review of Sociology* 11, no. 1 (1986), pp. 25–44.

86. J. Hagan and A. Palloni, " 'Club Fed' and the Sentencing of White-Collar Offenders Before and After Watergate," *Criminology* 24, no. 4 (1986), pp. 616–617. See also J. Hagan and P. Parker, "White-Collar Crime and Punishment: The Class Structure and Legal Sanctioning of Securities Violations," *American Sociological Review* 50 (1985), pp. 302–316.

87. *Justice in Sentencing: Papers and Proceedings of the Sentencing Institute for the First and Second U.S. Judicial Circuits*, eds., Leonard Orland and Harold R. Tyler, Jr. (Mineola, N.Y.: Foundation Press, 1974), pp. 159–160 (emphasis added).

88. Michael C. Jensen, "Watergate Donors Still Riding High," *New York Times*, August 24, 1975, sec. 3, pp. 1, 7. Copyright © 1975 by The New York Times Company. Reprinted by permission.

89. Tom Wicker, *A Time to Die* (New York: Quadrangle, 1975), pp. 311, 314.

90. Ibid., p. 310.

91. Sourcebook-1987, p. 486; U.S. Department of Justice, Bureau of Justice Statistics, *Correctional Populations in the United States, 1985* (Washington, D.C., 1987), p. 10, Table no. 2.6; StatAbst-1988, p. 13. Table no. 13.

92. U.S. Department of Justice, Bureau of Justice Statistics, *Profile of State Prison Inmates, 1986* (Washington, D.C., 1988), p. 3, Tables nos. 1 and 2; StatAbst-1988, p. 175, Table no. 304, and p. 432, Table no. 710; *Economic Report of the President, 1988* Washington, D.C.: U.S. Gov't Printing Office, 1988), p. 292, Table no. B-39.

NOTES TO CHAPTER 4

1. *Challenge*, p. 44.

2. U.S. Department of Justice, *Criminal Victimization in the United States, 1979* (A National Crime Survey Report), September 1981, p. 4.

3. Ibid., p. 5.

4. U.S. Department of Justice, Bureau of Justice Statistics, *Criminal Victimization in the United States, 1986* (Washington, D.C., 1988), pp. 26–27, Table no. 14; and pp. 34–35, Table no. 23.

5. A report to the Federal Communications Commission estimates that by the time the average American child reaches age fourteen, he or she has seen 13,000 human beings killed by violence on television. Although a few of these are probably killed by science fiction monsters, the figure still suggests that the extent of the impact of the televised portrayal of crime and the struggle against it on the imaginations of Americans is nothing short of astounding. See Eve Merriam, "We're Teaching Our Children That Violence Is Fun," in *Violence: An Element of American Life*, eds., K. Taylor and F. Soady, Jr. (Boston: Holbrook Press, 1972), p. 155. For a list of the twenty police programs (which does not include detective programs and other shows in which the fight against crime is the theme) aired on ABC, CBS, and NBC, the three major networks, see Center for Research on Criminal Justice, *The Iron Fist and the Velvet Glove: An Analysis of the U.S. Police* (Berkeley, Calif.: 1975), pp. 194–195.

6. Richard A. Cloward and Lloyd E. Ohlin, *Delinquency and Opportunity: A Theory of Delinquent Gangs* (New York: Free Press, 1960), esp. pp. 77–107.

7. Ibid., p. 81.

8. Ibid., p. 105.

9. Ibid., p. 107.

10. Ibid., p. 105.

11. Willem Bonger, *Criminality and Economic Conditions*, abridged and with an introduction by Austin T. Turk (Bloomington: Indiana University Press, 1969), pp. 7–12, 40–47. Willem Adriaan Bonger was born in Holland in 1876 and died by his own hand in 1940 rather than submit to the Nazis. His *Criminalité et conditions économiques* first appeared in 1905. It was translated into English and published in the United States in 1916. Ibid., pp. 3–4.

12. David M. Gordon, "Capitalism, Class and Crime in America," *Crime and Delinquency* (April 1973), p. 174.

13. Ibid.

14. William and Mary Morris, *Dictionary of Word and Phrase Origins*, vol. 2 (New York: Harper and Row, 1967), p. 282.

15. Sourcebook-1974, pp. 203, 204, 207, 223; Sourcebook-1981, pp. 192, 205, 210–211; Sourcebook-1987, pp. 142–143, 160–161.

16. Historical documentation of this can be found in David J. Rothman, *The Discovery of the Asylum: Social Order and Disorder in the New Republic* (Boston: Little, Brown, 1971); and in Frances Fox Piven and Richard A. Cloward, *Regulating the Poor: The Functions of Public Welfare* (New York: Pantheon, 1971), which carries the analysis up to the present.

17. *The Republic of Plato*, trans. F. M. Cornford (New York: Oxford University Press, 1945), p. 18 [I. 338]. Plato was born in Athens in the year 428 B.C. (or 427, depending on the reckoning) and died there in 348 B.C. (or

347). Scholars generally agree that at least Book One of *The Republic* (the section in which Thrasymachus speaks) was written between the death of Socrates in 399 B.C. and Plato's first journey to Sicily, from which he returned in 388 B.C. (or 387). See Frederick Copleston, S.J., *A History of Philosophy, Volume I: Greece and Rome* (Westminster, Maryland: Newman Press, 1946), pp. 127–141.

18. Karl Marx and Friedrich Engels, *Manifesto of the Communist Party*, in *The Marx-Engels Reader*, ed., Robert C. Tucker (New York: W. W. Norton, 1972), p. 337. Marx was born in Trier, Prussia (now in West Germany) on May 5, 1818, and died on March 14, 1883. The *Manifesto* was first published in London in February, 1848—when Marx was nearly thirty years old. Ibid., pp. xi–xiv.

19. An article on congressional ethics in *Newsweek* (June 14, 1976) makes the point so graphically that it is worth quoting at length:

> ... *Some of the Hill's most powerful veterans have long earned part of their income from outside business interests—and may be tempted to vote with their own bank accounts in mind when legislation affecting those interests has come before Congress. House whip Thomas P. (Tip) O'Neill is active in real estate and insurance in Massachusetts, Minority Leader John Rhodes of Arizona is a director and vice-president of a life insurance company and scores of other senior members are involved with the banking industry, oil and gas companies and farming operations. Do these connections destroy their judgment? Not necessarily, argues Russell Long of Louisiana, chairman of the powerful Senate Finance Committee and a reliable defender of oil interests—who nevertheless refuses to disclose the size of his personal oil and gas holdings, most of them inherited from his father, former Gov. Huey Long. "A long time ago I became convinced that if you have financial interests completely parallel to your state, then you have no problem," says Long. "If I didn't represent the oil and gas industry, I wouldn't represent the state of Louisiana."*
>
> *Even more difficult to trace is the influence of representatives who keep their law practices—and their clients, many of whom do business with the Federal government—when they become members of Congress. [p. 25]*

See Richard Quinney, *Critique of Legal Order: Crime Control in Capitalist Society* (Boston: Little, Brown, 1973), pp. 82–84, for an account of the financial interests and corporate connections of the members of the influential Committee for Economic Development—the domestic policy counterpart of the Council on Foreign Relations. For similar information on the members of various committees and councils that shape American foreign policy, see G. William Domhoff, "Who Made American Foreign Policy, 1945–1963?" in *Corporations and the Cold*

War, ed., David Horowitz (New York: Monthly Review Press, 1969), pp. 25–69.

20. J. A. Schmidhauser, "The Justices of the Supreme Court: A Collective Portrait," *Midwest Journal of Political Science* 3 (1959), pp. 2–37, 40–49, cited in William J. Chambliss and Robert B. Seidman, *Law, Order, and Power* (Reading, Mass.: Addison-Wesley, 1971), p. 96; and Richard Quinney, *Critique of Legal Order: Crime Control in Capitalist Society* (Boston: Little, Brown, 1973), pp. 60–82, 86–92.

21. "F.B.I. Burglarized Leftist Offices Here 92 Times in 1960–66, Official Files Show," *New York Times*, March 29, 1976, p. 1; "Burglaries by FBI Listed in Hundreds," *Washington Post*, July 16, 1975, p. 1. See also *Cointelpro: The FBI's Secret War on Political Freedom*, ed., Cathy Perkus, introduction by Noam Chomsky (New York: Monad Press, 1975).

22. "Hill Panel Raps FBI's Anti-Panthers Tactics," *Washington Post*, May 7, 1976, pp. A1, A22.

23. "FBI Labeled King 'Communist' in '62," *Washington Post*, May 6, 1976, pp. A1, A26.

24. "Kelley Says FBI Is 'Truly Sorry' for Past Abuses," *Washington Post*, May 9, 1976, pp. A1, A14; "FBI Break-Ins Still Go On, Panel Reports," *Washington Post*, May 11, 1976, pp. A1, A16; and "The FBI: Bag Jobs," *Newsweek*, July 4, 1976, pp. 84–85.

25. James F. Richardson, *Urban Police in the United States* (Port Washington, N.Y.: Kennikat Press, 1974), pp. 8–13, 22. See also Richardson's *The New York Police: Colonial Times to 1901* (New York: Oxford University Press, 1970).

26. Rothman, *The Discovery of the Asylum*, pp. 57–108, esp. pp. 79–81. Cf. Michel Foucault, *Discipline and Punish: The Birth of the Prison* (London: Allen Lane, 1977).

27. Richardson, *Urban Police*, pp. 158–161. See also R. Boyer and H. Morais, *Labor's Untold Story* (New York: United Electrical, Radio & Machine Workers of America, 1976).

28. Rothman, *The Discovery of the Asylum*, pp. 253–254.

29. Philip Taft and Philip Ross, "American Labor Violence: Its Causes, Character, and Outcome," in *The History of Violence in America*, eds., H. D. Graham and T. R. Gurr (New York: Bantam, 1969), pp. 281–395, esp. pp. 281, 380; and Richard E. Rubenstein, *Rebels in Eden: Mass Political Violence in the United States* (Boston: Little, Brown, 1970), p. 81 inter alia. See also Center for Research in Criminal Justice, *The Iron Fist and the Velvet Glove*, pp. 16–19.

30. Karl Marx, *The German Ideology*, in *The Marx-Engels Reader*, ed., Tucker, p. 136.

31. Each new ruling class "is compelled, merely in order to carry through its aim, to represent its interest as the common interest of all the members of society." Ibid., p. 138.

32. Marx was not the first to use the term *ideology*. The term was coined by Antoine Destutt de Tracy, who was among the intellectuals named in 1795 to direct the researches of the newly founded Institut de France. The idéologues of the Institut generally believed that existing ideas were prejudices rooted in individual psychology or in political conditions and that the path to liberation from these prejudices and thus toward a rational society lay in a science of ideas (literally, an "ideaology"), which made human beings aware of the sources of their ideas. Thomas Jefferson introduced the theory of ideology in America. He tried (albeit unsuccessfully) to have Destutt de Tracy's theory made part of the original curriculum of the University of Virginia. See George Lichtheim, "The Concept of Ideology," *History and Theory* 4, no. 2 (1965), pp. 164–195; and *Ideology, Politics, and Political Theory*, ed., Richard H. Cox (Belmont, Calif.: Wadsworth, 1969), pp. 7–8. Needless to say, Marx used the term *ideology* in ways that neither Destutt de Tracy nor Jefferson anticipated.

33. Lichtheim's essay provides a good discussion of the philosophical antecedents of the gradual separation of the notion of *ideology* from that of *false consciousness*. Undoubtedly, this separation is of a piece with the current wisdom that insists that all views of the world are conditioned and rendered partial by the limits of the viewer's historical and social vantage point, and thus shrinks from trying to say anything *true* about the human condition. An illuminating contemporary example of this "current wisdom" applied to the criminal justice system is Walter B. Miller, "Ideology and Criminal Justice Policy: Some Current Issues," *Journal of Criminal Law and Criminology* 64, no. 2 (1973), pp. 141–162. I shall use the concept of ideology in the Marxian sense, that is, to include that of false consciousness.

34. What follows is just a smattering of the literature documenting the wide and abiding disparities of wealth in America or the existence of a very small, not necessarily organized, group of individuals who, in addition to being extremely wealthy, make most of the economic and political decisions that shape America's destiny: G. William Domhoff, *Who Rules America?* (Englewood Cliffs, N.J.: Prentice-Hall, 1967); Richard C. Edwards, Michael Reich, and Thomas E. Weisskopf, *The Capitalist System: A Radical Analysis of American Society* (Englewood Cliffs, N.J.: Prentice-Hall, 1972); John Kenneth Galbraith, *The New Industrial State* (New York: Signet Books, 1968); Edward S. Greenberg, *Serving the Few: Corporate Capitalism and the Bias of Government Policy* (New York: John Wiley, 1974); Gabriel Kolko, *Wealth and Power in America: An Analysis of Social Class and Income Distribution* (New York: Praeger, 1962); C. Wright Mills, *The Power Elite* (New York: Oxford University Press, 1956); Joseph Pechman and Benjamin A. Okner, *Who Bears the Tax Burden?* (Washington, D.C.: Brookings Institution, 1974); Philip M. Stern, *The Rape of the Taxpayer* (New York: Vintage Books, 1974).

35. StatAbst-1988, p. 428, Table no. 701.
36. Alan S. Blinder, "The Level and Distribution of Economic Well-Being," in *The American Economy in Transition,* ed., Martin Feldstein (Chicago: University of Chicago Press, 1980), p. 466.
37. Marshall E. Blume, Jean Crockett, and Irwin Friend, "Stock-Ownership in the United States: Characteristics and Trends," *Survey of Current Business* 54, no. 11 (November 1974), p. 17 (emphasis added).
38. Undoubtedly, the most interesting recent work on this topic is John Rawls's *A Theory of Justice* (Cambridge, Mass.: Harvard University Press, 1971). The noted British philosopher Stuart Hampshire has called it the most important work in moral philosophy since the Second World War. It is sure to exert considerable influence on theoretical discussions of political, legal, and economic justice. Rawls's approach is essentially "naturalistic." That is, he takes the "good" to be that which people rationally desire, and the "moral good" to be that which would best serve *all* people's rational desires. Based on this, he takes justice to be those social (legal, political, economic) arrangements that best serve the interests of all. To reach specific principles of justice, he asks for those principles that it would be rational for all people to agree to if each could not use force or influence to tailor the principles to his or her own interest. On the question of the distribution of income or wealth, this way of questioning leads to the principle that economic inequalities are only just if they work to everyone's advantage, for instance, as incentives that work to raise the level of productivity and thus the level of well-being for all. It would be the task of government to rectify inequalities that exceed this point, by means of taxes and transfers. I cannot, of course, do justice here to what Rawls takes 600 pages to explain and defend. However, I offer this short summary to suggest that the disparities of income in America are far from just in the light of contemporary moral philosophy. Clearly, those disparities are far greater than anything that could be claimed to be *necessary* to increase the well-being of all. Indeed, one would have to be blind not to see that they are not increasing the well-being of all. Robert Nozick has replied to Rawls in a book titled *Anarchy, State and Utopia* (New York: Basic Books, 1974), which no doubt represents the free enterprise system's theory of justice. Nozick holds that no theory (such as Rawls's) that calls for government intervention to rectify income distribution can be just. His argument is that if people acquire their property (including money) legitimately, then they have the right to spend or sell it as they wish. If this leads to disparities in wealth, one cannot alter this outcome without denying that those spenders or sellers had the right to dispose of their property or money as they saw fit. I shall not try to answer Nozick here. It should be noted, however, that his view starts from the assumption that the property or money that is sold or spent was acquired legitimately. In light of the fact that

so much American property was stolen at gunpoint from Indians or Mexicans and so much wealth taken from the hides of black slaves, it is questionable whether Nozick's theory can be applied in the American context. It might require a redistribution of wealth just so that we could reach the starting point at which we could say that individuals own what they own legitimately. For an extended discussion of these theories of justice, see Jeffrey Reiman, *Justice and Modern Moral Philosophy* (New Haven, Conn.: Yale University Press, 1990).

39. StatAbst-1988, p. 437, Table no. 721.

40. One study reports that "among high school graduates with *equal* academic ability, the proportion going on to college averages nearly 25 percentage points lower for males (and nearly 35 for females) in the bottom socioeconomic quarter of the population than in the top quarter." Another indicates that "the sons of families in the top fifth of the socioeconomic pyramid have average incomes 75 percent higher than those coming from the bottom fifth." Arthur M. Okun, *Equality and Efficiency* (Washington, D.C.: Brookings Institution, 1975), pp. 81, 75.

NOTES TO CONCLUSION

1. Although I think this way of looking at the legal system, at justice, and at the moral legitimacy of the law, is common to most moral and legal philosophers, it should be acknowledged that my own formulation bears a heavy debt to the conceptions of justice and morality developed by John Rawls, Kurt Baier, and Herbert Morris. See John Rawls, *A Theory of Justice* (Cambridge, Mass.: Harvard University Press, 1971); Kurt Baier, *The Moral Point of View: A Rational Basis of Ethics* (New York: Random House, 1965); and Herbert Morris, "Persons and Punishment," in *Human Rights*, ed., A. I. Melden (Belmont, Calif.: Wadsworth, 1970), pp. 111–134. On the issue of the legitimacy of states (i.e., political-legal systems), see Robert Paul Wolff, *In Defense of Anarchism* (New York: Harper and Row, 1970 and 1976), Jeffrey H. Reiman, *In Defense of Political Philosophy* (New York: Harper & Row, 1972), Reiman, "Autonomy, Authority, and Universalizability," *The Personalist* (January 1978), pp. 85–92; and Reiman "Anarchism and Nominalism: Wolff's Latest Obituary for Political Philosophy," *Ethics* (October 1978). On the issue of the legitimacy and moral justification of police authority in particular, see Jeffrey H. Reiman, "Police Autonomy vs. Police Authority: A Philosophical Perspective," in *The Police Community*, eds., Jack Goldsmith and Sharon S. Goldsmith (Pacific Palisades, Calif.: Palisades Publishers, 1974), pp. 225–233; and Roger Wertheimer, "Are the Police Necessary?" in *The Police in Society*, eds., Emilio C. Viano and Jeffrey H. Reiman (Lexington, Mass.: Lexington Books, 1975), pp. 49–60.

2. See the thoughtful recommendations for gun control and their rationale in Norval Morris and Gordon Hawkins, *The Honest Politician's Guide to Crime Control* (Chicago: University of Chicago Press, 1970), pp. 63–71.

3. Ibid., pp. 3, 8–10; Arnold S. Trebach, *The Heroin Solution* (New Haven, Conn.: Yale University Press, 1982), pp. 267–270; and Philip C. Baridon, *Addiction, Crime, and Social Policy* (Lexington, Mass.: Lexington Books, 1976), p. 88.

4. For an argument that there is no moral difference between directly caused and indirectly caused harm, see John Harris, "The Marxist Conception of Violence," *Philosophy & Public Affairs* 3, no. 2 (Winter 1974), pp. 192–220; and Jonathan Glover, *Causing Death and Saving Lives* (Hammondsworth, England: Penguin, 1977), pp. 92–112.

5. These are the words of a former director of the fraud division of the Department of Justice:

> *No one in direct contact with the living reality of business conduct in the United States is unaware of the effect the imprisonment of seven high officials in the Electrical Machinery Industry in 1960 had on the conspiratorial price fixing in many areas of our economy; similar sentences in a few cases each decade would almost completely cleanse our economy of the cancer of collusive price fixing and the mere prospect of such sentences is itself the strongest available deterrent to such activities.*

Gordon B. Spivak, "Antitrust Enforcement in the United States: A Primer," *Connecticut Bar Journal* 37 (September 1963), p. 382.

6. See Chapter 1, "The Overreach of the Criminal Law," in Morris and Hawkins, *The Honest Politician's Guide to Crime Control*, pp. 1–28; Herbert Packer, *The Limits of the Criminal Sanction* (Stanford, Calif.: Stanford University Press, 1968); and Jeffrey H. Reiman, "Can We Avoid the Legislation of Morality?" in *Legality, Morality and Ethics in Criminal Justice*, eds., Nicholas N. Kittrie and Jackwell Susman (New York: Praeger, 1979), pp. 130–141.

7. John Stuart Mill, *On Liberty* (1859) (New York: Appleton-Century-Crofts, 1973), p. 9.

8. See, for example, Gerald Dworkin, "Paternalism," in *Morality and the Law*, ed., Richard Wasserstrom (Belmont, Calif.: Wadsworth, 1971), pp. 107–126; and Joel Feinberg, "Legal Paternalism," in *Today's Moral Problems*, ed., Richard Wasserstrom (New York: Macmillan, 1975), pp. 33–50.

9. See, for instance, the excellent discussion of the principle in Peter T. Manicas, *The Death of the State* (New York: Putnam, 1974), Chapter 5: "The Liberal Moral Ideal," pp. 194–241; and H.L.A. Hart, *Law, Liberty and Morality* (New York: Vintage Books, 1963).

10. The standard laid down in *Conally* v. *General Constr. Co.*, 269 U.S. 385,

391, 70 L. Ed. 322, 46 S. Ct. 126 (1926) is "whether or not the vagueness
is of such a character 'that men of common intelligence must necessarily guess at its meaning.' " See also *Lanzetta et al. v. State of New Jersey,*
306, U.S. 451, 83 L. Ed. 888, 59 S. Ct. 618 (1939), where the Supreme
Court struck down a New Jersey statute that made it a felony for
anyone not engaged in any lawful occupation to be a member of a gang
and so on because the terms of the statute were "vague, indefinite and
uncertain" and thus "repugnant to the due process clause of the Four-
teenth Amendment." Both cases are cited and discussed in Jerome
Hall, *General Principles of Criminal Law,* 2d ed. (New York: Bobbs-
Merrill, 1960), pp. 36–48. For a constitutional and philosophical argument for treating Mills's harm principle as an implied constitutional
principle, see David A. J. Richards, *Sex, Drugs, Death, and the Law: An
Essay on Human Rights and Overcriminalization* (Totowa, N.J.: Rowman and Littlefield, 1982), pp. 1–34 inter alia.

11. See *Robinson v. California,* 370 U.S. 66 (1962), where the court held
that a state law penalizing a person for a "status" such as addiction
constitutes "cruel and unusual punishment" in violation of the Eighth
Amendment. Cited and discussed in Nicholas N. Kittrie, *The Right to
Be Different: Deviance and Enforced Therapy* (Baltimore: Johns Hop-
kins Press, 1971), pp. 35–36 inter alia.

12. I have already pointed out that the vast majority of persons convicted
of crimes in the United States are convicted by juries. They plead
guilty as the result of a "bargain" with the prosecutor (underwritten
by the judge), in which the prosecutor agrees to drop other charges in
return for the guilty plea. Kenneth Kipnis argues that the entire system of bargain justice is a violation of the ideal of justice because it
amounts to coercing a guilty plea and often to punishing an offender
for a crime other than the one he or she has committed. It is an argument worth considering. See Kenneth Kipnis, "Criminal Justice and
the Negotiated Plea," *Ethics* 86, no. 2 (January 1976), pp. 93–106.

13. "Justices Uphold Disputed System of U.S. Sentencing," *New York
Times,* January 19, 1989, p. A1.

NOTES TO THE APPENDIX

1. This essay is a revised and shortened version of an article that appeared in *Criminal Justice Ethics* 6, no. 1 (Winter/Spring 1987). Peter
Darvas assisted me with the research for that article.

2. Frederick Engels, "Letter to Conrad Schmidt, October 27, 1890), in
Karl Marx, Selected Works, ed., V. Adoratsky (Moscow: Cooperative Publishing Society of Foreign Workers in the USSR, 1935), vol. 1, p. 386.

3. Karl Marx, *Capital* (New York: International Publishers, 1967), vol. 3,
p. 819.

4. Note that Marx does not hold that the value of a commodity is equiva-

lent to the *actual* amount of labor-time that goes into producing it. On that view, commodities would increase in value the more inefficiently they were produced. Instead, recognizing that a commodity will command a price no higher than that for which commodities like it are selling, Marx takes the commodity's value to be determined by the average or socially necessary labor-time it takes to produce commodities of its kind. See *Capital*, vol. 1, p. 189. Furthermore, although Marx claims that value is equivalent to average labor-time, he only assumes that values and market prices coincide for the purposes of the argument of volume 1 of *Capital* about the fundamental nature of capitalism. In the subsequent volumes, Marx shows at length the mechanisms in capitalism that lead prices to diverge from values. Even after these common misinterpretations of the theory are eliminated, it must be admitted that Marx's labor theory of value has come in for so much criticism in recent years, that many, even many Marxists, have given it up for dead.

5. See, for example, G. William Domhoff, *Who Rules America?* (Englewood Cliffs, N.J.: Prentice-Hall, 1967); M. Green, J. Fallows, and D. Zwick, *Who Runs Congress?* (*The Ralph Nader Congress Project*) (New York: Grossman, 1972); Edward S. Greenberg, *Serving the Few: Corporate Capitalism and the Bias of Government Policy* (New York: Wiley, 1974); and Ralph Miliband, *The State in Capitalist Society* (New York: Basic Books, 1969).

6. Karl Marx, "Preface to *A Contribution to a Critique of Political Economy*," in *The Marx-Engels Reader*, 2d ed., ed., Robert Tucker (New York: Norton, 1978), p. 5.

7. Karl Marx and Friedrich Engels, *The German Ideology*, parts 1 and 3 (New York: International Publishers, 1947), p. 14.

8. Op. cit., note 6, p. 4.

9. Ibid.

10. "It is not the subject who deceives himself, but *reality* which deceives *him*," Maurice Godelier, "Structure and Contradiction in *Capital*," in *Ideology in Social Science*, ed., Robin Blackburn (Glasgow: Fontana/Collins, 1977), p. 337.

11. Examples of theories of ideology that trace its distortions to subjective illusions are the attempt by some members of the Frankfurt School to explain the affection of German laborers for fascism by means of a Freudian account of the persistence of irrational authoritarian attitudes and the attempt of some sociologists to trace ideology to an existential need to reify a mythic worldview as protection against the terrors of meaninglessness. For the former, see Martin Jay, *The Dialectical Imagination: A History of the Frankfurt School and the Institute for Social Research, 1923–1950* (Boston: Little, Brown, 1973). For the latter, see Peter Berger and Thomas Luckmann, *The Social Construction of Reality* (New York: Doubleday, 1966).

12. Karl Marx, *The Poverty of Philosophy* (Moscow: Progress Publishers, 1955), p. 75.
13. Evgeny B. Pashukanis, *Law and Marxism: A General Theory*, trans. by B. Einhorn, ed., C. Arthur (London: Ink Links, 1978).
14. "The labor contract is to be freely entered into by both parties. But it is considered to have been freely entered into as soon as the law makes both parties equal *on paper*. The power conferred on the one party by the difference of class position, the pressure thereby brought to bear on the other party—the real economic position of both—that is not the law's business." Frederick Engels, *The Origin of the Family, Private Property, and the State* (New York: International Publishers, 1942), p. 64.
15. Pashukanis, *Law and Marxism*, pp. 112–113, inter alia.
16. Pashukanis approvingly attributes to Aristotle "the definition of crime as an involuntarily concluded contract" (ibid., p. 169).
17. Pashukanis observes that the exchange contract or *pactum* derives from *pax* or peace (ibid., p. 167).
18. Ibid., p. 169; see also Alan Norrie, "Pashukanis and 'the Commodity Form Theory': A Reply to Warrington," *International Journal of the Sociology of Law* 10 (1982), pp. 431–434.
19. Pashukanis, *Law and Marxism*, p. 177.
20. See Georg Rusch and Otto Kirchheimer, *Punishment and Social Structure* (New York: Russell & Russell, 1968), for a classic Marxian-inspired historical study of the relationship between penal policy and the supply and demand for labor.
21. This is the view of, for example, Allen Buchanan in *Marx and Justice* (Totowa, N.J.: Rowman and Littlefield, 1982).
22. This is essentially the view argued for by, for example, Allen Wood, in "The Marxian Critique of Justice," *Philosophy & Public Affairs* 1, no. 3 (Spring 1972), pp. 244–282.
23. This is the view of, for example, G. A. Cohen in "Freedom, Justice and Capitalism," *New Left Review* 126 (March/April 1981), pp. 3–16. There is, by the way, a substantial literature on the question of whether Marxism holds that capitalism is wrong because it is unjust or that justice is part of what's wrong with capitalism. See articles in M. Cohen, T. Nagel, T. Scanlon, eds., *Marx, Justice, and History* (Princeton, N.J.: Princeton University Press, 1980); K. Nielsen and S. Patten, eds., *Marx and Morality* (*Canadian Journal of Philosophy*, supplemental vol. 7, 1981), and J. Pennock and J. Chapman, eds., *Nomos XXVI: Marxism* (New York: New York University Press, 1983); as well as Norman Geras's review of the whole discussion, "The Controversy About Marx and Justice," *New Left Review* 150 (March/April 1985), pp. 47–85. My own views are presented in "The Possibility of a Marxian Theory of Justice," in *Marx and Morality*, eds., Nielsen and Patten, pp. 307–322.

Index

A

Aarons, Leroy, 22–23
Accidents. *See* Occupational hazards
Acquittal, legal counsel and, 97
Addictions
  antidrug policy, failure of, 33–34
  treatment as medical problem, 147–148
  types of, 28–29
  See also specific addictions.
Aerojet-General Corporation, 71
Age, young people as criminals, 19–22
Air pollution, cancer, 70–71
Alcohol use, 28
Althusser, Louis, 8
Anaconda Company, 70
Angel dust, 148
Antitrust violations, sentencing and, 102–103
Arrest
  blacks, 42
  economic bias, 85–94
Arrest records, information derived from, 43
Asbestosis, 62
Attica Prison uprising, 108, 113

B

Bail, significance of, 94–95
Baldwin, James, 143, 144, 145
Baridon, Philip, 147
Belgium, homicide rate, 17
Birth defects, yearly statistics, 73
Black lung disease, 62
Black Panthers, 134
Blacks
  arrests, 42
  cancer survival, 78
  discrimination and arrests, 82–84
  infant mortality, 77
  life expectancy, 78
  prison population, 81
  sentencing, 100–101
Blaming the Victim (Ryan), 75
Blumberg, Abraham S., 94, 96
Bonger, Willem, 128
Britton, Herschell, 90
Brown lung, 62
Burford, Anne, 71
Byssinosis, 62

C

Caffeine addiction, 28
Cameron, Mary Owen, 101

About the Author

Jeffrey Reiman was born in Brooklyn, New York in 1942. He received his B.A. in Philosophy from Queens College in 1963, and his Ph.D. in Philosophy from The Pennsylvania State University in 1968. He joined the faculty of The American University's School of Justice in Washington, D.C. in 1970, when it was called the Center for the Administration of Justice. The School of Justice is a multi-disciplinary department devoted to teaching and research in all areas of social justice with special emphasis on criminal justice. Dr. Reiman taught in the School of Justice (now called the Department of Justice, Law and Society) until 1988, when he moved over to American University's Department of Philosophy and Religion, where he is currently Professor of Philosophy. In addition to *The*

Rich Get Richer and the Poor Get Prison, he is author of *In Defense of Political Philosophy, Justice and Modern Moral Philosophy,* and numerous articles in philosophy and criminal justice journals and anthologies.